CLASSIC COOKING FROM INDIA

BY DHARAM JIT SINGH

CLASSIC COOKING FROM *India*

DECORATIONS BY WILLIAM BARSS

HOUGHTON MIFFLIN COMPANY BOSTON
THE RIVERSIDE PRESS CAMBRIDGE
1956

Library of Congress catalogue card no. 56-9601
First printing November 1956

The Riverside Press
CAMBRIDGE • MASSACHUSETTS
PRINTED IN THE U.S.A.

To my father
for his unfailing good taste

Acknowledgments

MY EARNEST THANKS to my friends below for their encouragement in writing this book; for their guidance and suggestions, and for submitting to my cooking.

Monsieur et Madame Charles Gratry, Paris, France; Mr. and Mrs. J. S. Mamik, Harrow, England; Mrs. Henrietta Ten Eyck, New York and Rumson, New Jersey; Mr. Frank Harper, author, New York; Mr. Carl B. Hess, New York; Miss Helen McCully, Food Editor, *McCall's* Magazine and *McCall's* kitchens, for letting me taste-test recipes in this book; The Waring Products for their equipment that made my taste-testing chores much easier; Mr. and Mrs. Avtar Singh, New Delhi, India; and, grateful thanks to Laurette Murdock, Houghton Mifflin Company, for her editing of a very complicated manuscript.

Contents

CLASSIC COOKING FROM INDIA

CHAPTER 1

Spices, Herbs and Sizzling Miracles

The Tradition in India

"IF YOU would be a king," they say in India, "you must eat like a king." This tradition is almost as old as Indian cooking. Happily and without fuss the people of India can and do eat like kings. Indian food has great variety and is not difficult to prepare. Whether made in the Indian or the American kitchen, this food needs neither magical incantations nor the elaborateness exacted by the two Roman playboys, Lucullus and Vitellus, who liked a dish of two thousand larks' tongues served by a hundred beautiful naked girls.

The purpose of this book is to make the American housewife familiar with authentic cooking from India. With her pioneering tradition of adapting new culinary ideas to her own needs, she will find much from India to welcome into her kitchen.

The Indians believe that their cuisine is the "diamond solitaire" of all cuisines. In my opinion, it ranks with the French and the Chinese as the greatest of all times. Its cooking methods include any found elsewhere in the world. Its influence has spread throughout the lands of the Monsoon climate, the Middle East, Europe and the West Indies. At home, it remains pristine and cannot be confused with any other type of cooking.

Contrary to popular belief, Indian food is not acrid, searing or sharp. Nor is it the gummy, pasty mess known here as curry, which to the Indian is strange. Good seasoning can be either hot or bland within the limits of good taste.

The approach to food in India is characteristic. Indians give to their cooking the same devotion as to their worship, the same care and skill as to their love, and the same sensitivity as to their art. I refer to the best tradition, which sees no real difference between these activities. What a person requires is a perfection in working, whether it is cooking or the search for truth. Man's freedom and fulfillment lies in achieving this perfection. There is no perfection save through the yoking (yoga) or union of each individual's real self with the life and power that pervades all different forms of creation.

In India even the poorest cook, with his alchemy of spices and respect for quality, can coax the most Cinderella of vegetables to appear on the table with elegance. The humble lentil is transformed into a savory delight for the most sophisticated taste. With meat, fish and fowl, the modest home in India can present a dish succulent enough to make the gourmet crow with delight or blow a flourish on silver trumpets as the French do to celebrate good food. And as you try the recipes in this book, you will learn for the first time what a glory vegetables can be. You will open up a new savory world of rice cookery and reach new dimensions in lentil and meat cooking.

As this is going to be a practical cookbook, I will stress that spices are the vital core of Indian cooking. From the uplands of the Himalayas to Cape Comorin, from the wheat fields of the Punjab to the lush rice paddies of Bengal, herbs are used everywhere and in the same manner. The many spices from the precious groves and fragrant hillsides find their way to the cavernous shops and chapmen's booths. Under the striped awnings the dealers sit handling their wares with the care of a jeweler. The spices are displayed in their original bags. To transfer them would be to waste them. From these bazaars the spices find their way to the kitchen with its spice chest of good grained wood, incised stone or the popular metal jars. The dozen or more powders are arranged within the honeycombed interior of the spice chest to form a constellation of colors. The use of the spice chest goes back to at least 4000 B.C.

Today these spices are available in most dime stores, supermarkets and grocery stores throughout the United States. The necessary kitchen equipment is found in every American home. Combining a little trial and error with the recipes here, you will soon turn into a born cook. That is how cooks are "born." It requires only a little effort, is not an occult process. As a saying from India would have it, "No deed comes to fruition without effort. You cannot clap a single hand, nor effortless, do what you planned."

Indian cuisine is highly developed but not intricate. Neither stewed tiger livers nor shark-fin soups nor stuffed peacocks will be treated in this book. Also there is no cooking with wine or alcohol. The meats, vegetables and ingredients pressed into use are reared or grown in every country.

There is more variety in Indian food than any one Indian can hope to taste in a lifetime, or compress into one book. The dishes are carefully and precisely created and an abundance of joy goes into the simplest ones. There is the ambrosial Rice Briani with a treasure of sea food under it; the rich Kormas — noble elder brothers of the quotidian curries; spiced game rotated on the spit, or the clean taste of smoked eggplant flavored with a few dried pomegranate seeds and finished off with a whiff of saffron ground in rose water.

I remember a feast in the house of a friend where nuggets of spring lamb were spiced and each cooked separately in a big hollowed onion. At Srinagar, the capital of Kashmir, I once tasted superb spiced koftas or croquettes. One pound of butter had been pounded heroically into every pound of meat — and the dish turned out to be crisply dry. Most of all I recall a visit to the Himalayan kingdom of a friend, where a grouse was stuffed with fragrant herbs, lightly touched with spices, encased in dough and cooked underground with a day-long gently insistent fire above. The meat emerged as delicate as a rose leaf. There are elaborate recipes like these, and very simple ones too, which will change your idea of Indian food from something to serve once-in-a-while to a perennial favorite on your table.

Which brings me to the main point. Indian food is not just "curry" and Indian cooking depends on a personal measure of spices. The packaged curry powder is not used in India. The exported variety is often not made from the best spices, or the best combinations of them. The readily available individual spices, as easy to use as salt and pepper, are listed, with their qualities, in the chapter on meat cooking. The uses of the herbs and aromatics have been listed in the Rules for the Hearth.

Curry is a word which comes from the Hindustani: turcarri. In the colloquial it is shortened to "turri," which in the Anglo-Saxon usage is called "curry." The Indian makes his with separate spices. Once you have tried this you will no more use the packaged curry powder than you would accept another person's taste in the choice of your clothes. It is also easier and more economical to use individual spices. Instead of the monotony that comes from using ready-made curry powder, you will discover something that will make the mind soar. And that is what good food should do.

Knowing the spices will make your Indian cooking more fun and more varied. No two dishes on a menu will taste the same, because no two are spiced in the same way. Also, formal and informal entertaining will cease to be a chore. Indian food can, if necessary, be prepared the day before and kept in the deep-freeze or refrigerator. To do this, it is best to slightly undercook the dish by a few minutes, and place it in an airtight jar or cover it with foil. The time used in gently reheating (preferably in a double boiler or a chafing dish) will bring it to the finished state. Frozen cooked food can never be better than fresh-cooked food, but the slight deterioration is not really noticeable: it is more than offset by the time saved. When using food to be deep-frozen, reduce the quantity of spices given in the recipes by a fraction, as some spices may tend to intensify with the freezing.

Some of the best of the recipes which follow are from the Punjab, which is the Cordon Bleu region of Indian cooking. Others are from neighboring Kashmir with a distinguished and refined manner of dressing meat. From Bengal with its plethora of fine fish there are great delicacies. The cuisines of the Gangetic plain, the Deccan and South India are represented here. These authentic recipes will not be found in any one home in India. They are the result of assiduous tasting (which was supremely easy) and an industrious ferreting out of secrets. Many of the recipes are rare; from the time of the Mogul and earlier.

The tradition in India of cooking as a fine art is as old as the pre-Aryan Indus Empire contemporary with Egypt and Sumer. We have direct evidence from the Aryans who came into India about 2300 B.C. The Aryan hearth, as today, was the center of importance in family and community life. Then as now, the Aryans seemed inordinately fond of milk, cream, yoghurt and curds, butter and *ghee* (a clarified butter). Wild boar and other meats, game, fish, fowl and vegetables were cooked in the *caru* — a big black iron caldron. Many descriptions in the Veda depict a scene where flesh on forks hisses over the open fire. Other vessels bubble with broth and green herbs. Fish from the river is in the warming pots. Big-bellied brass and copper vessels are working their slow magic over many vegetables. The aroma of spices is everywhere, carving boards groan with their meats. In the *tandur*, the upright clay oven, whole-wheat, barley and other breads are being baked. These people who laid the foundations of Indian cooking knew the joy of living.

Food in India today is always good in the home, and rarely so in the restaurant. Many people hold restaurants in disdain, but the last few years have seen great improvements. For excellent food, however, superlative in refinement or good taste, it is the home one resorts to.

That is the way I learned good taste in food and other things: in the kitchen. There is in my memory the kitchen at home and the constant nocturnal forays I made through it savoring the fragrance of cooking food and observing the spicer, or *massalchi*, at work. These impressions of drying vegetables and prawns in the sun, of macerating and settling the pickles and chutneys, spring up full blown.

My Grandfather's Kitchen

But the influence I cherish most is the great kitchen and the hearth in my grandparents' house. It was a dream house, full five floors high, with innumerable rooms which lent themselves to endless games. The three-foot-thick walls and the dungeonlike staircases of stone furnished all the imps and goblins that a child wants and keeps as his own. There were quiet awesome corners with piles of books, closets full of bottles, dark jars, clocks that had stopped ticking; and many things each of which led into a private garden of speculation. During one of these explorations of rummaging, ferreting, dust-blowing and reading I managed to discover the catch of a secret door panel and a real secret passage, much to my grandfather's displeasure.

Shivering with excitement and private bliss, I would creep into the kitchen to eat. Most of us in the house did not eat in the dining room. My aunts and uncles sat, at least during those days, in the kitchen, an immense room with smoky beams and mellowed ceiling. At one end was the hearth, presided over by the cook whom we called Big Brother Dilla. With caste in India, class differences are few and slight. For children and grownups it was obligatory to address him with deference. Indeed he was charged with not only cooking, but mending our manners, lending his opinion in family affairs and keeping an inflexibly sharp eye on our general behavior.

The house was always full of guests, as many as half a dozen at a time. Some stayed for days and others for months. Some were busy with special affairs while others were marking time till plans should crystallize. Almost daily, clansmen and family friends drifted in with a felicitous lack of formality just before lunch or dinnertime. This was expected. Our kitchen formed the hub of a very Indian, happily haphazard and enormously vital life. On holidays there might have been more than twenty people for meals which I remember as gay, bantering and full of raillery.

The kitchen was a place of warmth and happy extroverted fun. We could enter it from eleven to two in the afternoons and Big Brother Dilla, comforting, solid, burly, with his generous hand and overflowing ladle of wonderful things, was the king of the festive hubbub. Only my grandfather, a patriarch with unique energy, had the greater voice. It was for him that Big Brother Dilla exhibited his culinary skill. For forty years (till the holocaust of India's division threw us all askew) he was part of all our childhood, adolescence and manhood. At his hands I have tasted better food than any; more delicious bread than is conceivable . . . and known the joys of discovery.

In Big Brother Dilla's kitchen, as in the traditional Indian kitchen, we sat on the ground, on carpets or rush mats gaily woven with strips of madder red, sienna and white. Food was served on big circular trays called *thāli* made of burnished steel, hammered brass or copper or polished silver. On them were several metal bowls, *katoris*. These were for the food. They may have contained meat, chicken, some vegetables, perhaps rice. There was whipped yoghurt in cool, fresh unglazed earthenware which was broken after each meal by the spicer (the *Saucier* in a French kitchen). I remember a little refrain about that.

Like pots of clay, the wicked friend
Is quick to smash and hard to mend:
Like pots of gold the righteous flash,
As quick to mend, as hard to smash.

I often sneaked the clay bowl out of the kitchen to break it ringingly against the garden wall. There were bowls for condiments, and a place for the dessert. The bread is laid on the thāli. It is served smoking hot, never cold. So was the food in our kitchen where it did not have to be transferred to a serving dish. Eating in a dining room, the food traditionally is carried in from the kitchen in just the quantity required. Food keeps hot in the *degchi,* or cooking casserole. Each thāli or circular tray takes the place of a table setting.

As in other homes, we ate with the forepart of the first two fingers and the thumb. Eating with knife and fork is unsuited to Indian food, people think, and not quite chic. So it becomes taboo to touch the cooking vessel or the thāli of another with either the eating hand or the other. The Indian does not, like the Chinese or the Arab, eat from a communal dish. Hands are washed, and feet too, before a person sits down for food. Orthodox people may even wash and bathe before meals and change all clothes worn in the street. This is all part of the Indian ritual. It is not rare to see religion in the kitchen. To repeat another of the verses from fables I listened to sitting in the kitchen, long before meals:

In case of horse or book or sword,
Of woman, man, lute or word,
The use or the uselessness depends,
On qualities the user lends.

No shoes were allowed in our kitchen, for one sat facing the hearth which was on the ground. When carpets were used one trod them with unsandaled feet, for carpets were never made to be walked on with shoes. Hands and mouth were washed before and after meals, as hygiene and as part of a ritual that most Indians perform. If done with honesty and with understanding it does vouchsafe an awareness of the interrelation of human activities and saves food from becoming an end in itself. This was one of the discoveries I made in my visits to my grandparents' home and Big Brother Dilla's kitchen.

I have never seen Big Brother Dilla appearing to do just nothing. Even when he was silent, which he mostly was, he was more communicative than most. With few words, he maintained intact the atmosphere of the kitchen; it was all of a piece.

Every day, with an air of infallibility, he made his way to the five-foot-high ocher clay tandur, set behind a sweet-smelling hedge at one end of the garden. With an enormous tray, balanced high on one brawny arm, the other free swinging, he carried the dough.

His bread-making was more than half the feast. The resinous headiness of the wood charred in the belly of the oven as the heat arose and swelled in trembling waves. Seen through it, the trees and the sky shook and pranced. In the huge, deep tray of little-hammer-tap brass polished to a milky patina with wood ashes, the dough had been made into smooth balls. The clay lid was on the oven and Big Brother Dilla, as usual giving no sign of my presence, waited for the heat to mount and bank as he liked it. All this was a matter of gently befriending the fire.

Then with a quick movement the lid was off. The pink mouth of the oven cradled its brightness. It gave off a muted hum. Flattening the dough, Big Brother Dilla poised over the oven mouth the wet white-moon of a cake. There was a hush, a moment, and he turned his hand briefly in the horrendous oven and stuck the dough to the side. Then another and another. Easily done, it was like going into the mouth of a dragon by invitation and emerging unhurt. Often he would remain hovering over the oven, dough in hand, waiting for the small fractional moment when the fire and heat would accept him. Again in, with the bare hand right in the mouth of the coiled fire which I could feel and hear singing. There was that moment when he could step over the line and back again: a wedge into something unknown and mystifying. How easy, how graceful, and so miraculous.

A little boy who found it easy to get into a new world suddenly, swiftly, found it impossible to return from these wonder-touching experiences without wanting to share them. A wonderland is lonely and a child has no way of knowing that loneliness is the path to this world of wonderful things nor how that loneliness can be reconciled with happiness.

There was Big Brother Dilla working an act of secret magic, opening up his own world and managing to share it also with us all. With hand and touch and sight, his was a felicity that belonged to both worlds; of other men and his own.

Watching him, I saw suddenly how he made the fire innocuous; how he made a wedge in the obdurateness of something inhuman. That day I was suddenly very happy. Laughter burst out of me. "Yes, yes, yes," I said irrepressibly, and stood still. From high overhead came the cry of a free-wheeling hawk, piercing the frail integument of smoke, shimmering haze, heat of the tandur and magic-making. I ran into the house for lunch, happy with the recognition.

Food that day, I remember well, had never tasted so good. Many other things became sweeter. People and their voices turned nicer and clearer.

It is a discovery that may take a lifetime to complete. Its meaning comes, sometimes slowly, imperceptibly, at other times quite forgotten. But when it is there it makes everything happier, and brightens me with a feeling of glee.

And that is the happy factor in Indian cooking, and in life. An old saying goes, "All this must be done with great glee." That is how the Indians take their cooking and eating. So here, with great glee, are laid bare the simple secrets of this food.

CHAPTER 2

Rules for the Hearth

ONCE I knew a cook in India who could carve a braised grouse and make it seem like plucking a delicate spray of flowers. It is to him that I owe the keen edge of my appreciation of spices. These aromatics, spices and condiments are the essence of good Indian cooking. It is essential to know something about them, and also keep them on your kitchen shelves. Among these spices there are many that are regularly used in the American kitchen.

The main spices are turmeric (haldi), coriander (dhanyia), cummin or cumin (zeera), fresh green ginger (adrak), dry ground ginger (sundth), cloves (laung), cinnamon (dal chini), cardamon (elachi), mustard seed (rai), fennel (sounf), lovage (ajwain), poppy seeds (khus-khus), and black onion seeds. The last three are little used. Spices are always stronger in dried form than in fresh. The spice in seed form keeps better than in powdered, but is liable to rot in a damp place. Spices can be powdered through a fine grinder, in a mortar and pestle, and excellently with the modern blender.

Turmeric is always powdered fine. Coriander used in these recipes is powdered fine, bruised, or crushed in mortar and pestle, except where otherwise noted. Cummin is also used finely powdered, bruised or crushed. Dried ginger is always used in powdered form. Green or fresh ginger is used as in recipes.

Among the aromatics or herbs are sage, rosemary and thyme, all robust like orégano. These are best used with meats. Delicate ones like sweet basil, which the Indians grow prettily green in the courtyards of their houses and in gardens, are considered auspicious. Oddly enough the Ancient Greeks regarded this herb as evil. Chervil, tarragon and parsley are in this delicate group, as are poppy seeds and sesame seeds. There are a few not to be found outside India. They are too rarefied and need not worry us. The laurel or bay leaf (tej-pata) is also in this group of herbs which give a gentle, aromatic rather than a savory spiced fragrance.

In the sweet seasonings I would include nutmeg and mace, for they are rarely used with salt in Indian cooking. Honey, white sugar, brown sugar and confectioner's sugar are the basic items in sweet seasonings.

The saline or the salt seasonings are the sea salts, rock salts and various spiced salts. In using them it is well to remember that some free-pouring salts may have a small addition of perfectly harmless chemical powders to enable them to withstand humidity. These salts are less saline. For this reason I have not as a rule indicated the exact amount to use in the recipes. I personally prefer the flavor and effect of crushed rock salt crystals of the kosher type.

Acid seasonings may be unflavored vinegar and tarragon vinegar, used for both cooking and dressings — other vinegars are not used for cooking — or lemon and lime juice, which are used most of all in Indian cooking. There are three others which can occasionally be found in New York markets and I mention them in case the gourmet likes to have these on his kitchen shelves: dried pomegranate seeds, dried tamarind, and the powder of tart, green mangoes. Their use will be given with the recipes.

Hot seasonings are cayenne, dried red chili, chili powder,

paprika, black and white pepper, and green chili peppers.

Chief among the pungent seasonings are various types of onions. The small white and the yellow ones are used in Indian cooking. The Spanish onion has practically no flavor. Shallots, horseradish and garlic conclude this list. Onions are used for practically every one of the recipes in this book. Those who do not like onions need not quake, for the onions in the finished recipe have no smell or raw taste. They are meant to add to the flavor. Garlic is used sparingly in the best Indian cooking. Indeed many assert that garlic must be in evidence only as an indefinable flavor. Some recipes frankly avail themselves of garlic, and in certain parts of India garlic is used in a way reminiscent of the Calabrians and the Sicilians who even eat it raw on bread.

Garlic is well known for its properties that contribute to well-being in man, but it is difficult to realize its potency. I found this out not in cooking but trying to scare up some recalcitrant partridges in a remote section of northern India. With a few friends, I had been after some partridges for a small banquet where the main dish was to be a special Partridge Pellao. Having lingered too long over the pre-dawn breakfast, we arrived late and spent several futile hours in the fields. Eventually we wandered into a small village where a farmer, noting our chagrin, promised us partridge if we would stay and share his midday meal of creamy lentils and smoking-hot whole-wheat bread.

While we sat and talked the farmer's wife boiled a small pan of garlic bulbs. Taking these to a nearby field he strewed them around indiscriminately. Presently the partridges came out of hiding. From a distance we watched the birds tearing down the field and pecking with relish at the savory food. After a quick, hectic gobbling (these birds were no gourmets, I decided) they all scattered, skittering across the field instead of flying off. But before they could make cover at least a dozen slowed down, went groggily around in circles and lay down. With a cry the farmer ran to the field and scooped up the stupefied birds in a cloth. "Boiled garlic," he laughed, "does not sprout in the fields, but it lays these tricky rascals out in rows." He kept two and offered us the rest, saying, "I'm no hunter but I know my game."

"And your onions," I added.

We were no hunters that day but we had our banquet and a lesson in the use of garlic.

Onions too, when not cooked with spices, are powerful aromatics. The story from India of "The Onion Thief" has also found its way to the West. A man caught stealing onions was given the choice of paying a hundred rupees, getting a hundred cudgel blows, or eating a hundred onions; he chose at first the onions and with eyes streaming and stomach in torment, begged for the cudgeling, and with the first stroke chose the money fine.

Spices, onions, garlic and all aromatics in India are cooked with ghee (clarified butter). Butter is the nearest substitute but burns more easily. Oil is not much used in Indian cooking, except for fish. Gourmets know the wonderful taste oil can give to fish. The best of all these oils is the mustard oil of northern India. There is no other oil in India or elsewhere which will bear comparison. However, there are certain sections of India where oil is used as much as ghee.

Indian cooking is like French cooking. It is butter cooking as contrasted to the oil cooking of the Italians. This is naturally a matter of taste. The Indians believe that oil, save for special cases (notably in fish cookery), has a strong odor of its own which can overwhelm the fragrance of spices and the taste of the food. Ghee has the advantage of a much higher burning point than oil, and the mellowness of the essence of butter which it is. Ghee, from the health point of view, is excellent for the blood and an incomparable body builder. From the times of the Vedic Age the people of India have been singing the praises of ghee and discovering in it properties for the body and the brain, quite apart from its food value. It is ghee that has made the North Indian Sikhs the healthiest men in the world and their physical stamina a byword.

As a Sikh and a North Indian I cannot subscribe to oil. But many Indians do. One man's viewpoint is as valid as another's. So if oil is what you use in cooking, keep it always at hand. The oils that can be used are the usual ones: olive oil, cottonseed oil, vegetable oils, all other edible oils and margarine. Margarine and vegetable shortening are a good substitute for both butter and ghee.

The flours are the same as in the United States: white flour, whole-wheat flour, farina. The Indians also use maize (sweet corn flour), but whole-wheat flour is most commonly used. With it one makes an unleavened bread and the recipes will delight most people. Flour should be sifted finely before being used to make the dough.

Lemons and occasionally oranges are used in Indian cooking. Lemon rinds come in often for kababs, and stuffing for certain meats. This rind is used like the zest, meaning only the uppermost rind free of the white membrane. Lemon skins are sometimes sun-dried and kept for use. Some households scald, drain and dry them thoroughly and store them. Usually lemons are prepared fresh and at the last moment. Most Indian lemons are the shape of the American lime, but canary-yellow in color. The skin is much more delicate, and one variety called *kagazi-nimbu*, or chiffon lemons, have skins delicate and tender enough to be eaten. With a grilled or poached fish this is a great pleasure.

Despite the spread of modern knowledge many people still hold spices to be harmful. Spices however are antiseptic, soothing, and carminative in effect. That, as much as taste, was probably responsible originally for their use with food. Dining with a friend in Paris, I was aghast to hear that he had never touched black pepper. My efforts to explain the goodness of peperin in pepper made little headway.

Information about the medicinal qualities of spices was more prevalent a few hundred years ago than in this age of universal education. Ginger is a wonderful stomachic. Henry the Eighth of England was well aware of this and on one occasion sent it to the poor and sick of London. Turmeric is used for sterilizing. Cummin was especially imported by the Ancient Egyptians from India in the days of the great Indus Valley empire of 4000 B.C. to preserve their mummies. It was some of these spices that Sheba bore as gifts to Solomon. The Greeks no less than the Jews used spices for medicine. Spices became known to Europe of the Middle Ages as a preservative of food and meat in the days of no refrigeration. Indians, by the way, do not preserve their food. The many uses of spices in perfumes, medicine and some of the celebrated liqueurs of Europe is a fascinating subject.

All the spices are pure vegetable stuff with no synthetic qualities. Saffron, one of the few spices with no real nutritive or antiseptic qualities, can color 700,000 times its own weight in water. It takes the stigmata of 70,000 flowers to yield one ounce of the precious stuff. Like turmeric and most spices saffron is used for dyeing, and enters intimately into much of life in India.

The medicinal quality of spices in Europe was discovered in France in the early eighteenth century. During a visitation of bubonic plague, there went about in the streets of Paris four enterprising young men rifling the houses of the dead and dying. When caught they were asked to account for their immunity to the dreaded plague. On promise of clemency they gave out their secret: drinking copiously of a concoction made from cinnamon, cloves, camphor, pepper, garlic and wine mixed with vinegar. This is the story known as "The Vinegar of the Four Thieves." These reprehensible but clever young men were the precursors of Lister and Pasteur and the development of modern antiseptics.

The kitchen equipment and utensils used in Indian cooking are basically the same as in American and European cooking. Some casseroles of the 1½ quart, 2½ quart, and larger sizes, will be required. Dutch ovens (lined) of the same capacity, for cooking on the fire, will also be used. (Earthenware casseroles of the heavy type lend themselves admirably.) I would eschew cast-iron vessels entirely. The spices may produce a reaction from the unlined metal; vinegar, lemon juice, acids, tomatoes and garlic invariably do. In India brass, burnished steel and copper vessels are used for cooking. These are always lined with silver or tin which is renewed as soon as it shows signs of wearing off. Today aluminum is being used by some. I have tried them myself and found them satisfactory. But as substitutes only. It is necessary that all vessels used be of the thickest base and sides available. When we discuss the principles of Indian cooking techniques you will see why. Apart from the cooking vessels, cooking spoons, ladles, wooden ladles, and the usual sieves, graters, food grinders, etc., are all that we will need. All this and more is generally found in an American kitchen.

In the *samband* or *mise en place* I would recommend keeping the following always in stock for permanent use: the main spices listed above, lemon rind, fresh lemons, milk and yoghurt, butter or shortening or cooking oil, flour, both refined and whole wheat; also split-pea flour. If this is not procurable locally, it can be made by roasting split peas (yellow) in an ungreased skillet and evenly browning them. Then pulverize in a mortar and pestle or the modern blender. A meat grinder does equally well. Sift fine and keep in a jar for future use. I recommend split-pea flour as it is infinitely superior to refined flour in making sauces, roux and for other preparations for binding food. You will find this flour of great help in purely American cooking.

Other essentials are saffron, rose water, coconut, salt, pepper, various cayennes and both whole chilis and ground chili powder, dried garlic, and dehydrated onion flakes for the times you find yourself short. A few nuts such as blanched almonds should be always at hand. For the method of blanching them the Indian way, see page 267. If you can get some tamarind imported from India, lay aside a little of this. Fairly good tamarind, from Jamaica, of Indian transplanting (as are the mangoes, ginger and some other ingredients) is usually available in New York and some other American cities.

Here I would like to add that ginger figures much in Indian cooking. Where fresh or green ginger is not available, powdered ginger may be substituted, keeping in mind the difference in quality. A 1-inch square of green ginger root equals approximately a level ¼ teaspoon of powdered ginger.

In the following recipes, the spices or seeds should be ground for use. The ready-ground form in a recipe is indicated by the letter (P).

Just another word about spices and their use. Taste them individually in food and you will get to know them.

Tarragon and marjoram, for instance, are wonderful with spinach, salads and stews. Also use them with tomatoes, squash and green vegetables.

Try marjoram on hashed brown potatoes.

Fennel and anise cut the salt in herring and salmon.

Nutmeg is good in creamed dishes, soups and cooked oysters.

Allspice is fine for beef stews.

Ginger on a leg of lamb, rubbed in with oil or butter, is delicious.

Try using a little turmeric with buttery carrots.

Dill goes with yoghurt, sour cream and cream, and hot or cold cooked beets.

Poppy seeds for boiled potatoes, salads and string beans . . . try others yourself, for this is one place where familiarity does not breed contempt.

Remember that strong spices like cummin and coriander

can be used in the same dish, but the more delicate aromatics and herbs tend to cancel each other. The latter are a jealous tribe despite their sweetness. Few dishes can be made with more than one herb. This paradox is like many we encounter in life. One of India's many animal fables tells us:

> The fruit tree's branch by very wealth
> Of fruit is bended low;
> The peacock's feathered pride compels
> A sluggish gait and slow;
> The blooded horse that wins his race
> Must like a cow be led;
> The good in goodness often finds
> An enemy to dread.

When using oil for cooking, warm it, and cook it gently for a few minutes to allow the raw taste to escape. This will make an appreciable difference.

CHAPTER 3

Indian Cooking Techniques and Styles

(The Preparation)

THE TECHNIQUES listed here constitute the basic principles of Indian cooking. Many of these styles of dressing and preparing food are similar to those in American and European cooking. The cooking styles and the recipes are dependent on various cooking techniques, which I will deal with briefly here.

The basic curry, called *Turcarri* or *Turri,* is the one from which all others stem. The basic curry of meat or egg or vegetable is light, employs few spices and has much thin, not thickened gravy. The gravy is often more delicious than the food cooked in it. This curry is the cheapest and one of the best. It is never found in Western restaurants.

Variations from the basic curry include the rich, unctuous *Korma* curries. These styles are with little gravy. More spices are used and also more butter. Little water or liquid is used in the preparation. It is dry cooking. The Korma has infinite variations and methods of finishing.

The *Doh-Peeazah* means literally two (*doh*) and onions (*peeaz*). This refers to a dry curry made with plenty of onions. The classic Doh-Peeazah uses a certain quantity of ground onions and an equal quantity of sliced onions at a later stage. This is a doubling of the onion contents in the meat.

Bhoona meats are fried and then steamed under tight cover in their own juices. The oven-baked meats are the same as in America. They are cooked in the *tandur* (clay oven) or in a heavy pot of thickest metal with a fire below and on the lid which is clapped tight during the cooking.

The meats cooked on the spit over an open fire or on a barbecue grill furnish some of the fanciest Indian dishes.

The *Koftas* are meat balls and croquettes. They are prepared variously; broiled, baked, fried, as curry, as Korma, barbecued and other ways as shown in the recipes.

The *Kababs* form an important section of this book and of Indian cookery. This term refers to cooking chicken or meat whole or in small pieces on the spit or in the tandur. Also many are made from ground meat and meat mixed with lentils. The latter are generally called *Keema* (ground meat) Kababs to distinguish them from Whole Kababs. Kababs are never used in a curry.

Preparations

THE NAMES of the principal cooking techniques are: *Sookha Bhoona* (Sauté), *Geela Bhoona* (Braised), and *Puccka Bhoona* (Poeled, or dry fried).

Poaching and steaming is the same as in other cuisines. Steaming is often used in Indian cooking but poaching rarely. The Indians believe that food should never be served "plain boiled" except for the ill.

The rice cookery of India is unique. The three main styles, the many variations, and the techniques of cooking are described in the chapter on rice. This should be of absorbing interest to Americans and all gourmets.

Batter frying is used for savories, and sometimes fish.

Sweets and desserts, chutneys and pickles have their own

methods of preparation which are best described along with the recipes.

I will recapitulate for ourselves the important points of each style of food preparation. There is also one special Indian technique called *Bhogar,* listed here, which I have not found outside India, and not in many Indian kitchens.

Since the technique for cooking meats and vegetables is the same, I shall refer to methods of cooking meat in this section as covering all food. When butter is called for, any cooking fat of good flavoring can be used.

In the basic curry, the meat is gently fried and well browned in butter. Water is added. After a brisk boil the whole is simmered, covered, till done.

In the *Korma* curry, the meat is similarly fried and browned, but water is only sprinkled in, a spoonful at a time, to prevent the meat from scorching. The slight moisture is reduced to a glaze. At that moment, and not earlier, some more water is sprinkled in. The process is repeated until the food is cooked.

The *Sookha Bhoona* or sauté is made as follows. Butter is heated and the meat is frizzled. This is dry frying of meat cut in small pieces. It is necessary to *sear* the meat then finish the cooking on lower heat. In some cases the Sookha Bhoona may be finished in the oven. This type of Bhoona requires that the cooking be done quickly. Naturally only thin small pieces of meat will do here. The French sauté requires that the meat be lifted from the vessel and the pan washed out with some liquid like wine for finishing the gravy. Sookha Bhoona, the Indian sauté, never employs any liquid for dissolving the gravy.

The *Geela Bhoona* or braising is the same as in other cuisines. This technique is often poorly executed. It requires attention and care. Above all it requires "touch" meaning plenty of practice and the resolve to do it well. The Geela Bhoona does not require that the meat be cut in small pieces. Less butter than in the sauté is needed. Unlike the French braising, Indian braising does not make use of larding. The small amount of butter does the job. Also Indian meat is always lean, never fat. All skin or fell is removed before cooking, especially in braising. The meat is seldom marinated as sometimes is done in the French braising. Indian braising requires *dry* meat. If meat has to be marinated for special recipes (as often indicated for meats cooked on the rotisserie or open fire) the marinade is drained and the meat carefully dried.

Geela Bhoona is one of the most important ways of preparing Indian meats. First the butter to be used is heated, and when hot the herbs, aromatics and spices are added. These are gently fried and kept turning all the time. Overfrying spices will make the dish pungent and bitter. Now the meat is placed on the spices and fried also. Another method combines the meat and spices and fries them till they are ready for the braising liquid. In the second method the meat will get a longer frying period. This makes for a difference in taste.

After the frying is completed and the meat is well browned — but never scorched — the braising liquid, an Indian court-bouillon or plain water is put in, a few spoonfuls at a time. The lid is secured tight. When the liquid in the cooking vessel has been reduced to a minimum, some more liquid is put in. This process is repeated three or four times. After the fourth time, and according to the quantity of the meat, water or court-bouillon, enough to partly cover it, is added and the meat will be finished when this moisture is reduced to a minimum. Finally, the Geela Bhoona can be glazed by uncovering it and letting it stand on the merest suspicion of a fire for a few minutes, or placed in a moderate oven for a similar time.

This technique is not very different from braising as practiced in Western cooking. But where most people go wrong in braising is in adding all the braising liquid to the meat at one time. And in one fell swoop the meat has had its quietus.

When vegetables are to be added to the meat, in Indian cooking, they may be browned separately and then added or they may be browned with the meat, or, again, the vegetables may be placed with the meat for braising without browning them first. This is determined by the quality and the texture of the vegetable and the style of cooking desired. The recipes in the book will show all three variations in cooking (braising) meat and vegetables together.

As in French braising, so in Indian: at the last stage of braising, when the liquid is almost dried, we must watch it carefully. Now the meat must be turned all the time to prevent it from scorching or sticking to the vessel. The meat will be thoroughly impregnated with the spices and the sauce. The last of the braising moisture remains like a coating on the meat instead of evaporating. This is true for both Indian food and any kind of braised American food. Remember to start moistening, after the initial browning, with a *little* liquid. Repeat three times. Moisten again and cook *covered,* as throughout the whole process. Stir thoroughly each time the liquid is added, and more often if required. Remember also the hint for the last few minutes before the braise is ready. Also, never let the spices burn or overcook. Furthermore, use the smallest vessel you can. A large vessel necessitates the use of too much liquid for the amount of meat. One last word — white meats, young lamb, tender chicken if overcooked will be spoiled. Older and all red meat will not. Some meats (the quantity matters here also) require a long cooking time. In this case do not hesitate to repeat the moistening more than four times — but always with little liquid at a time.

The *Puccka Bhoona* (Poeled) indicates meat prepared by dry frying. It is cooked in butter and no liquid is added. If any liquid is used, it is to cook the herbs and spices and the base of onions or tomatoes. The meat is not added until any liquid has dried. The sliced onions are mixed with the requisite spices and herbs. These are gently fried in butter and any water or liquid used to cook and bind the spices must be dried out by further cooking. The meat is placed in this base and fried with it till nicely brown. Cover and cook in a very low oven. No moisture in the meat is permitted. The vessel is uncovered for the last few minutes, returned to the oven and left there to brown nicely before serving.

The treatment of grills, barbecues and food cooked on the spit over an open fire is discussed in the chapter on this kind of food.

We have seen that these types of cooking are radically different from the usual kind that passes for Indian food. No flour is used to thicken the gravy or to make the sauces. Thickening is achieved by the mode of preparation and the ingredients selected for a certain style of cooking.

One of the most unusual and cleverest methods of preparing food is the technique of *Bhogar*. It is simple and the results are exceptionally good. There is no better way of locking in the flavor of the meat. The Bhogar may be tried not with Indian food but American also.

The word *bhogar* is derived from the Sanskrit and here it means to assimilate and bring about a transformation. The word has many other meanings and subtle ramifications.

The Bhogar Technique: the meat is placed in a heavy, thick casserole where the butter had been gently melted. The spices are added and the food is simmered over low heat with the lid of the vessel sealed so that it is airtight. This "hermetic" sealing is essential to the method. No steam from within is allowed to escape. After a few minutes of cooking gently, the vessel is given a good shake and replaced on the heat. The effect of this is to drive the heat upward and the closed lid in turn drives it back. The savor and fragrance penetrate the meat. This bhogar is repeated from three to five times during the cooking period. The proper bhogar requires heat on the *lid* also to enable the flavor of the food to be really driven back into the food. The favorite Indian method is to place some live coals on the lid of the vessel. The lid is generally flat, not concave. This part with the live coals will not be easy to achieve in modern kitchens and may, alas, be eliminated.

The bhogar is not a stirring and a tossing but a gentle definite forward and backward shaking. It releases the aroma and the hermetically sealed lid drives it back. Indian cooks use thick dough to seal the joint of the lid and the vessel. If dough is not at hand, use a tape which will do a good job. Make the tape fold tight, and many times around the part to be sealed. For this kind of bhogar the vessel is not opened, or the bhogar is ruined, till it is cooked. This is *waterless* bhogar. It requires practice and confidence, for the meat cooks unseen. You may experiment a few times by opening the lid and taking a quick look to see if the meat is in danger of scorching. One or two attempts will promote enough confidence to try it on your choicest meat without having to open the lid.

Another bhogar is for cooking with liquids. The way to do it in specific cases is given with the recipes. The technique is as follows. Fry the meat with some of the spices in one vessel. Add the liquid and simmer for a while. Then remove and strain the gravy or liquid into another vessel. Keep aside. Also keep meat aside. In the vessel in which the meat was fried, melt a little butter and fry some of the spices. Add the meat. Cover and bhogar it a few times, till the meat is cooked. *Now* uncover and add the gravy which has been set aside, and finish cooking them together till the food is properly cooked.

It will be observed that in the dry bhogar the food is fried, covered, sealed and given several bhogars till it is properly cooked. In the second bhogar, the meat is fried, simmered a little while with some liquid. Then it is removed, and the gravy is also set aside. This is the crucial moment, when the meat is given several bhogars in a sealed vessel. The liquid is replaced and the cooking finished.

This technique is simpler than its description. It entails a little more trouble than usual methods. But the bhogar is not for every recipe. It is reserved for some delectable creations that demand the bhogar to manifest their finest flavor.

CHAPTER 4

Stocks, Sauces and Binding Agents, Soups

SOUPS have never played a large part in Indian cuisine. The menu does not seem to need them. The use of soups is bitterly debated by many famous gourmets in Europe. One opinion has it that soups do not belong to *haute cuisine* and may never be served with dinner and only occasionally for lunch. The modern soup as known in Europe and in France has been in existence not more than one hundred years. Before that time it was the whole meal. Nothing else was served with it in an average home. The few Indian soups are interesting and very good. All of them will also lend themselves to the American dinner.

There are few sauces, for each Indian dish has its own sauce which it develops at the time it is cooking. Unlike the French cuisine where the stocks and sauces are the essentials of good cooking, Indian cooking does not rely on separate stocks except in special instances. Sauces are made for certain steamed foods and others that are cooked on the spit or barbecued. In French cooking, without proper stocks you cannot make good food. In Indian cooking you risk bad food by not properly cooking the spices and the liquids. Indian stocks *are* used, however, for the ambrosial *Pellaos* and other rice creations. In point of truth, most Indian rice recipes lean heavily on the stocks of varying consistency called *Yakhni* and glazes called *Garhi Yakhni*. These are not to be confused with an Indian court-bouillon called *Akni*.

Stocks

AKNI I

This is a court-bouillon used for cooking, and for steaming fish, vegetables and meat. Whenever a recipe requires water, have some Akni ready and use it instead. A safe guide is to gauge the amount of spices being used in the recipe. Akni is best where the food is meant to be cooked with very few spices. Certain recipes in this book that require Akni have this indicated.

1 small onion
1 clove garlic
1⅛ tablespoons green ginger (⅛ teaspoon powdered)
1½ teaspoons coriander seeds
1½ teaspoons fennel seeds

Cut the onion fine; mash the garlic and ginger together in a mortar and pestle. Also crush the coriander and fennel seeds. Place these in a small bag of muslin or any other close-woven but diaphanous material and boil it in a quart of cold water. Simmer for ¼ hour and cool. The liquid may be kept in a jar for some days if required. The bag is to be thrown away.

AKNI II

½ teaspoon cummin
½ teaspoon mustard seeds
1½ teaspoons thyme (P)
1 small onion
1⅛ tablespoons green ginger (⅛ teaspoon powdered)
6 bay leaves

Pound the cummin, mustard seeds and thyme in the mortar and pestle. Bruise the onion and ginger. Add the bay leaves and tie up the whole in a small muslin bag. Place in a quart of cold water and boil for ¼ hour. Cool and bottle for use. May be kept a few days.

Sauces

LIVER PARSLEY SAUCE

1 pound liver
Akni (p. 28)
2 medium-sized onions
4 tablespoons butter
1 clove garlic
1 cup stock (beef, lamb, veal, or use bouillon cubes)
3 peppercorns
1 teaspoon parsley
salt

Clean and boil the liver in just enough Akni to cover. Replenish liquid when required. When tender, strain the liver through a sieve, or use an electric blender, or a meat grinder with a fine adjustment.

Slice and fry the onions in butter. Add the garlic, well bruised, after 5 minutes' frying. Cook for 5 minutes more. Then add the stock and simmer for ½ hour. Strain the liquid and pour over liver, adding the peppercorns, ground, and the parsley. Cook until parsley is tender, no longer. Serve hot.

Instead of adding parsley, substitute 1 teaspoon grated lemon rind (yellow skin, not the white membrane) and ½ teaspoon lemon juice. Into this mixture put 1 teaspoon butter dipped in flour or rice flour (p. 33), and salt. Add 3 ground peppercorns. Simmer 10 minutes and serve hot.

These sauces, like the others, are meant for recipes in this book. They may also be used for American food and made the base for dips with cocktail snacks. The Liver Parsley sauce is exceptionally good and tastes like liquid pâté de foie gras.

CURRY SAUCE FOR LEFTOVERS OR COLD MEATS

1 tablespoon butter
2 onions
½ teaspoon turmeric
1 tablespoon flour or rice flour (p. 33)
¾ tablespoon green ginger (¼ teaspoon powdered)
1 clove garlic
2 inches stick cinnamon
½ tablespoon cummin
2 cups stock
salt
pinch of cayenne

Melt the butter in a skillet or double boiler. Brown onions, chopped fine. Add turmeric, flour or rice flour, ginger, garlic, well bruised, cinnamon and cummin. Fry gently for 3 minutes and add stock. Simmer and thicken by reducing. When about ready add salt and cayenne. Cool and pour over leftovers. The meat can be warmed in a double boiler and the sauce served hot.

ESSENCE OF CHILI SAUCE

¼ pound whole dried red chilis
1 teaspoon salt
vinegar to make a paste

Roast chilis in an iron skillet. Pound very fine. A blender is excellent here. Put the powdered chilis in a bottle with stopper, with the salt and as much vinegar as needed to make a paste. Expose to the sun for 5 days, or place in a gently preheated oven (100°) for an hour every day. If the oven has been heated for cooking, use the expiring oven. An oven with a pilot light is very good, for this heat (if sunshine is not available) is the best for curing this sauce and many others in this book. After this heat treatment of the chilis, pass them through a muslin cloth or cheesecloth folded four times. Add more vinegar to make the consistency that of a thick sauce. Keep for use with other sauces and gravies; also for adding to the Indian recipes in this book.

PARSLEY SAUCE

4 tablespoons butter
¾ tablespoon green ginger
bunch of parsley
2 tablespoons capers
1 cup white stock (or chicken bouillon cubes)
2 tablespoons flour or rice flour (p. 33)
pinch of black pepper
salt

Heat butter and lightly brown onion. Meanwhile place parsley and capers (Indians use tamarind) in a bowl. To the browned onion in the saucepan add the stock, free of all fat. Thicken with flour or rice flour. Add pinch of pepper and salt. Simmer to the right consistency, then add parsley and capers. Cook for no more than a minute, since parsley overcooked is an abomination.

LOBSTER SAUCE

1 2-pound cooked lobster, with coral
¼ pound butter
salt
pinch of cayenne
1 tablespoon mustard seeds

Pound the coral and rub through a sieve or use an electric blender. Mix with the butter, then add the lobster meat cut fine and pounded (or use blender). Add salt, cayenne, crushed mustard seeds and simmer together. Do not boil. Serve hot.

INDIAN WORCESTERSHIRE SAUCE

This recipe also was given to me by a cook in India who knew both Indian and Continental cuisine.

1 quart vinegar
4 ounces raisins
4 blades mace
1 ounce garlic
1 teaspoon pepper (P)
12 cloves
2 tablespoons green ginger (¾ teaspoon P)
8 dried whole red chilis
1 tablespoon salt
¾ pound sugar
2 inches stick cinnamon

Grind fine all ingredients except the sugar. The blender, mortar and pestle or a grinder will do. Moisten the ingredients with some of the vinegar as you grind them with one-half the sugar. Brown the remaining sugar, then add the rest of the vinegar and the ground ingredients. Boil them gently for 10 minutes. Strain through fine cloth. Cool and keep for use.

Binding Agents (Powders and Flours)

HERE are the recipes for split-pea flour, rice flour and powdered shrimps. Split-pea flour and also chick-pea flour are available in many stores, including the New York Armenian grocery stores. The dried shrimps, imported from India, may be somewhat harder to obtain. It is worth the slight trouble to make them. They will be endlessly useful for soups, canapés, cream and cheese dips, quick chafing dish dinners, a kind of Indian shrimp and cheese fondue, mushroom dishes and many others you will think of yourself.

CHENNAH *(Split-Pea Flour)*

Roast a pound (or any quantity) of yellow split peas or chick peas in a heavy skillet, preferably of cast iron. Keep turning them to prevent scorching and to roast them evenly. Cool. Put through a grinder 4 times, and then through a fine sieve. Place in a tight, covered jar. Keep for future use. This chennah is remarkable for fish cookery. Recipes in the book will tell how to wash fish with it. No better method exists for ridding fish of its smell and unwanted oils and exudations. As a binder for making a roux in a sauce, it will provide a pleasant change. It has no pasty flavor.

Chennah is made from many kinds of dried peas and lentil-type beans. Lima beans, chick peas and marrow beans may also be used and kept in stock in the kitchen.

RICE FLOUR

Roast a pound of rice in a heavy cast-iron skillet. Handle the roasting with care, for the rice must be dried without coloring it unevenly. Cool it and pass through a fine grinder. The blender does well too. Powder it very fine and sift thoroughly. Preserve in a jar, well stoppered.

SHRIMP POWDER

Prawns or shrimps are used for this recipe. To dry shrimps, shell raw shrimps and cover in plenty of salt for 1 day. Then string the shrimps, using a big needle and thread. Hang them to dry in the sun for 15 to 20 days. This is the best method, as the sun has gentle heat and is also sterilizing in its effect. Where it is not possible to dry the shrimps in the sun, use may be made of the oven. One with a pilot light will serve nicely. In the absence of this, it may be done by heating the oven gently and then turning off the heat. Place the shrimps in the oven and leave there to dry. This may be repeated for some days till the shrimps are completely dried out.

To make the powder, roast the dried shrimps in a heavy cast-iron skillet. Remove and pound fine in a blender, mortar and pestle, or grind fine. While pounding add 8 peppercorns and 1 teaspoon grated nutmeg for every pound of shrimp. After pounding pass through a fine sieve. Bottle for future use.

It may seem odd to say that the finest taste in food can never be known till sensation is abandoned. One must develop the power to escape from both apathy and abandonment to sensation; to be superior to both and so discover the real savor in art and food and all else. The person with only an aesthetic appreciation of what pleases the eye or ear or the taste is merely a man who is too weak to stand up against pleasure and pain, thus suffering a loss in true and boundless pleasure. In India we hear much about true pleasure. "A woman in love shall not be shaken by pleasure and pain. She must refuse nothing (to the one she loves) and yet never fall" — is a viewpoint that touches on all other matters.

Without superior discrimination there is no superior taste. To me, the real connoisseur, in some ways, is the common man in India. Hapless and without money or merely not within reaching distance of food, he will sit down to eat a scrap of bread or a few berries, a handful of roasted peas with a bowl of fresh, cool water and consider it a banquet, a bounty of nature and eminently satisfying. When there is good food he will have it "with great glee." In this manner the whole question of good taste and good food seem to fall into place.

Soups

ALTHOUGH there is not much variety in Indian soups, I hope our gourmets will be pleased with them. They have not been greatly developed, for reasons explained, and are very much in the position of a beautiful woman with no poet passing by.

The first is an almond soup that I tasted during a journey to the Himalaya, one of the best.

BADAM SHOURWA (*Almond Soup*)

1 knuckle veal
2 slices ham
thyme
pepper
1 chicken, simmered in Akni (p. 28)
¼ pound blanched almonds
6½ tablespoons cream
1 tablespoon arrowroot

Make a stock (enough for six people) of veal knuckle and ham. Season with thyme and freshly ground black pepper. The stock, as in French cooking, is of primary importance in Indian soups. Make your stock simmer, skim and clear, strain and finish carefully and with love.

Take the meat off the chicken; slice and pound in a mortar and pestle (or use blender or grinder). Pound the almonds and mix with pounded meat, adding the cream (or milk blended with 2 egg yolks). *Force* this mixture through a cloth. Mix the arrowroot with a little stock to form a paste; then gradually add the rest of the stock, stirring carefully. Do not allow to boil. Serve immediately. For 6.

If arrowroot is not available, 2 or 3 tablespoons of butter will do.

COCONUT SOUP

- 2 coconuts
- 2 quarts clear white stock
- 4 egg yolks
- 1 tablespoon arrowroot or rice flour (p. 33)
- 1 blade mace

This soup really requires fresh coconut, but if canned or packaged coconut is used it should be blanched in boiling water and washed thoroughly, unless there is a packaged coconut with no addition of sugar.

Grate the coconuts fine. Place in saucepan with the stock and mace. Simmer gently ½ hour. Strain through a cloth. Have ready the beaten egg yolks (or ½ pint of cream), a little of the stock and the arrowroot or rice flour to thicken it. Mix this into a smooth batter and add gradually to the soup. Heat, without boiling, and serve at once. For 6.

MULLIGATAWNY SOUP

- 4 onions
- 1 clove garlic
- ¼ pound butter
- 2 stewing hens or a rabbit
- salt
- 1 tablespoon turmeric
- cayenne
- ½ teaspoon black pepper
- 2 tablespoons coriander
- 2 quarts clear stock
- ½ tablespoon flour
- juice of 1 lemon

Put the onions and garlic, well pounded, into a saucepan with the butter. Season the chickens or rabbit with black pepper. Lay on the onions, which have been sliced in rounds. Cook together, covered, for 20 minutes on lowest heat. Then take off the meat and cut into small pieces.

Grind the turmeric, cayenne, pepper, and coriander and add to the meat with the stock; bring to a boil and simmer gently for 40 minutes. Remove from heat and take off any scum.

Cook another 5 minutes, adding the flour and lemon juice mixed to a paste. Strain the soup, replacing the best parts of the meat. Serves 6 to 8.

This is a tangy vegetable punch for those who like capers, gherkins, olives and all things briny.

KANJI (*Carrot and Mustard Seed Punch*)

4 pounds carrots
½ pound mustard seeds
⅛ pound red chilis
½ pound salt
mint leaves

Scrape carrots and divide down the center; quarter them. Place in large glass or earthenware jar. Half fill with cold boiled water. Add all other ingredients. Let stand for 1 week, stirring occasionally. Serve with a mint leaf in each glass, slightly chilled.

This drink may be thinned or used concentrated, according to personal taste. The above quantity of carrots will make about 12 quarts if diluted. Of a deep claret color, with bright stars of mustard seeds floating in it, Kanji is made from purple Indian carrots. I have not seen these grown elsewhere. Lacking these, the trick is to put a few slices of boiled beets with the carrots and keep them together during the maturing period.

CHAPTER 5

Meats

Now we come to the traditional Indian ways of preparing meat. These are good and unique, like some people we meet who are persons rather than people. This has been so from the beginning of Indian cooking. How people become persons rather than people is somewhat of a mystery, but it is always through some intense creative work on their part. It is as a creation full-blown that this food is introduced.

All meat used in these recipes should be lean, free of fat and the skin and fell that covers it. Except where noted, the meat is cut into pieces of 1½ to 2½ inches. Lamb is most often used. Mutton is also much favored, as it is in Europe. With certain types of recipes, mutton develops a savor that lamb cannot. A great deal of lamb is very fatty, and is good for broiling or cooking on a spit where the fat can drain away. Where beef or veal has not been mentioned in any recipe, it does not mean that they cannot be used. However, most beef should be cooked rare, which these recipes do not permit. Beef stewing meat is tougher than lamb or mutton and lacks the delicacy of flavor and texture. Those who prefer beef may, on occasion, like to substitute it for the meats indicated. Remember, however, to give the prolonged cooking time which beef and the darker meats require to break down the fiber and make them edible. In the section on barbecuing, more recipes using beef will be given.

The amount of salt used in these recipes should be the same as in an American recipe, since there is a difference in the saline content of the packaged salts.

This chapter will also introduce you to the use of yoghurt in Indian cooking. Indians use it as the French do wine. Yoghurt has some remarkable properties for assimilating spices, removing any excessive pungency, and impregnating the food with the flavor of the ingredients used. Also, yoghurt does not curdle or separate as cream does in cooking. Yoghurt never obtrudes; it leaves no taste. It loses its own to intensify other flavors. There is no residue, fat, oil or sludge left from it. A recipe for making yoghurt painlessly is given in the Appendix.

Here is the basic curry (turcarri).

SIMPLE MEAT CURRY

(*Lamb or Mutton*)

2 small onions
2 tablespoons butter
1 pound leg or shoulder of lamb
¾ tablespoon coriander
3 crushed peppercorns
¼ tablespoon turmeric
salt

Brown the onions, thinly sliced, to a pale gold in the butter. Add the meat, diced, with the spices, except the salt. Brown the meat over a brisk flame, turning it all the time. Fry 10 minutes and add 1½ quarts of water. Add salt. Bring to a boil and cook covered till tender. Uncover for the last 10 minutes and simmer over the lowest heat. Keep liquid quantity level.

This light and delicate curry has lots of liquid gravy. It should cover all the pieces of meat. A quarter pound of sliced potatoes may be added 15 minutes before serving. For 2.

ROGAN JAUSH (*Color-Passion Curry*)

5 tablespoons butter
6 medium onions
2 pounds lamb
¾ tablespoons turmeric
1½ tablespoons coriander
½ tablespoon cummin
¾ tablespoons green ginger
(¼ teaspoon powdered)
¼ teaspoon red chili (P)
salt
6 tablespoons yoghurt
3 ripe tomatoes

Heat the butter in a heavy casserole. Brown the onions, finely chopped, till an even dark brown. Add the lamb, free of fat, cut in pieces 2 to 3 inches. Add the turmeric, coriander, cummin, ginger and fry for 12 minutes; stir all the time and take care not to burn or scorch the meat. Now add chili, salt and yoghurt. Crush the tomatoes on the meat. Stir well and cook till all the moisture and the yoghurt have been dried to a glaze. Add ½ cup of water. Cover and cook till water is reduced. Repeat till meat is tender. Cook uncovered over very low flame for last five minutes.

This Rogan Jaush is an epicurean dish, and one of the best of all Indian recipes. Unctuous and rich, it will seduce you with its ineffable savor.

Here, as with most Indian recipes of this kind, the salt is added after 40 per cent of the cooking time. Salt added too soon makes the meat exude moisture, hinders dry frying and toughens the meat. Chili, paprika and cayenne added after 20 per cent of cooking time give a red coloring to the dish. The onions are dissolved with the ingredients to make the gravy. In the finished dish they are difficult to distinguish. Serves 4.

The Rogan Jaush can be made in many ways. A variation on the above recipe is to proceed as above to the point where the water is added to the meat. Instead of adding ½ cup of water and repeating this, add enough to cover the meat. Cook covered except for the last 20 minutes. Reduce the liquid to a thick gravy.

The second method is easier, as it requires less attention. Its flavor, however, is less refined.

KHARE MASSALE KA KORMA

(Lamb with Happy Spices)

2 pounds lamb
3 tablespoons butter
1 teaspoon turmeric
strong pinch of ginger (P)
1 clove garlic
3 cloves
3 cardamons (seeds of)
1 inch stick cinnamon
2 onions
⅛ teaspoon cayenne
salt

Cut the lamb in pieces the size of almonds. Melt the butter in a heavy skillet with cover, or a small casserole, and sear the meat in it. Add the spices: turmeric, ginger, cloves, cardamon seeds, and cinnamon, splintered. Fry the meat over a low fire for 10 minutes. Now slice the onions fine and crush the garlic. Scatter over the meat, adding the cayenne and salt. Close the lid tight. Give it a good shake and cook on low fire for 35 minutes. Shake the vessel two or three times during this period.

This is a dish without any liquid. The technique was a Sookha Bhoona or sauté, just as the technique for the Rogan Jaush was Geela Bhoona or braise. To get the best flavor of food cooked according to Geela Bhoona, and especially for Sookha Bhoona, use a vessel with a hermetically tight lid. If steam escapes, it is a loss in flavor and also tends to dry the meat which uses no liquid anyway. Serves 4.

MALAI KORMA

(*Lamb with Cream and Almonds*)

3 tablespoons butter
½ pound onions
¾ tablespoon green ginger
  (¼ teaspoon powdered)
2 pounds lamb
1¼ tablespoons turmeric
½ pint jar yoghurt
3 ounces blanched almonds
4 ounces heavy cream
2 bay leaves
¼ teaspoon chili (P)
salt

Melt the butter in a heavy casserole. Slice half the onions and the ginger. Fry them light brown. Strain any remaining butter and reserve, keeping it warm. Also reserve the onions and ginger. Dice the meat small and season with half the turmeric, remaining onions, well bruised, and rest of ginger. Mix them into the meat with enough yoghurt to moisten. Heat the butter (add more if necessary) and fry the meat 3 minutes. Add the rest of the yoghurt and boil meat till dry. Continue to fry meat with little sprinklings of water. Cook covered till tender. Repeat the braising as often as necessary. Then grind the almonds and mix them with the cream, rest of turmeric, bay leaves and chili powder, adding the onions reserved, and pour over the meat. Cook, without boiling, for 12 gentle minutes. A real gourmet's recipe. Serves 4.

KORMA BARRE DARAYHEE

("*On a Riverbank Grove*")

2 pounds lamb
2 tablespoons green ginger
  (¾ teaspoon powdered)
1 pound yoghurt
9 tablespoons butter
salt
4 onions
2¼ tablespoons coriander
½ tablespoon cinnamon
¾ tablespoon each cardamon
  seeds and cloves
2 eggs
1 beetroot sliced
½ teaspoon turmeric

Cut the meat into 1-inch squares. Season with a mixture of green ginger ground fine with yoghurt and salt. Bhogar (shake) the meat in a little warm melted butter and 2 of the onions, sliced. Then sprinkle the coriander over the meat, also 4 tablespoons water. Boil gently till meat is dry. Now add all spices and ingredients except the turmeric. Give the casserole a good shake and leave covered on low fire for 5 minutes. Then remove meat and reserve it.

Boil the eggs and onions together with the beets, cut so they may bleed, until the eggs are hard. Cut eggs and onions into rounds the same size. String them on small skewers: meat, egg, onion, beet. Place the skewers in rest of butter, sprinkle with turmeric and fry in a skillet till done. Serves 4.

A Riverbank Grove

This is a particularly fine recipe; though to my way of thinking it might have been more appropriate with the kababs in this section. However, the method of cooking is a combination of Kabab cookery and the Korma technique.

The recipe is called "from," or on, "a riverbank grove." This refers to nothing more than the Indian fondness of visiting a river grove for a picnic. Today and for all time, a riverbank grove has a particular mesmeric attraction for the Indian. It is a desirable site for hermitages, schools of yoga, gatherings for poetic recitals, religious meditations, prayers, and among many other things, the visit with favorite persons for no other reason than being together in a lovely spot. The beauty of nature is felt and expressed not by a minute examination of the flora and fauna in these surroundings, but by a surrender to this beauty so that it expresses itself in many convivial ways, by talk, by the sharing of picnic foods, high wit, spirited and extempore poetry, and deep reflection. An anonymous Sanskrit poet left us his word on it long ago. ". . . There are only two things irreplaceable, when everything in this world has vanished: poetry and a friend." It was on a riverbank grove that a remarkable man, also anonymous, exclaimed deliciously that there was no delight greater than friendship; in a grove, quiet and sheltered, by the cool bank of a running river, the seed of amity flowers best, and, ". . . Six things are done by friends: To take and give again; to listen and to talk; to dine, to entertain." These words are perhaps more true today when most of us have begun to use distractions not to supplement friendship but as a substitute for it.

Good and superb food, no matter what its savor, depends for taste on the goodhearted conviviality and bonhomie that trusted friends create. Friendship seems to spice it best: "Better lose your life than friends; life returns when this life ends. Not the sympathy that blends," is what another wise person said. I don't know what he shared for his repast in a forest or riverbank grove. Our recipe for the Korma Barre Darayhee would have pleased him much. He would have been in good company.

Indians love parables, stories and anecdotes and will reel off one to fit any situation. More than these, they love dining with a guest. To eat alone is the act of a savage, although there is one part of India where they eat alone, or facing away from other persons present, thinking it an act of gross vulgarity to be caught chewing away; not a lovely act from anyone's point of view. I must have been trying to steer a course delicately balanced between these two at a famous pleasure garden in northern India called Pinjor.

The cousin of a cousin of one of the employees in the Department of Information for the Government of The Patiala and East Punjab States Union, of which I was Deputy Director, got wind that I was touring the district. He was there, standing like a benign basilisk extending with his smile of welcome his invitation to dinner. Since I wished to see properly the Garden of Pinjor, which is one of the least known and one of the best in India, I turned away his invitation.

Pinjor is on the foothills bordering the higher mountains. I made a plea of work higher up the road. But as I drove off, a demented fury of a sudden hailstorm and monsoon rain sent me back to the village. At the rickety bazaar, under the awning of a tea shop, sat my host, nodding sagely as I drove past. With a wave and a bleat of my klaxon I spun down the road to the plains. Five miles away the road was awash and it would take the waters several hours to subside sufficiently. Turning back, once more I drove for the Garden. While waiting under the cornice of the Elephant Gate, hoping the rain would slacken and I could call the keeper to let me in, down the road came my host, wet, straggly, but smiling a smile of pure welcome. It was rather hard to battle with such kindness, and I gave in and to my delight sat down a while later to a delicious meal. While I ate, my host told the following story: "Once there was a parrot called Blossom. This parrot had supreme beauty, grace, wit, and his intelligence had not been warped by his great attainments.

"One day Blossom, nestling in the hands of his king, happy and care-free, was discoursing at great length. Suddenly he caught sight of Yama, lord of death. Blossom edged away and made a spirited attempt to put a distance between himself and the deadly messenger. All the people who had collected to hear the wise parrot asked, 'Sir, why do you move away?'

" 'He brings harm to all living creatures,' said Blossom. Upon this they all calmed him and begged Yama to spare Blossom. 'You must not, please, kill this parrot.' Yama replied, 'It's not I who decide but Time who makes the decision.' They took poor Blossom with them and asked Time to relent. Likewise, Time said, 'It is Death who is posted in these matters. I beg you all to speak to him.'

But meantime the parrot had dropped dead in fright. The distressed populace asked Yama what it all meant. To which Yama replied, "It was fated thus." My host smiled a fat and victorious smile.

I took his recipe and considered the whole affair a draw.

DOH-PEEAZAH (*"Not Bad at All"*)

2 pounds meat (lamb or veal)
2 tablespoons butter
2 onions
3 cloves garlic
salt
6 cardamons (seeds of)
12 cloves
¾ pound blanched almonds
1½ cups cream
1 quart milk
1 teaspoon turmeric
6 peppercorns

Cut the meat into small pieces. Wash and simmer in a little water for ¼ hour. Remove, drain and cool the meat, reserving the liquid. Melt half the butter, adding the onions, garlic and salt, all well pounded. Mix the meat with this and cook till lightly browned. Then take another skillet or casserole and melt the other half of the butter. Gently heat the cardamon seeds and cloves. When they sizzle, put the meat in. Close the lid and give it a bhogar (shake). Grind the almonds, mix with cream and milk, and strain through a coarse cloth into the meat right after it has been given a bhogar. Close the lid again, raise the heat and bhogar them together. Then uncover and bring to a boil 3 times, stirring often. Add the turmeric, peppercorns and the gravy which was reserved. Simmer till the liquid has been reduced by less than half. Serve with pride for 4.

KORMA DOH-PEEAZAH

The Doh-Peeazah style of cooking will be dealt with later, but meanwhile we have this recipe for a combination of it and the Korma style.

2 pounds lean pork
1 pound onions
1½ tablespoons coriander
salt
1 pound yoghurt
3 tablespoons butter
12 peppercorns
1 tablespoon turmeric

Cut the meat into 1-inch strips. Prick well with a sharp-tined fork or a knife. Rub into the meat a mixture of 1 onion, coriander, salt, with enough yoghurt to moisten. Rub this over the meat. Let stand for ½ hour. Then warm butter, and brown to a delicate gold the onions sliced medium thick. Remove onions and put aside. Fry the meat and give it a bhogar (shake) with black peppercorns crushed fine. Add 4 tablespoons water and dry it. Keep on frying the meat and turning all the time. When the meat is well browned, add the onions, crushed and pounded with the remaining yoghurt. Sprinkle in the turmeric. Mix well. Simmer a short while and serve. For 4.

VINDALOO

2 pounds fat beef or pork
1 heaping tablespoon coriander
3¼ tablespoons green ginger
  (2 teaspoons powdered)
1 tablespoon turmeric
1 teaspoon cummin
salt
4 cloves garlic
2 medium-sized onions
¾ cup vinegar
3 tablespoons butter
6 bay leaves

Cut the beef (chuck steak does very well) in pieces about 3 to 4 inches each. Smear well with a paste made of all the spices, garlic and onions ground down with vinegar. Stand the meat in this for 24 hours. Then cook in butter and bay leaves. Uncover for the last few minutes. Use a gentle fire all the time. Cook till the vinegar has evaporated.

The Vindaloo is equally good with fatty duck. That is given in the section on poultry. Vindaloo paste made with oil may be kept for the times you like to make this dish. Serves 4.

EK-AUR KORMA

(Literally: One More Recipe for Korma Curry)

The preceding recipes have been variations of Korma. This is not a variation but one of the traditional sort:

1 pound lamb
1½ tablespoons green ginger
  (½ teaspoon powdered)
salt
¼ pint buttermilk
4 tablespoons heavy cream
1 onion
3 tablespoons butter
12 cloves
¼ teaspoon saffron
1 teaspoon black pepper
juice of 1 lemon

Dice, wash and dry the meat. Place it aside with the ginger and salt pounded together. Strain the buttermilk and the cream through a fine cloth. Fry the onion brown in the butter, add the cloves and the meat. After 10 minutes add the buttermilk and cream mixture. Cook these together, covered, till they begin to dry. When meat dries add some water and cook covered. When meat is tender, lower the fire and add the saffron and pepper with lemon juice. Leave covered, on the lowest heat that you can manage, or in a warm place for a few minutes. Shake the cooking vessel and serve it up. For 2.

CURRY KULLEAH DIL-PASANDH

(To Tickle Your Heart)

2 pounds lamb or steak
5 tablespoons butter
¼ pound onions
2¼ tablespoons green ginger
  (¼ teaspoon powdered)
salt
1½ tablespoons coriander
flour
1 pound carrots
1 tablespoon garlic, chopped
rice water, rice flour (p. 33)
  or cornstarch
1 quart yoghurt
6 cloves
1 teaspoon turmeric
½ teaspoon cayenne
8 peppercorns

This one is really fine. It happened to be the first recipe I ever collected at Ellora, a great temple center fifty-five miles from Ajanta with its remarkable cave paintings. I will give the directions first and let the incident come as a post-prandial relish. A relish can always be left aside:

Cube 1½ pounds of the meat. Warm the butter, brown the sliced onions. Add ginger and bhogar (shake) the meat in this. Then open the casserole cover and add salt and coriander. Finish the cooking with a little sprinkle of water if necessary.

Grind the rest of the meat, or have it ready ground. Boil it till half cooked. Mix it with a little of the suet and 2 tablespoons white flour. Clean carrots; split them lengthwise and quarter them. Emball them with the ground meat. Then fry them in a little butter. When the carrots in the ground meat are done, place them atop the meat cooked with coriander. Cover and cook 12 minutes.

Pound the garlic in a mortar and pestle and mix with it a little rice water or ½ tablespoon of rice flour (p. 33), or failing that, a little cornstarch. Add the yoghurt to it. Warm 1 teaspoon of butter and fry the cloves for 5 minutes. Bhogar (shake) the yoghurt mixture in this. Add turmeric, cayenne, and peppercorns, crushed. Cook briskly 10 minutes. This recipe is served by pouring the yoghurt sauce over the meat and carrots, or it may be served in a sauceboat for ladling over the food. It must be served hot. These diverse preparations seem more complicated in reading than in mixing. Serves 4.

The Curry Kulleah to "tickle your heart" can also be made substituting cooked beets and eggplant for the carrots. The carrots, in this recipe, were raw. They may be parboiled to make them tender. This to my mind does not help the dish. The raw carrots have a pleasant texture, a surprising taste, and are much healthier that way.

CURRY KULLEAH SAFFRON

(No saffron is used in this; turmeric is!)

1 pound lamb or good beef
½ teaspoon parsley
salt
2 eggs
¼ pint yoghurt
butter
4 ounces blanched almonds
½ tablespoon turmeric
½ tablespoon lime juice

Grind the meat and mix with the parsley, chopped fine, salt, the beaten eggs, and yoghurt. Form these into meat balls and fry them in butter till they are well browned. Continue cooking till they begin to split open. Make a paste of the ground almonds and turmeric in water and sprinkle this over the meat balls. Cover, shake gently a few times and serve, when dry, with lime juice sprinkled over it all. Serves 2.

The Pandit of Ellora

This dish should belong to the Kabab section in this chapter, though the method of cooking may have earned it its place here. I got it — a good introduction to the Kabab style of cooking — also at Ellora.

This, my first recipe, came fortuitously — in 1943, many years before I learned to wield the chopper and flourish the ladle in Paris. I began learning French and Indian cuisine simultaneously there. Then many of the recipes, including my first from Ellora, that I had gathered with no apparent purpose, came miraculously to my aid.

Ellora is one of the most fascinating places on earth, quite unknown to the outside world and to most Indians. Ajanta, a twin wonder of cave temple architecture, only fifty-five miles away, is world-famous and much visited.

When I first saw Ellora, it was, as a writer several hundreds of years ago had described it, quiet, unhurried, lost to the world, and seeming to belong to another dimension. From a distance the crescent-shaped mountain scarp with its thirty-six amazing temples is awesome. I arrived there at a time when the sun was setting. Shadows were thickening under the cornices of the temples. As the light paled fitfully, it ran over the red stones like molten glass. It grew darker and the surface seemed actually to move.

The cave temples themselves were enough to astound the imagination. The incalculable expenditure of human energy, the architectural and sculptural uniqueness, and the genius of engineering involved in fashioning the hard rock culminated in what Indians call Samvega or aesthetic shock. Sunlight is used in a masterly way, so that the scene changes hourly. In the middle of the cave formations, a waterfall thunders down, arching over the cliff to smash pulverizingly on the rocks below. Against a background of tropical greenery, soft monsoon skies with their racing thunderclouds, the crest jewel of the temples, the Kailas, is set. Here a whole mountaintop has been *lifted* and carried away to let in the sun on the temple, carved in one piece with small, delicate chisels; one mistake in calculation would have ruined the whole edifice. The master plan is of epic envisioning, and correct in every embellishment. Bigger than the Parthenon, and in its way as fine, it imposes an oblique approach on a person. A too blasé, or too naïve, or too romantic way of viewing it would ruin its meaning. The hundreds of photographs I took for a book on Ellora have been lost with the exodus from what is now Pakistan and was once India.

Next morning I walked down to the small village and on the way was greeted by a man, the Pandit or learned man, who wished me a good stay.

And in the days that followed, the Pandit came often to see me and open up his inexhaustible scholarship on the philosophical and psychological meaning of the sculptures. On the second day, the Pandit invited me to eat with him. I accepted with delight. The cuisine in the Pandit's home was simple and frugal. Also, as a practicing student of Yoga, a principle which much influences Indian life, he ate no meat and permitted none in his home. He abstained from smoking and drinking, and since his family had grown up, had been a celibate for many years. The food had the cleanness of unmuddled cooking; there appeared to be a great respect for the goodness of the simple material used; no attempt was made to hide it by oversaucing or overspicing. It was to be taken as it stood . . . very much like the Pandit himself. He was a tall man, and spare. His voice, the arrangement of his draperies, every gesture he made was of a certain correct measure. His manner was not quiet, but calm. During the long telling of his stories and discourses, there came to me a sharing and participation in that calmness.

Before I left Ellora, I told the Pandit that I intended to spend one night awake in the inner part of the temple. This was to experience the place without the noise, the light of the sun and the voices of people. I tried it too, but gave up after three hours. In the silence the thousands of fancies that invade the mind, deprived of its normal supports and crutches, were too much. Fear and a vague alarm made me uneasy. Never have I known anything more deafening than that silence and the thronging of so many things waiting admittance. I weakened and left, and admitted my failure to the Pandit the next morning.

He said nothing, but a few days later, in one of the cave temples of the Buddhist period, he stopped before a life-size sculptured panel depicting the Temptation of Buddha and the assault on him by the forces of Mara. The Pandit said in his quiet, even voice, "This is what you were fighting the other night in the Kailas temple."

"Buddha knew," he went on, "that the frightening shadows and the tumult unleashed against him were no more than the reflections of his own psyche . . . his tendencies. The fire he saw, the hot ashes, the flaming rocks, as well as the alluring temptations, were the last agitations within him of his own unreconciled nature, the antagonisms that had not been solved. If he had been shaken even once, momentarily, his release from them would have been impossible. So when the horrors assailing him entered his field of concentration, they became flowers . . ."

The Pandit turned away from the panel. "What we see outside is the reflection of our own nature. The exterior world is no less real than the one inside. But it is a true reflection, like all reflections inverted. What is apparent and obvious may be really the opposite of the truth. And that," he said, looking me directly in the eyes, "is all there is. *There* lies the personal struggle, and the cause of our unhappiness to which we ascribe a thousand reasons save the one real one."

The last day before I left Ellora, I met the Pandit; he was sitting under the shade of a medieval temple. As I stopped to greet him, he took me aside and sat down. From his immaculate white draped shawl he took out a bundle of papers. He gave them to me and asked me to copy down certain material. The document was apparently of the seventeenth century. It contained much mathematical calculation — astrological perhaps. There was a mass of commentary on philosophical ideas. He turned to fourteen pages of recipes for food. These papers he said had come into his family several hundred years ago, in this same village. And noticing the look of bewilderment on my face, for I was thinking what exactly I would do with these recipes, he told me. "Ah," he said softly, "knowledge is dead matter if no use is made of it. I cannot, but you may make it fit where it should. No one can say what good this is going to be for you. Keep it however. Don't lose it."

His voice closed on a note of farewell. Returning his adieu with folded hands, I left him; a remote, white-robed, very human figure, sitting under the camphor cool of a pipal tree. A scene as old as India itself.

This next recipe is also from the Pandit of Ellora.

KORMA CURRY ELLORA

(One More on the Theme)

2 pounds lamb
1 tablespoon green ginger (⅜ teaspoon P)
4 tablespoons butter
salt
½ pound onions
1 pound yoghurt
½ pound blanched almonds
1 cup cream
pinch of saffron
5 limes (juice of)
12 peppercorns, ground fine

Slice the meat and wash several times. Dry in paper toweling. Pound the ginger with a little butter and salt. Rub this into the meat. Warm the rest of the butter and lightly brown the onions sliced in it. Add the meat and fry it well on all sides. Mix the pepper with 6 tablespoons water and add to the meat. Cook the meat covered. When the liquid has dried, put in the saffron and the yoghurt. Mix them well and cook till the yoghurt is practically dry. Now mix the almonds, well pounded, with the cream, the pinch of saffron and the lime juice. Put these in with the meat. Remove from heat and mix them well. Cover and keep warm on the lowest heat possible for 20 to 25 minutes. Serves 4.

SPECIAL MANNER OF MAKING A CURRY

3 tablespoons butter
4½ teaspoons turmeric
1½ tablespoons coriander
1½ tablespoons green ginger (¼ teaspoon powdered)
3 tablespoons yoghurt
1 teaspoon poppy seeds
1 teaspoon sesame seeds
12 blanched almonds
2 tablespoons coconut
12 cloves
juice of 1 lime
salt

Use this for any meat (2½ pounds), fowl or fish that you like.

Make all the ingredients into a paste, using mortar and pestle. Slice the meat, fowl, fish, or vegetable into shape. Brown an onion in butter. Add the meat with the paste. Cook till dry and add coconut milk, or water made by soaking packaged coconut overnight and reserving the water, or pouring boiling water over the grated coconut, letting remain for 5 minutes, and reserving the liquor.

Or the meat and the paste can be cooked with good stock, or bouillon cubes dissolved in a little water.

If it is desired to acidulate the curry, capers, lemon juice, tamarind or pomegranate juice may be added near the finishing of the preparation.

A different and very good taste in curry can be had if the ingredients in this recipe are added to the meat by making half of them into a paste and adding the other half slightly bruised but dry. Serves 4.

ANOTHER SPECIAL MANNER OF PREPARING A CURRY

For each pound of food:

milk from 1 coconut
2 onions
1 tablespoon chili
1 tablespoon turmeric
2 tablespoons garlic, chopped
salt
2 tablespoons butter
1½ teaspoons lemon juice

Drain off the coconut milk, or make your coconut liquor as explained in the preceding recipe. Add the onions, chili powder, turmeric, garlic, and salt. Soak the meat in this mixture 15 minutes, and then place all in cooking vessel. Cook till the meat is partly done. Then add the butter. Add some more coconut milk and as it begins to boil, add the lemon juice and finish cooking.

If the curry is too thin, make a roux with butter and flour, rice flour (p. 33) or cornstarch before adding to the meat. Serves 2.

Liver is much prized in India, and used both for cooking on the revolving spit, and in the casserole. For those who like liver, to have a finger in this pie is to have a hand in it, "all five fingers," it is said in India.

CURRY OF LIVER AND PEAS

2 pounds liver
2 tablespoons butter
1½ teaspoons turmeric
4 peppercorns
1½ tablespoons coriander
2 teaspoons mustard seeds
salt
1 tablespoon green ginger
  (½ teaspoon powdered)
½ pound shelled green peas

Wash, dice and dry the liver. Fry in a skillet without any butter. Turn it on all sides. Then remove and scrape the meat with a knife. Heat the butter in the skillet; add the spices — salt, bruised mustard seeds and the ginger cut in thin strips (or add powdered ginger). After 10 minutes of very gentle frying, add the liver to the spices. Cook it covered till almost done. Then add the peas with the pepper. Mix well, and cook covered, with a sprinkling of water or by covering the whole with two whole lettuce leaves. Shake a few times till the peas are done, bright green and crisp; not too soft. Serves 4.

Among these recipes, we have already used a few where the meat is accompanied by a small portion of vegetable. In this case, these vegetables were for the coloring or for helping the braising method.

Supreme among the curries of any kind are those where the meat and the vegetables play equally important parts. The result is a perfect marrying of the two. The flavor of one ingredient is absorbed by the other. In return it lends its savor in a fashion that gives us a new, delicious dish. The vegetables are not a garnish, as they are in a stew, where they only steal some of the flavor of the meat used. The Indian recipes of this kind owe their excellence to a final result which is neither one nor the other, and yet is both.

This next is an exciting alliance of spinach with lamb. If you have never liked spinach before, now you will learn to love it.

SAGH MHAS (*Spinach Meat*)

- 2 onions
- 4 tablespoons butter
- 2 pounds lamb (lean as always)
- 1 teaspoon turmeric
- 2 teaspoons coriander
- ¾ tablespoon ginger (P)
- ½ teaspoon chili (P)
- 1 pound spinach
- 2 tablespoons yoghurt
- pinch of thyme
- 1 tablespoon mustard seeds
- salt

Slice the onions very fine and fry them in the butter, adding the meat cut in 2½ inch pieces, at the same time, with the turmeric, coriander, ginger and chili. Mix them well and fry over medium heat for 10 to 12 minutes. Scatter the spinach, shredded fine, over the meat, with the yoghurt, thyme, mustard seeds and salt. Mix well. Now cook it covered, taking care to shake the casserole several times, adding ½ cup of water as the moisture dries out. Then finish over gentle heat till all the moisture is dried. The spinach should be in the nature of a thick purée, completely mixed with the meat and the finished dish should have no moisture.

The best way is to open the cover for the last few minutes and, over a brisk flame, bring the whole to a glaze. When the mixture begins to stick, it is ready to serve. While the gravy is being brought to a glaze, the food must be kept turning frequently.

This technique can be employed with any, or most Indian recipes with gravy. If the gravy is reduced to a glaze, it has another taste and savor. Remember to finish the last 5 minutes on brisk, even high heat; keep turning, not stirring, the food, and when it begins to stick, off with it. Do not keep too long before serving, as moisture will begin to collect again. Serves 4 to 6.

Now to go on to another exceptional marriage of meat and vegetables. This was Big Brother Dilla's best. I do not have his recipe, but my result is very much like his.

GOBHI MHAS (*Meat with Cauliflower*)

4 tablespoons butter
3 onions
2 pounds lamb
1 tablespoon turmeric
1 tablespoon coriander
3 tablespoons green ginger (1⅛ teaspoon powdered)
2 small tomatoes
4 ounces yoghurt (optional)
1 pound cauliflower
1 teaspoon chili
salt

Melt the butter in a heavy saucepan. Slice onions and fry them dark brown. Add then the meat, the turmeric, coriander and ginger. Fry these together 10 minutes. Add the tomatoes and yoghurt. Cook till tomatoes are somewhat done. Arrange the cauliflower, cut in small pieces, over the meat. Mix well, adding salt and chili. Cover and cook. When dry, put in ½ cup water. Cover and cook till the cauliflower is perfectly soft. Simmer 5 minutes over low fire, uncovered. All liquid should be reduced before presenting to the table. Serves 4 to 6.

The best way, and the most delicious, is to cook the cauliflower to a purée.

You may, however, prefer to have the cauliflower keep its shape. For this, cut it into medium-sized flowerets. Add to the meat at the stage indicated in this recipe. Mix well with the meat and spices. Add a little water. Cover firmly and steam over very low heat till done. The meat and cauliflower must be both well cooked and tender. The cauliflower should be added about 20 to 25 minutes before serving.

SHALGAM MHAS (*Lamb with Baby Turnips*)

¾ pound butter
3 onions
2 pounds lamb
¾ tablespoon turmeric
1 tablespoon cummin
5 whole red chili peppers
8 small turnips
2 cloves garlic
1 teaspoon ginger (P)
1 tomato
salt

Heat the butter, as for all Indian cooking, in a heavy casserole or cooking vessel. Chop the onion coarsely and fry it a pale gold. Add the lamb which has been cut into pieces of 2 to 3 inches. Put in the turmeric, cummin and whole red peppers bruised well. Fry the meat, stirring all the time, for 10 minutes. Put in the turnips (if you can't find baby turnips, halve or quarter them) and fry together for another 5 minutes.

Pound the garlic with the ginger and the tomato in a little water to make a paste. Put this in with the rest. Add the salt, and boil the whole for a minute or so. Lower the fire and add a small amount of water (3 or 4 tablespoons) with a sprinkle and a splash. Cover the casserole tight and cook over the gentlest heat you can manage. Add more water and braise again. Repeat if necessary till the meat is tender and turnips cooked. Shake the casserole during this time, once or twice. Do not stir much.

The turnips will have absorbed much of the spices, butter, and the flavor of the meat. The meat will have carried the taste of turnips, which should be whole and never purëed or broken.

This is a rather tasty dish. Serves 4.

It is said that fortune is a dame whose noddle is bald at the back. If you do not catch her by the forelock, it is impossible to grasp her by the noddle. In fact, I said these very thoughts (which are Francis Bacon's) by quoting from an Indian writer. It happened in a forest clearing, where a lone forest ranger was cooking his midday meal. Halting at the edge of the clearing, under a leafy banyan tree, I was caught by the indescribable fragrance. A tiny twist of smoke hung over the chimney; the door was agape, and the forest charming enough to embolden me to anything. I was also hungry.

I made for the door of the ranger's hut. By way of introducing myself I quoted a verse from the Panchtantra — India's compendium of animal fables — which have traveled to every country in the world and are found in Aesop, in La Fontaine's third volume. This from the original.

> "If a man be a fatalist and slacker,
> Irresolute and sang-froid lacker,
> Him Fortune — as a bouncing miss,
> Her aged lover — hates to kiss."

To my utter surprise, the answer from the same book came:

> "A guest in need
> Is a guest indeed."

And that is how I tasted and came away with this recipe.

SUBH-DEHG, OR THE BLESSED POT

2 pounds lamb
2 cloves garlic
4 peppercorns
2 onions
1 medium cucumber
8 tablespoons butter (¼ pound)
1 tablespoon turmeric
1 teaspoon cummin
1 pint yoghurt
1 tablespoon tomato paste
salt
1 pound white turnips
½ pound carrots
Akni (p. 28)
large piece of pumpkin or squash
2 or 3 zucchinis
2 tablespoons coriander

Wash and dry the lamb. Cube 1 pound lamb. Grind the rest. Pound in a mortar with pestle the garlic, peppercorns and 1 onion with salt. Mix this with the ground meat and make into meat balls.

Cut the second onion in thin slices and brown well in a casserole with butter. Add the cubed lamb and the meat balls. Put in the turmeric, coriander and cummin with the yoghurt and the tomato paste; salt also and stir well. Cook, turning the meat, for 10 minutes. When the liquid is dry, add turnips and carrots and cook together with the meat and ½ cup Akni one quarter hour. When meat and vegetables are tender, cut the pumpkin and zucchinis in large slices, and the cucumber in strips. Place these atop the meat. Seal hermetically. Remove from heat; shake the casserole well, keep on low heat and uncover after 10 minutes. Serves 6. This dish is traditionally made on feast days.

KORMA—LIKE NARCISSUS FLOWER

- 6 eggs
- ½ tablespoon coriander
- 2 cardamons (seeds of)
- ½ inch stick cinnamon
- 2¼ tablespoons green ginger (¼ teaspoon powdered)
- 2 pounds lamb
- 5 tablespoons butter
- 2 cups buttermilk
- salt
- 2½ tablespoons lentils
- ¼ pound spinach
- 3 carrots
- almonds
- 1 tablespoon pimentos (fresh or canned)
- 1 teaspoon turmeric
- pinch of cayenne

Hard-boil the eggs. Grind the following spices: coriander, cardamon seeds, cinnamon and ginger and mix with the meat cut in pieces. Fry together in butter. After 5 to 7 minutes, add the buttermilk and salt and cook briskly. Now put the lentils in a bag of cheesecloth, chop the spinach; dice the carrots. Put them in with the meat. When the meat and vegetables are tender, strain the gravy. Reserve meat and vegetables. Pound the lentils, after removing from bag, or better, work them through a blender. Put the lentils in the gravy and give it one bhogar (shake). Add the meat and vegetables and cook ¼ hour. Cut the eggs in half. Stick 3 almonds in the center of each egg. Place them upright on the meat and vegetables. Put in pimentos cut in delicate strips and strew the turmeric and cayenne evenly all over the dish. Cover and cook for a few minutes till done. Serves 4 to 6.

CURRY KULLEAH CUCUMBER

This can be made with any kind of long gourd vegetable.

- 1½ pounds meat (veal, pork)
- 4 onions
- ½ pound butter
- salt
- 1 pound cucumbers
- ½ pound yoghurt
- 2 tablespoons chopped dill
- 1½ tablespoons turmeric, or saffron

Chop the meat into tiny bits. Pound the onion well with a mortar and pestle. Heat butter and fry onions for a few seconds; add the meat and fry together 12 minutes. Add salt and braise with a little water till the meat is cooked.

Peel the cucumbers and split them lengthwise. Rub them with salt all over and put them in an expiring oven (heated and shut off) for ¼ hour. Wash them well in water; seed them and soak them in the yoghurt for 3 hours, or even overnight, in the refrigerator.

Stuff the cucumber, with the fried meat and chopped dill and a little yoghurt. Tie the cucumbers with strings or skewer with toothpicks. Sprinkle liberally with turmeric. Fry a few minutes in melted butter. Add the yoghurt. When this is dry, serve as it is or with a little saffron mixed with just enough butter to make it liquid. Or the saffron may be dissolved in hot water. In this case the moisture has to be dried before the dish is brought to the table with a flourish, and a smug smile. Serves 4.

Artichokes and meat make a fine combination. These two recipes show two different styles of cooking. Both may please you if you are fond of artichokes. This vegetable is less known in India than in the West. Those who know it believe "that mathematics fails to count its many goodnesses." It is good for the liver, fine for health, and has many of the properties of green food.

ARTICHOKE AND LAMB CURRY

6 large artichokes
lemon juice
5 tablespoons butter
1 teaspoon cummin
1 tablespoon coriander
1 teaspoon chili (P)
2 teaspoons turmeric
salt
1 tablespoon yoghurt
2 pounds lamb
1 tablespoon garlic
1 tablespoon green ginger
(⅜ teaspoon powdered)

Cook the artichokes in water and a little lemon juice until tender but not too soft. Remove leaves and reserve the hearts (bottoms). Heat the butter, add the spices and salt, with the yoghurt. When yoghurt begins to dry, put in the meat, cut in small strips. Fry the meat in the spices for 5 to 7 minutes, and then add the garlic and ginger well pounded and made into a paste with a little water. Add the artichoke hearts, mix well with the meat. Sprinkle with a little water. Hermetically seal the casserole. Give it a good shake and cook till done. Serves 6.

The artichoke hearts may be quartered if too large.

Here is another one with artichokes.

LAMB WITH ARTICHOKES

(*Castanets*)

6 artichokes
1½ pounds lamb
butter
1 onion, sliced
1 tablespoon coriander
6 peppercorns
⅛ teaspoon thyme (P)
3 tomatoes
1 pint yoghurt
1 tablespoon turmeric
salt

Steep large artichokes ½ hour in salt water. Bring water to a boil, cut off leaves and reserve the hearts (bottoms). Cut the meat into pieces the shape and size of almond halves. Melt butter and fry the sliced onion. Remove onion and reserve. Put in the meat and fry in butter with coriander, peppercorns, crushed, and thyme. After 12 minutes add the tomatoes crushed, and cook meat till done. Place a thick layer of the meat on an artichoke heart. Sprinkle with salt, and top this with another heart, hollow side down. Tie this together, or use toothpicks, to hold together. Handle them with great care. Take the onions reserved, put them in the casserole with just enough butter to moisten them; when these are warm, mash them with a fork and add the yoghurt. Add the turmeric; mix them well together. Place the artichokes (castanets) in the yoghurt and cook uncovered till most of the yoghurt is dry. If this dish is preferred without gravy, dry out all the yoghurt. When it glazes, turn the castanets once. Serves 4.

Now for the Doh-Peeazah style of cooking. This has been explained in the introduction to the meat section. I also spoke of eating a Doh-Peeazah in the house of a friend. For the success of that dish, nuggets of spring lamb appearing dramatically inside big hollowed out onions, the chef had to master-mind the entire operation; the recipe required that the Akni should be cooked dry at exactly the same moment the food was done to a pitch of savory perfection. The round, gleaming onions, with their treasure of lamb nuggets, arose from the depths of the vessel in a dramatic cloud of steam, carrying the essence, not just the fragrance. The onions were pearl white, modestly showing the delicate veining, and shot with many delicate tints from the spiced steam it had captured in passing.

That Doh-Peeazah is a challenge for anyone. Among the many other creations in this style, here is one; and some more.

CURRY DOH-PEEAZAH

1 pound lamb
2½ tablespoons butter
½ pint yoghurt
½ teaspoon turmeric
1 teaspoon cummin
1 tablespoon coriander
½ teaspoon cayenne
2 pounds onions
1 tablespoon green ginger
(⅜ teaspoon powdered)
2 tablespoons green pepper
4 medium tomatoes
juice of 1 lemon
salt

Put the lamb, cubed, into the casserole with the melting butter, the yoghurt and spices. Cook them well till almost dry. Take care not to scorch the meat or the spices. Cut the onions in quarters and separate them skin by skin. Sprinkle them over the meat. Over this add the ginger, slivered fine, the green peppers cut in little strips and mixed with ¼ cup of water, and the tomatoes, crushed. Cover tightly and cook over very low heat till done. Before serving, add lemon juice. For 2.

The following recipe gives a new and most practical way of steaming food: meat, fowl, fish or vegetable. You will like to use this method of steaming for many American dishes.

DOH-PEEAZAH KUSSAH

2 teaspoons ginger (P)
2 tablespoons coriander
salt
2 pounds lamb, pork or beef, ground
1 tablespoon thyme
1 teaspoon crushed black pepper
1 clove garlic
½ tablespoon fennel seed
1 tablespoon mustard seed
sprigs of parsley
½ pound butter
¼ pound onions
¾ cup yoghurt

Make a paste of the ginger, coriander, ground fine, and salt, with a little water. Form the meat into *one* large cake. Put in a kettle the thyme, black pepper, garlic, well crushed, fennel seeds, mustard seeds slightly bruised, parsley and greens. Pour in water, the amount depending on the size of the vessel. A 4-quart kettle will do nicely with 1 quart of water. Over the top of the kettle or saucepan tie cheesecloth folded 4 times. Bring the water to a boil and when steam issues, place the meat cake on the cloth, stretched tight. Cook for not less than 10 minutes; preferably 15. Turn meat cake to other side and steam the same length of time. The meat can be eaten now, but the Doh-Peeazah is finished in this manner:

Heat the butter in a heavy skillet; add onions, yoghurt and salt. Fry the meat cake on both sides till nicely brown. Serves 4.

With this method of steaming, you will notice that the meat shrinks in length and expands in thickness. The shrinkage is due to the draining away into the kettle, through the cloth, of the fat contents. The cheapest cuts of hamburger meat may be used satisfactorily in this manner. All the fat and other undesirable elements melt and drain away and the meat is left lean. Also, a hamburger cooked in this way makes good eating cold the next day. The texture of the ground meat becomes more like that of pot roast.

DOH-PEEAZAH WITH LENTILS

2 pounds lamb, or pork
¾ pound onions
1 tablespoon garlic
¾ tablespoon cummin
salt
¼ cup yoghurt
¼ to ½ pound butter
1½ pounds lentils
12 peppercorns
1 tablespoon turmeric (optional)

Wash and cut the meat in 2-inch strips. In a mortar and pestle thoroughly crush all but one onion, garlic and cummin. Mix this with the salt and yoghurt. Rub this well into meat and leave marinating for ½ hour, if time permits. Melt the butter; slice and make golden brown the forlorn onion; put in the meat and yoghurt marinade. Clap on the lid, give it one good bhogar (shake). Add the lentils (see directions for preparation on package) and enough water to cover. Cook over medium heat. Put in the crushed peppercorns and turmeric, mixing them well. Simmer till done. This may take 10 to 20 minutes, depending upon the thickness of the casserole. Serves 6.

A proper Doh-Peeazah has no gravy save that of the butter.

MOCK DOH-PEEAZAH WITH EGGS

2 pounds beef, veal or pork (fat-free)
¼ pound onion
2 tablespoons green ginger (¾ teaspoon powdered)
6 peppercorns
4 tablespoons butter
8 eggs
¼ teaspoon cayenne
2 cloves
2 teaspoons turmeric
salt

Dice the meat small and mix it well in a bowl with the onion, ginger and peppercorns ground down. Salt the meat. Cook it in a casserole with ¼ cup water till the water has dried. Then add butter and fry meat 10 minutes. Prepare the eggs in the following manner: Break them into another saucepan, with a little salt and about 6 to 8 tablespoons water. Keep stirring till they begin to set. Mix the eggs with the meat, adding another sprinkling of water, and simmer for 10 minutes. Now put in the cayenne, cloves and turmeric. Mix the whole well. Cover and simmer few minutes till ready to serve. For 4 to 6.

KEEMA KORMA CURRY

This one uses ground meat. Lamb or beef will do best. These must be made with lean, fat-free meat.

1 onion
2 tablespoons butter
2 pounds meat
1 teaspoon turmeric
½ teaspoon chili (P)
salt
4 tablespoons yoghurt
1 tablespoon coriander

Slice the onion and fry it a dark brown in the butter. Add the meat and all the spices with the salt. Fry well 10 minutes and add the yoghurt. Mix well. Cover and cook till done. Serves 4.

The Keema may be made with quartered potatoes, peeled and put in about 15 to 20 minutes before serving. Add 2 cups water for this.

Or mix ¾ pound green peas, about 10 to 12 minutes before serving. This is the best variation. Only ¾ cup water needed.

Another variation is with eggs well hard-boiled. Halve the eggs and place in the curry for 10 minutes before serving. The eggs may be placed when frying the meat. In this case do not halve them till the last 10 minutes. Then heap a little gravy over the eggs and do not disturb till serving.

Yet another variation is with sweet green peppers. Cut the peppers in strips 1½ inches wide and place atop the Keema curry. The peppers may be left in for 5 minutes, if desired crisp, or put in with the yoghurt if you like them soft and permeated with the spices.

KEEMA HUZOOR PASANDH

(Ground Meat to Please Your Noble Self)

2 pounds lean mutton or beef
2 teaspoons turmeric
8 peppercorns
salt
1 teaspoon mustard seeds
1½ pounds black-eyed peas (half cooked)
cooking oil (not olive) or sesame oil
10 onions, chopped

Grind the meat 3 times. Mix well with the turmeric, peppercorns, crushed. Salt, mustard seeds, bruised, and peas. Mix the meat and peas with the oil.

Fry the mixture with 4 of the onions heaped on top of the meat. Keep on low heat for 10 minutes. In an oven-proof dish, put in a layer of meat mixture, then a layer of the remaining 6 onions. Top with another meat layer. Press this down with a spatula and add on top a little more oil. Cook in a 375° oven for 40 minutes. If the dish gets too dry, place a bowl of water in the oven. Serve piping hot. For 6.

LEFTOVER BEEF

(or any other meat)

Mix 2 tablespoons rice flour (p. 33), or split-pea flour (p. 33), or flour with 1½ tablespoons turmeric, ½ teaspoon ginger (P), 1 crushed clove of garlic, ½ teaspoon cummin, ½ inch stick cinnamon. Warm these in a skillet, without using any butter. When it starts browning add, little by little, some stock, or infusion of bouillon cubes in water. Stir and thicken. When almost ready, add the salt and ½ teaspoon chili (P). Pour this over the leftovers (2 pounds of meat), or place the leftovers in the sauce to simmer for a few minutes only. Then serve with a squeeze of lemon juice. No butter has been used here. Serves 6.

The following are Kababs. These are meat balls and croquettes made with ground meat. Kababs are also made from cubed meat, cooked in the oven or a rotisserie; also barbecued. Some of the ground-meat kababs may be made from leftovers, but to be fair to yourself, make them with fresh meat.

KABAB ZEERA (*Kababs with Cummin*)

- 2 pounds lamb (leg or shoulder, ground)
- 1½ tablespoons cummin
- ½ teaspoon cayenne
- 2 onions, chopped or pounded
- 1 tablespoon parsley
- 1 tablespoon green herbs
- salt

Mix the ingredients thoroughly; roll into sausage-shaped kababs, each to be about ¾ inch in diameter by 4 inches in length. Handle them gently and broil or fry them in a lightly greased skillet over low heat. Serves 4.

MASSALE DARH KABABS (*Spicy Kababs*)

- 1 tablespoon green ginger (⅜ teaspoon powdered)
- 1 tablespoon turmeric
- 1 tablespoon coriander
- 3 peppercorns
- 1 teaspoon chili (P)
- salt
- 2 pounds meat (lamb or beef, ground)
- 3 medium onions
- 2 tablespoons butter
- yoghurt
- 2 tablespoons rice flour (p. 33)

Grind well all the spices and salt. Mix the meat thoroughly with them, and the onions, pounded. Add half the butter, melted, with enough yoghurt to moisten. Roll the meat and onion mixture into sausage shapes. Powder lightly with rice flour, and dip generously in a bowl of the yoghurt and fry them in butter in a heavy skillet. Handle very gently. When the kababs are set, turn them tenderly over to the other side and finish. For 4.

SHAMI KABABS

2 ounces yellow split peas
 (may be soaked overnight)
2 pounds beef or lamb ground
½ tablespoon ginger
¾ tablespoon coriander
¾ tablespoon cummin
2 mint leaves
2 cloves garlic
butter
1 onion

Boil the peas; add the meat and the spices. Cook in just enough water to be absorbed. Remove mixture; drain and cool. Add remaining ingredients except the butter and mix in a mortar and pestle so that all are thoroughly mixed. Make into small croquettes — about 1½ inches, circular shaped. Handle with great gentleness; fry in butter. Serves 4.

An exciting Shami Kabab is made by enclosing a few shreds of lemon rind in each croquette.

Liver makes another much appreciated kabab. Calf, beef, sheep or chicken liver may be used.

KOFTA KABABS STUFFED

8 eggs
2 cloves garlic (optional)
2 onions
3 tablespoons coriander
3 mint leaves (optional)
6 cloves
2 cardamons (seeds of)
salt
2 tablespoons tomato paste
2 pounds meat, ground
butter
1 pint yoghurt

Hard-boil the eggs. Cool and reserve. Pound half the garlic (if used), onion, coriander, mint leaves (if used), cloves and cardamon seeds ground fine, tomato paste and salt. Mix them well with the meat.

Shell and quarter the eggs. Carefully cover each section with a thick, smooth coating of the meat mixture. Place in a lightly buttered skillet and panbroil on low heat, turning once to cook on both sides. These are ready to serve, but may be extended thus:

Fry the other chopped onion in butter till well browned. Add yoghurt, the remaining ground spices and tomato paste to make a gravy. Place the koftas in it and simmer for 15 minutes. For 6.

KOFTA KABAB KHATAEE

2 pounds lamb, ground
1 tablespoon green ginger
  (⅜ teaspoon powdered)
1 teaspoon black pepper
4 tablespoons coriander
salt
1 teaspoon saffron (P)
½ cup yoghurt
1 cup cream
½ pound blanched almonds
juice of 4 lemons

Cook meat in water. Drain and pound well with pounded ginger, black pepper, coriander and salt. Mix with saffron. Strain yoghurt through coarse cloth, mix with cream and almonds. Mix with the meat. Make into balls and fry in a heavy skillet. Serve with lemon juice. For 4.

KOFTA DOH-PEEAZAH KHEER

(With Milk and Cream)

2 pounds veal, lamb or pork, ground
1 teaspoon black pepper
6 flakes thyme
6 cardamons (seeds of)
salt
capers or cocktail onions
3 tablespoons butter
1 onion
½ inch stick cinnamon
5 cloves
1 quart milk
½ cup cream
pinch of nutmeg

Make koftas (balls) of the meat, with pepper, thyme, finely crushed cardamon seeds and salt, enclosing 1 or 2 capers in the meat. Heat the casserole, and melt the butter. Fry the koftas until fairly brown. Then scatter the onion, sliced thick over them, with the splintered cinnamon and the cloves. Cook uncovered and shake it a few times. Add the milk and reduce the heat to the lowest point after boiling it for 5 minutes. This recipe requires frequent stirring of the milk and the meat. When the milk has almost evaporated, put in the cream and nutmeg. Cover; keep warm for 12 minutes. Shake it well and serve. For 4.

It will be found that the 2 cups of milk, because of the slow heat and frequent stirring, are reduced to a creamy paste. The heavy cream used for finishing the preparation adds to the texture and flavor.

Needless to say, this manner of preparing meat is not very common, or used frequently. It is authentic, however, and gives us a look at the diversity of Indian cuisine. This recipe is unctuously delicious.

In the Punjab, which among all the different parts of India has the finest food, a creamy paste — called *Malai* — is made separately. About 6 pints of milk may be reduced to only an inch of heavy layered cream. When the meat is ready, this cream is cut in plump strips, about 1 by ½ by 4 inches and laid on the meat for 2 minutes before serving. This Indian cream lends itself to endless uses: on toast, bread and muffins; on fruit with sugar and honey. On meat and vegetables, for it has the pliability of dough. It is velvety, coagulated, and is not liquid like cream in America and Europe. However, it is a laborious process. If you are counting minutes and dying to put your feet up and let down your hair, after a hard day, do not attempt it.

Sweet and Pungent

We come now to the *Chasneedarh* or Indian sweet and pungent meat recipes. These are best made from very lean pork, veal or lamb; in that order of preference. In Indian cuisine, chasneedarh recipes are served with various light, crisp vegetables and dry whole-wheat Indian bread, to counteract the sweetness of the syrup. Where it is not mentioned in the recipes, it may be understood that raw vegetables like celery, bamboo shoots, fresh young white cabbage may be added to the syrup and cooked for only a few minutes to let them retain their crispness. Celery should be diced small, cut on a slant. Cabbage should be cut in tiny shreds, bamboo shoots slivered, and so on. The small size enables the vegetables to absorb the spices and syrup without overcooking.

LANGAR CHASNEEDARH

(*Sweet-Pungent Recipe Hot from the Kitchen*)

2 pounds pork
1 pound beets
1 pound carrots
1¾ tablespoons coriander
12 peppercorns
1 tablespoon green ginger, (⅜ teaspoon powdered)
salt
1 pound sugar
1 pint lemon juice
1 pound onions
¼ pound butter
½ pound spinach, soya, kale or any other green
3 tablespoons pimentos
¼ teaspoon saffron

Cook the meat, cut into small pieces, with thin rounds of beets, diced carrots, the coriander, pepper, ginger and salt pounded and made into a paste with a little water. Boil the sugar and lemon juice for 5 minutes, to make the chasneedarh syrup.

When the meat is done, strain the gravy, and reserve. Lightly brown onions, sliced, in the butter. Add the meat and give it a bhogar (shake) in this. Fry it well. Then add the chopped spinach or other greens and pimentos to the gravy reserved. Cook them covered. When these are done, place the bhogared meat in it, sprinkle the saffron dissolved in a tablespoon of hot water over the whole. Take off the fire and add the syrup. Cook and serve after 10 minutes.

Some people like this served cold also. For 6 to 8.

FLOUR DUMPLINGS FOR INDIAN CURRIES

2 eggs
2 tablespoons butter
½ teaspoon salt
½ cup matzo meal
chicken or meat broth

Separate the eggs and beat the yolks, together with the butter and salt. Mix thoroughly with the matzo meal. Whisk the egg whites until they pyramid. Fold gently into the mixture. Chill 10 minutes. Shape into 1½ inch cakes or biscuits. Drop them into chicken or meat broth (or use bouillon cubes) and cook covered 20 minutes.

This is the basic recipe. Other pastes, like ravioli, can be used.

Here is another recipe for the Sweet and Pungent style of preparation. It is in the style called Aush — meaning with dumplings, lentils, vegetables and meat. Not all of the recipes using dumplings are sweet and pungent, however. This recipe for dumplings is especially good. There are many others, and different households have their own. Most of them are made with an Indian leaven called *Kheemer*. There is little difference between Indian and American dumplings. I give here a recipe using ingredients found in all American food stores.

KORMA RANGH-BRANGHI

(Dumplings Colorful)

1 pound sugar
1 pint lime juice
¼ pound onions
¼ pound butter
2 tablespoons coriander
salt
2 pounds pork
½ pound beets
1 pound carrots
¼ pound (each) spinach and other greens
2½ tablespoons white beans (marrow beans or others)
4 cardamons (seeds of)
¾ inch stick cinnamon
½ teaspoon chili (P)
8 dumplings (p. 75)
½ teaspoon saffron (P)
rose water

Fry the onions in the butter, put in the meat, cut medium fine, with the coriander and salt. Brown the meat well and add 3 cups of water. Simmer till done.

Boil the sugar and lime juice for 15 minutes to make the chasneedarh syrup.

In another vessel cook separately the beets; cook the carrots, spinach and beans along with the cardamon seeds, cinnamon, chili. Add the dumplings 15 or 20 minutes before the vegetables are done. Mix the vegetables with the meat. Before serving, add the syrup mixed with the saffron. Sprinkle with rose water. Serves 6.

Dumplings are also used in the next recipe. This one is called Aush Bhogar. It is a recipe for lamb, though pork, veal or rabbit will do equally well; or pheasant — though I was never advised to try pheasant for this recipe.

It just happened, motoring on an eerie Himalayan road at dark midnight, that the pheasant fairly fell into our cooking pot. My chauffeur and a photographer on a tour of official duty gaped to see a magnificent leopard walk out of the shadow of massive, silent deodar trees, look at the car with glinting eyes, and begin to amble with sang-froid ahead of the car. There were alarms and agitations in the car. After five minutes, tiring of this diversion, the beast gave a lithe shrug of his spotted shoulders, and slithered down the ravine.

Before we had time to compose ourselves, a gorgeous pheasant flew soundlessly into our lights and with a turgid *thwak* draped himself foolishly over the radiator. There was a well smoked, much used casserole in the luggage compartment and . . . Aush Bhogar Pheasant.

AUSH BHOGAR

2 pounds lamb
2 teaspoons turmeric
1 tablespoon coriander
1 teaspoon cummin
1 tablespoon green ginger
(3/8 teaspoon powdered)
salt
1 teaspoon chili (P)
½ tablespoon garlic
½ pound onions
3 tablespoons butter
10 dumplings (p. 75)

Cut the meat into medium-sized pieces. Pound in a mortar and pestle the turmeric, coriander, cummin, ginger, salt, chili, garlic and onions chopped, with a little water, into a paste. Cook, turning the meat, for 10 minutes. Then close the casserole tight and cook till meat has absorbed all the butter. Then add the water (about 1¾ cups) and cook till meat is tender. The dumplings are to be added 20 to 25 minutes before serving time. This recipe may be finished with plenty of gravy, or it may be served with just a few tablespoons of its juice, considerably reduced. Serves 4.

AUSH JAWAR (*Aush with Barley*)

1 pound barley
water or Akni (p. 28)
2 pounds lamb or pork
¼ pound onions
2 tomatoes
5 cloves
½ teaspoon cayenne
8 cardamons (seeds of)
salt
4 tablespoons butter
½ inch stick cinnamon

Bring the barley to a boil in water or Akni (p. 28) 4 times in just liquid water to cover it . . . Then add more liquid and cook till done.

Brown the diced meat with cinnamon, cloves, salt and cardamon seeds in 2 tablespoons butter. Add the barley after draining it. In another saucepan melt the remaining butter and fry the onions, sliced, and cayenne, adding tomatoes when onions are well browned. Add to the meat and barley. Firmly close the casserole. Give it 3 bhogars (shakes) in 3 minutes, and serve at once. For 4.

No dumplings were used with the preceding recipe; with the barley they would have been redundant. The next one has them again. This one is quite special.

KORMA BHURTA

(*With Eggplant and Dumplings*)

- 2 pounds lamb or pork
- ¼ pound plus 4 tablespoons butter
- 1 pound onions
- 1½ tablespoons coriander
- 1 tablespoon garlic
- ½ teaspoon chili (P)
- 1 small eggplant
- 2 teaspoons turmeric
- salt
- 4 cardamons (seeds of)
- 8 dumplings
- 1 pint yoghurt
- 2 tablespoons chick peas, soaked and parboiled (optional)

Dice 1 pound of the meat small, almond size. Grind the other pound fine. Fry the diced meat in 4 tablespoons butter, with onions sliced, coriander, pounded garlic, and chili. Fry the ground meat, mixed with well mashed, peeled eggplant, with 1 teaspoon of the turmeric, salt and crushed cardamon seeds. Reserve both the meats, keeping them separate.

Flatten the dumplings into cakes, square in shape, about 4

by 4 inches each. Place on them a little of the ground meat and eggplant mixture. Fold the dumpling cake so it makes a triangle. Press the sides down firmly, pinching them so that they will not open. Now fry the cakes in a little butter, browning on both sides. Then boil them in a mixture of the yoghurt with 1 cup water for ¼ hour. Reserve both the yoghurt and the cakes.

Add the yoghurt mixture (and chick peas if used) to the diced meat and cook briskly till the meat is tender. Then add the cakes. Sprinkle the other tablespoon of turmeric over it all. Mix well. Cover for 5 minutes, away from the fire and serve. For 4.

CHAPTER 6

Indian Rice Cookery

If Indian meat cooking is distinct from any other type of cooking, Indian rice preparation also resists comparison. There is not just boiled rice, or steamed rice, or even fried rice, but a system and taste that promises to be the apogee of pleasure and refinement.

Apart from boiled and steamed rice, Indian cuisine heralds and proclaims four other main modes of cooking.

The *Pellao* is generally made with butter and with vegetables, meat, fish, fowl and game. It may also be made plain. Sometimes only good stock and a few green herbs suffice.

The *Kitcheri* (or to use the Scotch appropriation and name of this cooking, Kedgeree) is made with rice and lentils. The cooking here is different from that of the Pellaos.

The spiced *Briani* is a fine and clever fusion of the principles of the many curry styles and of pellao cooking. Here, too, the Briani may be made plain with spices only, or with meat, fowl, game, fish and sea food. Many styles of preparation go to create the unique savor of this way of cooking rice.

The *Zarda, Meetha Pellao* and *Chasneedarh* are sweet. These are made with sugar, almonds, pistachio nuts, dried and fresh fruit. A generous addition of fragrant spices help to make the Zarda rice one of the most refined of all desserts. These are a far cry from the ordinary rice pudding.

The recipes have their cooking techniques explained with their preparation. The *Pellao, Briani, Kitcheri* and *Zarda,* made with either meat, vegetables or fruit, may be braised, steamed, baked or fried in a variety of ways. The meat may be prepared and added to the rice, and both finished together. Or both may be cooked together. Also, the stock of the meat cooked in water, court-bouillon or Akni is used to cook the rice. The meat and rice are combined at a certain stage and baked till done. Occasionally rice may be parboiled, then fried in the gravy of the meat, the meat fried separately, and the whole combined for the desired mode of preparation. There are times when half the rice may be fried, the other half boiled, and these finished with the meat (also fish, sea food, fowl or vegetables, and fruit for the sweet rice). Then again, the rice may be made plain, with the meat in this style: the meat is arranged in the center; melted butter is poured over both, and the cooking takes place in the oven. Rice can also be acidulated, if that taste is demanded. The Chasneedarh rice is used of course, in the Zarda variety. This is finished off in another style, and the chasnee is used to sweeten it. The chasnee is sweet-pungent, whereas the syrup for most sweet rice dishes is pure syrup.

In every case, the essence of the meat permeates the rice. Often the rice has *more* flavor than the meat used in or with it. And this is the delight — the common rice outshining the best meat — that awaits you in this chapter.

Rice in India, as in many countries in Asia, or what I would call the Monsoon lands, is of superlative quality. It is grown with the care lavished on rare flowers. There is connoisseurship in rice selection, as there is in wine tasting in Europe. The poorest man in India knows the grades and varieties of rice. Excellent rice is available in the United States. There is brown or unpolished rice which is less used although it has a pleasant, nutty flavor and retains most of its nourishment and there is fine long-grain white rice, long-grain fortified rice and converted rice. It is only in the United States and India that converted rice is now produced on a large scale. The process of converting rice is actually a parboiling which tends to drive the nutrients into the center of the rice grain and to harden its surface against loss of those nutrients during the polishing process. Converted rice looks amber in the polished grain but emerges white from cooking. Many good types of Indian rice may be aged for fifteen years, so it can be used for the best zarda and chasnee modes of preparations. The grain of the best Indian rice is a delight to see, and pleasing aesthetically: an inch long, curved like the new moon, and frail as a frost flower.

The origins of rice are unknown. It is reliably thought that it was first grown in northern India. The Indus Valley civilization — phase of 3600 B.C. — was using carefully cultivated rice. It was known in China at least as early as 2800 B.C. Rice has the most colorful history of any food. It was the subject of royal favor in many lands. Since then, and for centuries in Europe, it has been a favorite food.

The word curry has not only become a slander of Indian cooking but has served also to disseminate the accompanying sticky mess of rice that could do admirably for book-binders' paste.

First, here are a couple of ways to make faultless boiled rice.

CHAWAL (*Plain Boiled Rice*)

For ½ pound of rice, use a 2-quart open vessel. Any saucepan, casserole or Dutch oven will do. It is essential to have the vessel of thick metal. Thin and flimsy vessels are responsible for many failures to cook rice — *any* kind of rice.

Fill a 2-quart vessel three quarters full with cold water. Bring the water to a boil. When water is jumping briskly, add the rice. Stir a little and cook uncovered till done. This should take about 20 minutes. But the only accurate, and indispensable test is to try a grain of rice, with your thumb or your teeth. When it is cooked at the core, add 1 tablespoon salt and 1 cup cold water to the boiling rice. Remove immediately from the fire and straightaway drain in colander. The rice will be dry and ready to serve in a few minutes.

During cooking, stir the rice once. Overstirring is the main reason for pulpy rice. Indian rice is dry, fluffy, and perfectly cooked all the way through.

This method is the simplest, and is infallible. To recapitulate: for ½ pound of rice use a 2-quart vessel filled three quarters with cold water brought to a furious boil. Rice is added, stirred well *once only*, cooked uncovered. After about 20 minutes, *test by hand* a grain of rice. When done, add salt and 1 cup *cold* water. Quickly remove rice from fire, stir once again, and *immediately* drain in colander.

In general it is important that rice by this method be cooked in plenty of water. One pound of rice should be cooked so that it is about 6 to 10 inches under water.

TO REHEAT LEFTOVER BOILED RICE

If you have a little rice left over and want to combine it with freshly boiled rice, put into the vessel of boiling rice 5 seconds before adding the cup of cold water. Drain them together, and serve.

TO REHEAT LARGE QUANTITY OF LEFTOVER BOILED RICE

Heat plenty of cold water in a big vessel. When water is boiling fiercely, put the leftover rice in. Stir it once. Leave in water for not more than 3 to 5 *seconds*. Drain immediately in a colander. Your rice will be hot, and good as new.

PLAIN BOILED RICE, LITTLE WATER STYLE

This is another way of cooking, that I learned myself. No one ever taught me this. Best if stock is used instead of water.

Take a thick casserole — 3 to 4 quarts will do for 1 pound of rice or more — and put in the rice. Now add cold water or stock to cover the rice by a depth of 1¼ inches, no more. Bring to a boil. Keep boiling for 1 minute, roughly, then reduce the heat to very low. Cook till rice is done. All the water will have dried. Clap on the lid tight. Remove from heat for 5 to 7 minutes and serve. The rice will be light, dry, fluffy and each grain separate.

The thickness of the vessel will determine the exact amount of water needed. It is better to use less than required and add more. To determine if the rice is done, and dry, prod the rice with a knife to see if any moisture is left. Test with thumb.

Stirring is again forbidden, except in the beginning.

To obtain dazzling white boiled rice, squeeze in the juice of ¼ to ½ lemon when boiling it. This goes for any method of boiling rice.

But everything has its own good use; the plain boiled rice as much as the near bacchanalian raptures of the Pellao. We keep that in mind, for pleasure in food and good things lies not in satiation, but in "hitting the mark" in choice and judgment. "You would not take poison because a doctor lives in town," says an Indian proverb, "nor wear tiaras on the toes just because we can, my dear."

We approach the Pellaos.

PELLAO SADAH (*Pellao without Frills*)

1 onion	½ pound rice
3 tablespoons butter	1 teaspoon salt (about)

Slice the onion carefully into thin rings. Heat the butter. Brown and crisp the onion rings. Lift them out carefully and reserve. Add the rice to the butter and cook it over gentle heat for 7 to 10 minutes. The rice will absorb the butter; with constant stirring it will not have burned or scorched. Now add enough water to cover the rice by 1¼ inches, and the salt. Bring to a boil for 1 minute, reduce the heat to very low, and cook till all the water has been absorbed. (After the water has been added, the rice should not be stirred.) When the water has evaporated, cover tight, leave away from heat for 5 to 10 minutes; uncover and serve, with onion rings arranged over the rice.

This is the Little Water Method. Add salt to all pellaos with the water.

The seeds of 3 cardamons, 2 cloves and ¼ inch of stick cinnamon may be added to this recipe.

These recipes for Pellao, Briani, and the Chasnee Pellao are not arranged according to the main ingredient, but according to some identity of cooking style and of preparation. For instance, lamb and beef recipes will be found with fish and those for fowl. These are straightened out, according to category, in the all-knowing index!

MURGHI PELLAO KHASA

(*Chicken Pellao Somewhat Different*)

1 2-pound chicken
1½ teaspoons salt (about)
¼ tablespoon green ginger
(a good pinch of powdered)
2 onions
½ pound rice
5 tablespoons butter
5 peppercorns
2 blades mace
2 cardamons (seeds of)
4 eggs

Clean, wash thoroughly and truss the chicken. Cook in 2¼ cups water, salt, ginger and 1 onion, pounded together. Reserve chicken and stock.

In a heavy vessel, warm the butter; brown the other onion sliced very thin. Remove onions when golden, and reserve. Fry the rice in the butter with the crushed peppercorns, mace and cardamon seeds. Pour in just enough of the chicken stock to cover the rice and not a whit more. Simmer rice, very gently. Brown the chicken in some more butter. Hard-boil the eggs. When the rice is done, serve it with the whole chicken on top, with quartered eggs, or with chicken disjointed into 18 pieces. Decorate with fried onion, or strew it on top. Serves 4.

A Dusty Journey

The common spud and the familiar rice can make an unusual combination. Although you may object that this is starch mixed with starch, you will find that the food textures are different; also it is more interesting for the person who likes variety to eat a combination of two different things than just one by itself. When I first tasted this recipe, I was hungry, famished and parched by a dusty journey. I ate in one of the wayside foodstalls notorious in India for bad food. This one proved to be good. Sitting in the cool shade of the foodstall, I ate the Pellao with Potatoes served on a big plume of banana leaf, cool and green. The water I drank was drawn from a hillside, leaping fresh from spring into a porous clay cup like the one I had broken clatteringly, years ago, having stolen it from Big Brother Dilla's kitchen.

The few benches of rough-hewn sisoo wood were full of farmers, sitting astride as on horseback. Their white draperies and multicolored turbans, fiercely starched, nodded and swung as they bent their heads to the pellao.

They finished their pellao, threw the banana leaves into a tin canister, and asked for more. So did I. The stallkeeper was proud of his pellao. His wooden benches and tables were scoured with hot ashes and water till they shone like silver. The stall was, as usual, set in a small house with the tables out in the sunshine, over carefully swept ground. A bunch of hill flowers curved over the entrance. In the darkness of the shop interior glittered rows of copper and brass casseroles. His range of wood-burning grates were fresh painted with clay; over them the rows of warming pots and ovens sat like magnets for the roadsider. The long ladle reached with a clang into the pots, and the food turned with an Oh and an Ah into the sunny light.

The stallkeeper, who enjoyed the repeat calls, said he made so much every day and no more. To make more pellao would ruin the quality, and tire him unduly. I have tried to duplicate his pellao, but never been even remotely able to match it. Remembrance of that creamy-colored pellao, peaked high on the satiny, full-veined banana leaf, pleases me still.

That life tends to repeat itself somewhat may be apparent from a scene from one of India's finest classical dramas. In *The Little Clay Cart* one of the cast (whose predicament seems identical to mine, when I found the roadside foodstall) says that he has been working for so long that his eyes are dancing. He is so hungry that his eyes are crackling like lotus seeds dried in the fiercest rays of the summer sun . . . I'll ask my wife whether there is anything for breakfast or not. Hello! here I am. Merciful heavens! Why in the world has everything in our house been turned upside down? A long stream of rice water is flowing down the street . . . It smells so good that my hunger seems to blaze up and hurt me more than ever. Has some hidden treasure come to light or am I hungry enough to think the whole world is made of rice? There surely isn't breakfast in our house, and I'm starved to death . . . Well, I'll call my wife and learn the truth . . . "Mistress, will you come here a moment?"

The actor (to carry my abridged version further) asks if there is anything to eat.

"There is everything, sir."

"Well, what?"

"For instance," the actress says, "there is rice with sugar, rice with melted butter, rice with coagulated milk; rice: and altogether it makes a dish fit for heaven. May the gods be always thus gracious."

The actor cries, "All that in our house?"

"Oh no. It is in the market place, sir."

The actor, angrily (for heaven seems to have no fury like a hungry man, and an actor at that), scorned and outwitted by his wife, cries out a plea that her hopes be cut off similarly.

The actress begs forgiveness for the joke, but reminds her husband that it is a day of fast. This is a sacrifice for a handsome husband in the next life. The actor is wrathful again. Look, he says; she is sacrificing my food to get herself a handsome husband in the next life. But he calms down, and forgets his hunger, on learning that it is he his wife wants as a husband in the next life.

Hunger, and the size of the appetite, it seems, are ruled by more things than the stomach.

We, profiting from antiquity, will keep our rice always at home, and savor it at leisure.

PELLAO WITH POTATOES

1 pound small potatoes
1 onion
½ clove garlic (optional)
4 tablespoons butter
1 pound rice
1 tablespoon coriander
½ tablespoon parsley
½ tablespoon green ginger
(no substitute)
salt

Steep rice ½ hour in cold water. Wash, peel and quarter the potatoes. Warm the butter in a heavy casserole and lightly brown the onion thin sliced. Then add the rice, drained well, and the potatoes, with pounded garlic and pounded ginger. Stir the whole together for 10 minutes. Then add water to cover by 1¼ inches. Salt it. Bring to a boil, lower heat, and cook till dry. Serve with shredded parsley. For 6.

You may also try cooking the rice with 1 inch of water, covered, till the rice is dry and tender.

Green peas may be substituted for potatoes.

PELLAO WITH ASPARAGUS

½ pound asparagus
salt
1 pound rice
3 tablespoons butter
4 cardamons (seeds of)
2 peppercorns
½ cup heavy cream
½ tablespoon coriander

Clean, wash and cook the asparagus stalks in salted water till they are tender. Reserve asparagus and its liquor. Boil the rice in the asparagus water, adding more water if necessary. Reserve the liquor. Drain rice.

Melt the butter, fry the cardamon seeds and the peppercorns, crushed. Lightly fry the cooked asparagus, for not more than 5 minutes over a low flame. Remove asparagus casserole from the heat, put in ¼ cup asparagus liquor; add the rice; pour the cream over this, with the coriander. Mix them well, but tenderly. Cover hermetically and place over brisk heat for 5 minutes. Then remove to preheated (250°) oven for 20 minutes. Take out and serve a truly fragrant recipe. For 6.

PELLAO "EYE OF COAL"

(*With Stuffed Tomatoes*)

½ pound ground meat
6 tablespoons butter
6 peppercorns
salt
6 small tomatoes
1 pound rice
1 teaspoon mustard seeds
meat stock, or bouillon cube infusion

Cook the ground meat in a little water and butter with the crushed peppercorns and salt. Scoop out the tomatoes without damaging the skin. Mix the scooped out tomato with the ground meat. Stuff the tomato shells with this and skewer them tight with cocktail sticks. Reserve for the moment.

Melt the rest of the butter and brown the rice in it. When the rice has gently absorbed the butter, add the mustard seeds. Fry them well together (about 10 minutes for the rice and another 1 minute for the mustard seeds). When the first mustard seed snaps and crackles, pour in the stock to cover by 1½ inches. Gently and with care place the stuffed tomatoes. Bring the rice to a boil and then reduce heat to very low. Cook uncovered till done. Then cover for 5 to 7 minutes, away from the heat.

This pellao will have taken on a gentle pink color. The aroma of the tomatoes will have been carried to the rice. The tomatoes will have taken on the goodness of the rice and stock. Tomatoes well prepared will show themselves as good journeymen, not as sanguinary demons intent on devouring the flavor of their associates. Serves 6 to 8.

In the play I have just mentioned, there is a description of a scene which will give you an idea of the home and the hearth. This one concerns a courtesan. No matter, for the life we all lead is similiar in essentials and necessities. The old Indian courtesan — I am unable to compare her with anyone save the Japanese geisha — had to be every inch a lady, save in one respect. Like any cultured high-born woman, the courtesan mastered the Sixty-four Arts. These range from social manners, conversation, flower arrangements, entertaining, letter writing, understanding different human temperaments, subtlety in human relations, and, with her gifts for amorousness, to all the domestic talents of a housewife, including cooking.

In this play, *The Little Clay Cart,* one of the actors, on assignment for his best friend, goes to see the courtesan.

The gateway is sprinkled and clean. There are offerings of all sorts of fragrant flowers. It is adorned with strings of jasmine garlands that hang and toss about like the trunk of king elephants . . . holiday banners gleam red as great rubies . . . water jars of crystal in which are set bright green mango twigs.

. . . Here is the first court, with rows of balconies brilliant as the moon, or sea shells, or lotus stalks . . . There the porter sits and snoozes as comfortably as a professor.

Well! Here is the second court. The cart bullocks are tied. They grow fat with the pulse-stalks and grass brought them. Their horns are lacquered. Here is another bullock snorting like a gentleman insulted. And here is a fighting ram, having his neck rubbed like a prize fighter after the fight . . . here is a monkey, tied fast like a thief . . .

The third court: books for young gentlemen to read; a half-read book lying on the gaming tables. And the table itself has dice made out of gems. And here are the women of the place holding pictures painted in many colors (this was one of the Sixty-four Arts).

Then the fourth court, where drums are booming and cymbals are falling . . . the pipe makes music as the humming of bees, and here, again, courtesan girls who sing as charmingly as honey-drunk bees. Water coolers are hanging in the windows to catch the breeze. And there is the fifth court.

In the fifth court, the smell of spices and oil is attractive enough to make a poor devil's mouth water. The kitchen is kept hot all the time, and gusts of steam, laden with all sorts of good aromas, seem like sighs issuing from its mouthlike doors. The fragrance of the preparations of all kinds of food and sauces makes me smack my lips. And here is the butcher boy washing a mess of chitterlings. The cook is busy with all kinds of food. Sweetmeats are being confected, cakes are being baked. (To himself): I wonder if I am to get a chance to wash my feet and hands, and an invitation to eat what I can hold . . .

In the sixth court, the jewelers are testing the lapis lazuli, the pearls, the corals, the topazes, the sapphires, the cat's-eyes, the rubies, the emeralds.

Also more preparations for food and for perfumes are being made. (Spices have been always used for both.) Here musk is being moistened, wet bundles of saffron are being dried, sandal-wood is being ground to make sandal-water. Beetle leaves (an Indian aromatic mostly used as an after-dinner pleasure) and camphor are being given to courtesans and their guests. Coquet-tish glances are being exchanged . . . laughter is in the air.

And so on to the seventh court, where people are billing and cooing and the parrot in a cage, chanting like a Brahmin, with his belly full of rice and cream.

The play goes on with other things, and we have no means of knowing if he got the invitation to dine that he had so wanted.

But cooks and spicers, and all things nicer, are ours for the taking. Does fancy turn to a:

MASSALE DARH PELLAO

(*Intriguingly Spicy Pellao*)

1½ pounds rice
1 onion
5 tablespoons butter
4 small chickens, squabs, or game hens (about 1 pound each)
¾ tablespoon green ginger, (¼ teaspoon powdered)
1 tablespoon garlic
salt
1 pint yoghurt
stock (chicken or veal)
4 cardamons (seeds of)

Soak the rice 35 minutes in cold water; reserve. Brown the onion, sliced very thin, in butter and put in the birds. Pound the ginger with half the garlic and salt; add to the yoghurt. Add these to the butter and cook very gently for 5 minutes. Then place the birds in this mixture. Fry them well on all sides.

Grind with a mortar and pestle the remaining garlic with 1 cup stock or water. Add this to the birds with the cardamon seeds. Place the drained rice on top. Be sure the liquid level comes to about 1 inch above rice. Sprinkle in water if necessary. Close the lid hermetically and cook gently, after bringing it to a brief boil. Serves 8.

It may be repeated here that the quantity of water for the rice in this recipe, and all others, is approximate. About 1¼ or 1¾ inches may be correct. The variation depends on the thickness of the casserole and the exact quantity of heat applied. The kind of rice, and the tenderness of the squab used, can also influence the cooking time. The rice has to be perfectly tender, but dry and not mushy. Cooking rice a few times in the manner of these recipes will show you the exact amount of liquid required. Keep to the same casserole, and you should have little trouble.

And again: it is better to start with 1½ inches instead of the 1¾ inches called for in the recipe, if you feel uncertain. It is always easy to add more, if more liquid is required, but almost impossible to salvage over-inundated rice.

In this recipe it will be noticed that the preparation is according to the Little Water Method. Here 1 inch is used instead of the usual 1¼ inches of liquid over the surface of the rice, because it is cooked covered. If it is desired to cook the rice uncovered, use 1¼ inches of liquid.

CHICKEN AND SWEET GREEN PEPPER PELLAO

2 onions
½ cup butter
2 cloves garlic
salt
2 green peppers
1 pint yoghurt
1 4-pound fowl
2 pounds rice
7 cardamons (seeds of)
½ pimento (fresh or canned)

Lightly brown the onions, sliced very thin, in the butter. Crush and remove the onions, reserving them. Mash the garlic with the salt and mix with yoghurt. Add enough water to this mixture to cook the chicken as you would a stewed chicken. Enough liquid should remain to cook the rice. Reserve chicken cooked in this fashion.

Cook the rice about 10 minutes in the same chicken liquor. Place it atop the chicken, adding enough liquid to enable rice to finish cooking. About ½ cup should do here. Having arranged the rice over the chicken, sprinkle with cardamon seeds, crushed, and place on it the green peppers cut in rings. Cross these with strips of pimento. Close the lid tight and cook the rice over very low heat for about 25 minutes, or till cooked. Remove from heat and let stand for 5 minutes, keeping it covered. Serves 10.

There are many more recipes of Pellao, with vegetable, chicken or meat. These are distinct from the Briani, which is a combination of the pellao style and the curry technique, and the Chasnee Pellao which is always sweet, or sweet and pungent.

For a change here are a few pellaos with fish and with sea food.

MACHCHI PELLAO (*Fish Pellao*)

2 pounds salmon or any firm-textured other fish
6 tablespoons sesame, or peanut oil
split-pea flour (optional, p. 33)
salt
½ pound onion
½ teaspoon black pepper
½ cup yoghurt
butter
½ teaspoon cloves
4 ounces blanched almonds
1 tablespoon coriander
1 pound rice (boiled 10–12 minutes)
½ teaspoon cardamon seeds
1 inch stick cinnamon

This Pellao with Fish introduces two important stages of preparing fish the Indian way.

First, the fish is rubbed well with Bessan or split-pea flour, kept for a little while and then washed thoroughly. This process may be repeated, for certain recipes, by fastidious chefs. The result is to remove much of the fishy smell and some of the superfluous oils in the fish; it becomes much sweeter, more delicate.

Second, most Indians favor oil for fish, even the northern Indians in the Punjab who swear by clarified butter. Oil does give fish a certain savor. Indian mustard oil, which I have not found elsewhere, is excellent; in fact some fish prepared with this last oil is unbeatable. But not all fish in India is fried in oil.

Both of these steps may be dispensed with in preparing the Machchi Pellao.

Clean and wash the fish thoroughly, in several washes of running water. Dry it, and cut in thick steaks. Steep the fish in the oil for ½ to ¾ hour. Then wash it off (this is the place to use the bessan preparation: rub fish with split-pea flour, wash immediately; repeat 4 times). Then gently prick the fish all over with a silver fork. Pound in a mortar and pestle salt, the onion, pepper and yoghurt, and paste over the fish slices.

Melt the butter in a heavy saucepan, fry the cloves, and bhogar (shake) the fish in this. Open the cover and add the following to the fish: almonds, bruised, coriander and ½ cup of water from the rice. Simmer the fish gently till the gravy thickens. Put the rice in a casserole, place the fish in the center, cover with rest of the rice adding cardamon seeds and cinnamon. Over this pour the fish gravy (½ cup) and the butter. Hermetically close the casserole. Heat 3 minutes, then place in a preheated (275°) oven for another 10 minutes. Serves 6.

These pellaos are not difficult, although they do require meticulous timing and preparation. Once you have made a few, the rest will seem easy. A pellao of this kind is (or rather, can be) a one-dish meal. The cooking time is about ¾ hour, including all the preparations. For after-theater suppers, and other such occasions, resort to the pellao. All the ingredients can be laid out in advance. I have often made a pellao for more than six persons in twenty-five minutes, and left the guests to ponder on the ingenuity of the "Mysterious East."

SHRIMP PELLAO (*Rose Petal*)

1½ pounds raw shrimps (fresh or frozen)
5 tablespoons butter
1 pound rice
3 tablespoons hearts of celery, or bamboo shoots (canned)
salt
rose water

Rose petal refers to the manner of arranging the shrimps. Using a large needle and coarse thread, five shrimps are strung and tied, tails together — presented thus in the Pellao, opening out like a flower. Another manner of making the rose petal is to make butterfly shrimps (by slitting the front part and flattening them and then tying them around the middle, without threading them. This presentation can be dispensed with, of course, with a hangdog look.

Shell, wash and tie shrimps as desired, and dry in paper toweling. Fry them gently in 1 tablespoon butter for 1 minute, then cook in water and salt till done. Shrimps, depending on the size, should never be overcooked. Five to 10 minutes suffices. Reserve the shrimps and the liquor.

Melt the rest of the butter and fry the rice, stirring all the time. When the rice has absorbed the butter, place the shrimps on the rice, and cover with shrimp liquor to a depth of 1¼ inches. Add the celery or bamboo shoots, cut bite-size, and salt. Bring to a boil, then reduce heat to very low. When cooked, serve by sprinkling a little rose water over all. Serves 6.

PELLAO (*Culled from the Sea*)

½ pound scallops
½ pound shrimps
1 large crab or several small ones (to make ½ pound crabmeat)
¼ pint oysters or clams (fresh or frozen)
6 tablespoons butter
2 pounds rice
8 cardamons (seeds of)
½ tablespoon green ginger (good pinch of powdered)
salt
1 teaspoon sesame seeds
½ lemon (juice of)
1 tablespoon watercress

Cook the scallops and the shrimps, shelled, till half done, reserving the liquor. Cook the crab or crabs similarly and if possible extract the meat in one piece. Open the oysters and reserve, with their liquor, with the other fish. If the oysters are frozen, thaw them somewhat. Reserve the oyster liquor also.

Heat the butter, put in the rice with the cardamon seeds, ginger and salt pounded together. Fry till the butter is absorbed.

Then pour in enough of the reserved liquor to cook the rice. Place the shrimps and scallops on the rice. Add the oysters or clams with their juice. The liquor should cover the rice and sea food by 1¼ inches. Add the sesame seeds and bring the rice to a boil. Immediately reduce the heat to very low and cook. Five minutes before the rice is done, stir it a little and place the crab, in one piece if possible, in the center. Squeeze lemon juice over the top. When the Pellao is ready, serve with watercress over it. For 12 persons, who will love to dig under the rice for its hidden treasure of these fruits of the sea. Serves 6 to 8.

LOBSTER PELLAO

- 4 1-pound live lobsters
- salt
- Akni bouquet (p. 28)
- 12 bay leaves
- 1 onion
- 4 teaspoons coriander
- fish bones
- 1 teaspoon black pepper
- 3 tablespoons butter
- 2 pounds rice

Wash the lobsters thoroughly with salt and water. Boil the lobsters in Akni I or II, adding the bay leaves, onion, 3 teaspoons of the coriander and fish bones, bruised and placed in a separate cloth bag. When lobster is done, reserve it and the cooking liquor.

Shell the lobster reserving the coral. Bruise it with the remaining coriander, pepper and some of the liquor reserved.

Melt the butter and fry the rice as usual. When rice has absorbed the butter, add enough liquor to cover by 1½ inches; mix in the spiced coral paste. Boil up once and cook over the lowest heat. Five minutes before rice is ready, separate it lightly and place in the center the lobster broken into medium-sized pieces. Serves 8.

Here is a recipe quite different from the others. This one will make you feel like a frolic in spring.

PELLAO HUZOOR PASANDH

(*Pellao "To Please Your Noble Self"*)

2 pounds lamb or a 2-pound chicken, or 2 squabs, or 2 game hens
1 orange
½ cup grapes
¼ pound mangoes or papayas
1 tablespoon cashew nuts (unsalted)
2 tablespoons pistachio nuts (unsalted)
milk
4 tablespoons butter
1½ pint yoghurt
8 peppercorns
4 tablespoons blanched almonds
pinch of saffron (optional)
1 pound rice
1 tablespoon green ginger (⅜ teaspoon powdered)
salt
rose water (optional)

Wash and cut the lamb in pieces, about 1½ inches each. Keep the chicken or squab, if these are used, whole. Peel and cut the oranges in delicate rounds. Peel the grapes. Skin the mango or papaya (or try using an avocado; but *firm*, please). Reserve for the nonce.

Cook the shelled nuts in milk till they are tender. Reserve them and the milk.

Heat the butter and fry the meat till well browned all over. Add the yoghurt, peppercorns, crushed, ginger and salt pounded. Cook the meat in this for 10 minutes. Now place on top the rice which has been steeped in cold water for 35 minutes. Add enough milk to correct the amount of liquid necessary to cook rice (about ½ cup should be appropriate). Arrange the fruits prettily on top of the rice with all the nuts. Close the lid hermetically. Cook over a medium fire for 6 minutes. Then transfer the casserole to a preheated oven (250° to 275°) for 24 minutes. Rose water may be sprinkled over just before serving. Mix the pinch of saffron, if used, with rose water. For 6.

LAMB PELLAO WITH YAKHNI

1¾ pounds lamb
6 mint leaves
¼ pound butter
7 cardamons (seeds of)
2 lemons (juice of)
salt
1 cup heavy cream
½ cup yoghurt
½ pound rice (steeped 2 hours in cold water)
1 inch stick cinnamon
6 tablespoons spinach, cut in strips
6 cloves
rose water

Wash the meat well and sprinkle the mint leaves on it. Reserve. Heat 2 quarts water and cook the lamb, cubed, till liquid is reduced to 2 pints. This is the Yakhni. Clear and skim the stock. Strain and mix with the butter. When it bubbles add the cardamon seeds, and replace the meat in the stock. When the stock is reduced to 1 pint (2 cups), squeeze in the lemon juice, add the salt, and keep warm.

Mix the cream and the yoghurt and strain through a coarse cloth over the meat and sauce.

Drain the rice and boil it 10 minutes. Drain and pour rice over the meat and sauce. Put in the cinnamon, strips of spinach and the cloves. Close the lid hermetically. Cook over brisk fire for 6 minutes, shake once; finish off with 20 minutes in a preheated oven (250° to 275°).

Serve the Yakhni Pellao with a whisper of rose water. For 4 to 6.

From the Pandit of Ellora comes a magnificent pellao, one of the best dishes I have ever tasted in any cuisine. Despite the formidable amount of butter, cream and other ingredients, the pellao blooms into a dry, incredibly fragrant creation.

The recipe is named after Bandha Bahadur, a great hero among the warrior Sikhs of northern India. On his journey to Hyderabad in the Deccan, Bandha stopped at Ellora. This may or may not have been the favorite recipe of Bandha. Among Indians it is a common tradition to create dishes in honor of some one person. This recipe may have been dedicated by a great chef, turned mystic, an active disciple of a philosophical discipline and way of life.

The recipe is in the great tradition of medieval Punjabi cooking. In this form, like many of the Ellora Pandit's recipes distributed anonymously in the book, it dates to 1678.

So, whether Bandha Bahadur liked this recipe, or it was merely someone's inspiration from which we profit, this is the way to make it.

ALMOND CHICKEN YAKHNI PELLAO OF BANDHA BAHADUR

1 quart stock (beef, veal or chicken)
1 2-pound chicken (whole)
½ pint yoghurt
salt
1 cup heavy cream
½ pint milk
½ pound blanched almonds
2 lemons (juice of)
1 pound rice
¾ inch stick cinnamon
3 cloves
4 cardamons (seeds of)
12 anise seeds
2 tablespoons coriander
¼ to ½ pound butter
3 tablespoons green ginger (¾ teaspoon powdered)

It is best to make the stock from 2 pounds of stewing meat, which can be later ground and used for kababs or curry. Cook the meat in 2 quarts of water and remove when the stock has been reduced to half its quantity.

Thoroughly wash the chicken, and its cavity. Dry well with paper towels. Prick all over with a fork. Rub half the ginger pounded with salt inside the cavity and the other half, pounded with salt, outside.

Melt the butter in a *heavy* casserole or Dutch oven that can be sealed hermetically. Mix the yoghurt with the butter and, over low heat, brown the chicken all over. Then pour in ½ cup water. Remove from heat. Mix the cream and milk with the almonds well pounded or put in electric blender. Pour this over the chicken. Squeeze the lemon juice on top of this.

Boil the rice in the 1 quart of reserved stock till done (about 18 to 20 minutes). Strain off any liquid left and place rice on top of chicken. Strew over it the cinnamon, cloves, cardamon and anise seeds. Also sprinkle the coriander. Close the lid hermetically and cook briskly for 5 minutes over the fire. Then place for 25 minutes in a preheated oven (250° to 275°). For 8.

Game Pellao

THIS can be made with pheasant or game hen. If these are not available, use small pigeons. The following recipe is for the last named. Use any kind of game hen if it is in season and you are good with a gun.

PIGEON PELLAO (*Tease-Heart*)

3 small pigeons
½ pound onions
½ teaspoon saffron
2 cloves garlic (optional)
salt
1 cup yoghurt
1¾ pounds veal
¾ pound chick peas, soaked and parboiled
8 tablespoons butter
12 cloves
2 pounds rice
5 cardamons (seeds of)
2 tablespoons coriander
½ inch stick cinnamon
1 teaspoon black pepper

Wash, clean and dry pigeons. Split them down their length and flatten them well. Prick all over and cover with a paste of half the onions, saffron, the garlic well crushed (if desired), salt and yoghurt. Marinate the pigeons for 5 to 6 hours.

Mix the veal, sliced thin as for scaloppini, with the pigeons. Also mix in the chick peas. Cook them together in water, removing each when done sufficiently. The veal is to be pounded and made into a paste. Here the electric blender is excellent; use some cooking water to enable the veal to liquefy. Strain the liquefied veal through a coarse cloth. Bhogar (shake) it well with 2 tablespoons butter and 4 cloves, ground. Repeat bhogar three times. Now put the rice into the veal liquid and boil till rice is done.

Then take a heavy casserole and put a layer of rice on the bottom; sprinkle with 4 more ground cloves, some of the cardamon seeds and coriander, ground. Arrange the pigeons on this layer of rice, and over them spoon 2 tablespoons melted butter. Arrange on it thin-sliced, browned onion rings. Another layer of rice, cinnamon and cardamon seeds and 4 more ground cloves. Then the chick peas, a layer of rice with the remaining saffron, 4 tablespoons more butter and then the rest of the rice. The black pepper comes last. Cover the vessel hermetically, and keep on heat for 5 minutes. Now place in a barely warm oven or near heat for 65 minutes. Serve with reasonable pride and pleasure to a dinner party of 8 to 12.

Two Fables

Rice has always figured much in Indian life. Most religious ceremonies are symbolically performed with rice. The ideal offering, also the traditional, and moreover an ample one, is the Indian Kheer or Sheer (recipe included later). It is offered to all revered personages. Learned and holy men are welcomed into an Indian home with an offering of Kheer. Somehow Indians, adults and children, both find this dish a delectable pleasure. Properly made, it is one of the best sweets or desserts to be found. Many other kinds of rice preparations are used in Indian ritual. The first taste that Buddha had of food, after his rigorous meditation and enlightenment, was rice and milk.

I recall one of the multitudinous Indian fables that gives us an oblique glance at some part of Indian life, customs, and the ubiquitous rice. This story, like many Indian stories, does not depend on plot, or a trick ending. The aim is to display human life, and man's struggle to contain it in the wisest manner.

In India, the bird clans flocked together for deliberations. Swans, cranes and nightingales; peacocks, plovers and owls were there. Also present were doves, and pigeons, and partridges; blue jays, vultures and skylarks; starlings, demoiselles, cuckoos and woodpeckers were all there. Their plaint was that the lordly Golden Eagle was so intent on his meditations and religious work that he forgot his subjects. What use was a sham king? Wasn't there an old saying, People should avoid seven things — "leaky ships at sea, a dull professor, a priest without learning; a king who does not afford protection, a wife whose tongue can slash, a herdsman hankering after town life, and a barber after cash."

So it was decided to choose a new king. Then, observing that the owl had a dignified visage (Indians consider the owl stupid), they chose him and began preparations for all the prescribed ceremonies for anointing. Water from holy streams was brought. A bouquet of 108 roots, including the one marked with a wheel, were obtained. The throne was set, and a tiger skin spread before it. Golden jars were filled with five blossoms, sweet twigs, and grains. Bards chanted poetry. Maidens sang sweetly. In the forefront was prepared a grand vessel of consecrated rice, set off with white mustard, parched grain, golden saffron, wreaths of flowers, conch shells and more holiday drums rumbled . . .

At that moment a crow came into the assembly raucously announcing his own presence: "Well. Well! what's all this about?" When he was informed of the occasion, the crow laughed. He said, "Gentlemen, this is foolish. With eminent swans, shelldrakes and partridges . . . why anoint this ugly fellow who is blind in the daytime? It seems wrong. With his big hooked nose, eyes asquint, face without a hint of tenderness, he is fierce to see." And the perspicacious crow convinced them of the poor substitute.

And so, I hope the preceding recipes have aroused you to a full awareness of this golden eagle of rice cookery, and its superiority to the owl that is known all over the world as "Rice and Curry."

During a long stay in the Himalayan state called Chamba or Chamba Achamba (Chamba the Charming) I had gone out for a bear hunt. The *bhalu* had been troubling some villages. Cornfields had been despoiled, and one unwary farmer mauled badly.

There were two who set out for the bhalu, a *mian* or hill baron, and myself. The mian led the way, his white turban bobbing. We clambered over the rocks. In the cornfields the sun ran its warm fingers through the cool green. There was not a noise in the stillness save the mumble of the stream chiding the rocks. Ahead and quite close lay the pine forest where we presumed the bear lay drowsing the afternoon away. We were not trying to proceed silently as the bhalu, unlike the tiger, does not prowl or stalk humans.

Then we heard the noise, a slight scraping and snuffling. If it was the bear it wasn't a good place to be caught in. Nothing short of a double-barreled charge, which we were not carrying, would stop a bear at such short range.

As we stared and waited, another turban, and then a pair of eyes, slowly peeped over the ledge. Our "bear" suddenly gave cry with a very human throat:

"*Jai,*" he greeted us, leaping up with a smile.

I sat down on the grass laughing, and the mian ran down, confused with anger and sheepfacedness.

The farmer, barrel chested and swarthy jowled, under fierce imperial mustaches, looked like the bhalu's first cousin. But his smile was a smile of pure welcome. He held out a basket for me, full of apples, pears, mountain mulberries all purple, sweet green and red berries, choice walnuts, and some home-baked sweetmeats. This was his way of saying welcome, and he had run a mile over mountain paths to reach us in time. The Indians count hospitality as one of the greatest of virtues and pleasures.

I thanked him. Relaxing from the hard climb, we sat down near the stream and fed well on succulent fruit and delicious sweetmeats. We rinsed the purple from our mouths with the cool water, and drank only a little, for we had the climb ahead.

Getting the bear was similarly farcical. The young men of two mountain villages had turned out to beat the bear out of the forest. Drums boomed and horns raised a dreadful noise. There was a long, weary wait, and a tense cuddling of our rifles. Late in the afternoon, the bear emerged with a howl of rage, spreading utter confusion, for he was quite distant from where he was supposed to be. He broke in on a group of farmers, quietly smoking after their beat had finished, and sent them scattering like partridges all over the hillside. Both the mian and I tried to get a bead on the beast, who was more than three hundred yards away from us. I fired, and the bear spun around. But I had only pinked him in the rump and he was properly angry. Standing on the ledge he shook his fists at me and drummed on his chest. A moment later he was gone down the ravine. The villagers got him the next morning.

That evening, on our way down, the sky slowly grew darker. From the trenches behind the hills, massed battalions of clouds, with scarred and wind-swept banners, churned upward. The first drops fell solidly, making our ponies start with horsy restiveness. The downpour began. Rain in big plumes broke upon the rocks. The grass furrows became rivulets. Down the hillsides came new streams, rushing with a fearful clatter. Solid streaks of rain hid the mian, a few yards in front.

"You think, my mian," I shouted, "that the farmer, the bear — has a fire?"

"If there is a house left in this rain, there will be a fire."

With the sure instinct of the hill-born the mian sought the corridors between the darkness and the rain to our farmer's hillside house. The farmer, with a flash of white teeth in a blue-jowled face, rushed out, grabbing the reins, and shouted, "Good it is! fine it is! it's as I would have wished," and pushed us into the lighted hearth. While he took the horses in, the farmer's wife came to welcome us with folded hands.

She was beautiful, like many hill women in Chamba. With a voice which was soft, the most feminine in the whole world, she asked us to sit before the log fire.

In the Indian code of manners, which is abstemious, it may be insulting to offer drink to one who abhors it. Our host was biding his time. The mian asked if I was warm enough. "When is warmth enough?" I said. The mian threw up his hands in a graceful, helpless gesture, and the host rummaged within his great wooden chest and produced a bottle and three glasses, silvered, chased; his family heirlooms.

The taste wasn't bad, but it smelled decidedly odd. However, the fire in the front drew me and the cold in my back pushed me, and I finished half of the silver tumbler while I was making up my mind. A great glow pervaded my arms. Heat slowly mounted to my head. Pleasant tickles like tiny embers sat on my back, and a positive feeling of well-being slipped its hand in mine.

The mian, with a smile, said, "This is the speciality of our region, *Marul Huhm,* a whiskey made from wheat, rare Himalayan herbs, malt . . . and choice partridge." He sipped his and added, "It's a great tonic; some take it as that during the months of snow."

As the farmer's wife busied herself in the kitchen, the mian again raised the bottle, and the whiskey leaped out like an escaping salmon. We toasted each other. I sniffed my drink. There wasn't anything wrong with the smell, I decided. I was glowing, and this healthy feeling persisted for days afterwards.

The farmer put another log on the fire and we sat down to a pleasant dinner.

The next recipe is not from the farmer, but I owe it to him. He mentioned a man, a wandering recluse living in the forest near Chamba, who was known for his culinary skill and for his attainments in the classic music of India. As there is nothing I prize more than Indian music, I made a note to ferret out the man.

But first: the recipes for Pellaos from the Himalaya.

PORK PELLAO WITH PEPPER

3 pounds lean pork
1 tablespoon green ginger
(⅜ teaspoon powdered)
2 tablespoons crushed garlic
salt
4 teaspoons crushed peppercorns
6 tablespoons yoghurt
4 tablespoons butter
2 onions
½ pint buttermilk
1½ pounds rice
2 cardamons (seeds of)
8 cloves

Cut the pork into medium-sized pieces. In a mortar and pestle pound the ginger with the garlic and salt. Rub this into the pork. Now strew on the peppercorns, and beat the meat with a kitchen mallet. Rub the meat with yoghurt and leave aside for 1 hour.

Melt the butter, brown the onions, sliced, and fry the pork with its sauce in this. When it begins to dry, add the buttermilk. Cook till pork is tender. Reserve for the moment.

Half-cook the rice in water (10 minutes), drain it, and put on top of the pork and whatever remains of the buttermilk. Add the cardamon seeds and cloves. Pour on 1 cup water. Close the casserole firmly. Give it 4 minutes over a brisk heat. Then place in a 250° oven for 22 minutes. Serves 8.

PELLAO-RANG BRANGHI

(Pellao Colorful)

2 pounds pork or lamb
½ pound butter
½ pound onions
¼ pound kidney beans (precooked)
¼ pound chick peas (precooked)
¼ pound lentils (precooked)
2 beets
2 turnips
½ pound spinach
2 pounds rice
2 tablespoons green ginger (¾ teaspoon powdered)
½ teaspoon cummin
10 cloves
1½ inches stick cinnamon
1 tablespoon coriander
7 cardamon (seeds of)
1 teaspoon black pepper
3 cloves garlic

Brown the meat, diced medium, in half the butter, in a casserole, adding the onions at the same time. When the meat and onions are brown, add the kidney beans, the chick peas and the lentils. Stir the whole well. Add the beets, diced and cooked tender but firm, the turnips, sliced and cooked not too tender, and the spinach chopped very fine. Mix well again and add 2 cups water. Boil up once and simmer 5 minutes.

Drain the liquid from the meat and beans. Cook the rice with cardamon, cloves, cinnamon, black pepper, cummin, coriander and salt by the Little Water Method, adding water if necessary (to cover by 1¼ inches). Then arrange in a casserole: first the meat, then the rice, then the vegetables and beans, lentils, chick peas. Sprinkle with the remaining ¼ pound of butter, melted, and hermetically seal the lid. Simmer over the gentlest heat 7 to 10 minutes till rice has absorbed all moisture and is perfectly dry.

PULLET PELLAO HALF-MOON

(Indian Omelet, Rice and Fowl on a Spit)

1 pound ground meat
1 tablespoon coriander
salt
5 onions
5 tablespoons butter
6 eggs
½ teaspoon black pepper
¼ teaspoon saffron
1 3-pound pullet
4 cloves
6 cardamons (seeds of)
1½ pounds rice
½ inch stick cinnamon
¼ pound yoghurt

Mix the ground meat with coriander, salt, 2 onions, pounded, and fry it for 10 minutes, using 2 tablespoons of butter. Cool the meat and then mix well with egg whites beaten stiff. Make small meat balls the size of big marbles and fry again for few minutes on a greased skillet. Reserve.

Mix the egg yolks with pepper and salt. Melt the butter and lightly brown 2 more onions, sliced thin. Put in the eggs and make it as you would an omelet. Fold once only. Sprinkle the saffron on it, and reserve.

Rub the well-washed and dried pullet with salt and onion juice (made by grating an onion, or using the bottled variety), on the outside and inside of the cavity. Fill the pullet with the meat balls and cook on a spit; lacking that, roast the chicken. After 10 minutes of browning, baste the chicken with a sauce of the cloves and cardamon seeds well pounded and mixed with the yoghurt and 3 tablespoons of melted butter.

Half-cook the rice with cinnamon. Arrange the whole in this manner: rice, rest of butter, the half-moon omelet, and the chicken on top. Pour all the gravy from the chicken over the whole. Hermetically close the lid. Cook for 4 minutes over brisk heat, then over the lowest heat till done.

KITCHERI (*Kedgeree*)

1 pound lentils (the quick-cooking variety)	salt
1 pound rice	2 tablespoons butter
7 cups water	4 peppercorns
	2 bay leaves

This kitcheri is made of equal parts of lentils and rice. There is a variation that uses three parts rice to one part lentil. India has over 60 kinds of lentils, most of which are indigenous. They are all named, and the cooking time for these lentils is known. For the recipes in this book use any kind of lentil, but find out, by once cooking it, the time required to make them tender. If split-peas, green or yellow, are used, these will have another time factor. Some lentils have to be cooked with the rice all the way; others added to rice halfway through.

The consistency of a kitcheri is like porridge, unlike the pellaos you have been tasting.

This is a singularly good dish for invalids, and for children. Somehow the Indian parrots, who like to talk vociferously, have developed over the ages a liking for kitcheri.

Steep the lentils in water for ½ hour; drain. Bring water, in a heavy, deep casserole, to a furious boil and add the lentils and rice. Add the salt also. Cook gently, after 18 minutes, till the water had dried and the kitcheri is a velvety, smooth mixture. The lentils will be tender but not overdone. Now warm a casserole, melt the butter, add the peppercorns, crushed, and bay leaves. Put into kitcheri, mix well and cook for a bare minute. Serves 6.

The butter can also, if desired, have thin sliced browned onions.

The kitcheri can also be made with water just enough to cover it, instead of the 6 cups. For this style, cook covered, and stir a few times.

If made for invalids, leave out the butter. The kitcheri without butter is called *Geela* (softened) Kitcheri, and the kitcheri with butter is the Bhoona (sautéed) Kitcheri.

The Muni

Before I managed to cross the river and find the wandering recluse a month had passed from the time I heard about him at the farmer's hut on the rainy mountainside. He lived only across the river Ravi in Chamba town. That it took me a month to cross the river and find him is not odd, considering what happened.

In India there is always a river. Somehow the life of the Indian is always touched by the river.

There are rivers that are pathetic streams. Others swing over the horizon, and seem more like the sea in their expanse. From the alluvial deposits of millenniums of flowings have sprung rich, sprawling cities always by the side of the river.

Wherever the Indian has his river, his fields are full of abundance to which there seems no end. The great rolling rivers, parabolic arcs of shining water on their way to the sea, are strung with names like sweet-sounding bells. The famous places of pilgrimages are here. It is on the banks of these rivers that the mind and the feelings of the Indian were made. There is no temple that stands far from the river. It is at the river more than at the temples that the Indian sits and visualizes his God. Where the temples and the meditational groves and the humble homes are far from the river, the architectural marvels he has created always have a pool, for which the first water is brought from the nearest well-known river. Thereafter, the waters of the pool are symbolically those of the river.

It is said in India that there are two things pure in the world: Water and Woman. No matter what one heaps into them and on them, they remain essentially pure. This is no sentimentalization or mysticism. The matter cannot be gone into here. But water, to the Indian, is the tangible essence of the Divine Being. To this day, the most common object of worship may be a pitcher of water. It is the first and primary essence of creative energy: the world of limitless possibility.

What happened to a man in India a long time ago happened also that year at Chamba, after the mian and I spent the evening at the farmer's hut.

It happens, sometimes, that the rain that all Indian rivers await comes and stays. The thunderclouds lodge in the Himalaya, endless with their bounty. There comes a moment when an invisible line has been crossed. No longer do the clouds and rain come just to refresh the seared land. They have ceased to consider only man's needs, and pile in, thick, gray and potbellied. The Himalaya resounds day and night to the sound of waters shattering over its peaks. The sun has not shown itself. Now the rain has started to fall in lakes and seas throughout the fresh new forest growth. Storm after storm hurls itself across the sky; phosphorescent hailstones come in with the falling rain. Under the hard burrowing of the rain, the earth is bare and ugly. Whole mountainsides slide into the river, the sky seems upended into the earth, man stands disconsolate, looking at the water. When the waters can be held no longer in the hills, they come downward like a furious bear. Everywhere there is the roar of crashing hillsides, and of trees laid naked to their roots. The rain comes down inexorably. It is getting darker and colder.

Gale after gale shakes the denuded trees, making their ribs clatter. The waters with a million fingers probe into the inside, under houses, and man is left unhoused beneath the sky. Trees lean aslant, to grow that way for the rest of their life.

Long before this deluge, the birds have taken off in breathless flight, and the animals of the forest have scattered. There is no more noisy carnival in the trees, by the black-faced, silver-furred Langoor monkeys. No one is left to keep company with man.

Even the mountain bear has gone off. The Yak moves higher, to the snows, in an effort to escape the pitiless water. That lord of the forest, the tiger, roars no more. He moves about, with a passionate fury. His blood is chilled with the noise of the earth dissolving itself. Here is something that surpasses the savageness of the striped beast; infinitely more inhumane and impersonal.

Only man remains. Above the engorged, full-bellied river singing its song of murder and violence, he watches and thinks, for this is something he can do. The vision his thinking gives him is the compulsion of the earliest hunger known to man: to know *why?*

Far away, down in the plains, the river takes in fields and cities in its endless sweep. In the night the waters rise high, and the temples that man had built in joy and love for the bounty that the river gave him are shaken in their foundations. The strength that man has poured for generations into the soil, and his many works, are erased in a single starless night.

Prayers and supplications change nothing, for the violence behind the flood and the devastation demands more than faith and kneeling. With the debris there are left many questions that man has to answer, and there is little that he can make of the two faces of the river.

There was also a time when he thought the rains would never arrive. In India, when the year has metered and measured out half its length, the sun blazes red and hot. The mighty rivers shrink to a hairline of illusion. There is a draining away of the waters to the bowels of the earth where great fires, nourishing memories of the time when they once enveloped the earth, have retreated.

The breezes have dropped away. Only the heavy dust stirs faintly. The trees stand without shadow; all things lie thin like a meager rind. The bushes stand with a hard, brassy, lacquered varnish. The water buffaloes stand motionless in an eternity of waiting. Like bleached bones the stones by the roadside are bare and white. Overhead is always the noon-day sun . . . This is a scene that has repeated itself for all time.

But also perennial is the scene where, magically and unbelievably, a host of white clouds flood the sky. Like an endless procession of king elephants, they gambol over where the Himalayas sit straddling the land, and shatter themselves like a stack of withered sheaves. The water flows again. The sap mounts in land, forest and man. The lifeblood circulates freely . . .

The paradox of the river, of anything being two opposite things simultaneously, struck man with force. How to reconcile the two different, contradictory aspects of the same thing? The same river was life-giver and also death. A paradox, its laws seemed arbitrary and capricious. If this were true, why, then, it sundered him from his faith and his God.

He discovered then that he had no real freedom. It lay with life and nature, and other people's actions, so he set out to discover more. Now man desired to know the nature of everything without interpretations: things as they are and not as they seem.

The power that this catastrophe, or any other, had over man was the fact that it was unknown. "Does the river know me?" he asked in his agony. "Perhaps yes! But I do not know the river?" What is unknown mirrors an incapacity in man. In god-seeking, in man's love for woman, in man's relationship with the world, in his link with his work, the only and basic error comes from not knowing enough.

If he had to understand this calamity of the river, he had to free himself from both faces of the river; the smiling and the horrific. Free himself from the two parts inside him that smiled when the river smiled, and blanched in terror when the river showed its mask of horror. Truth lay not with one or the other but somewhere between, and included them both . . . And so began the long journey (of which the discipline is Yoga, the most objective of psychological systems) to freedom from both love and hate. For one has to be free from love also, not only hate, to be able to love. The rest is self-love, and not knowing enough.

And this is what most motivates the Indian. That is the reason he is often called mystical, and paradoxical. He has learned the paradoxical truth, that not till he has freed himself from emotion can he understand the nature and the value of emotion. Nothing is disparaged, nothing is overemphasized.

The result is an unchaining from every state of antagonism — heat and cold, for example. In this state of freedom, a new appraisal of life is taken, new values are formed, and the man becomes entirely transformed.

This is somewhat like the Pandit of Ellora, who abstained from most pleasures, yet made it a point to give me the recipes which form the core of this book and the classic system of Indian cookery. All things in life are interrelated, though everything modern is worked out as though it were absolute and independent.

How well this viewpoint can be practiced is a concern of the individual. But when you see an Indian behaving in a way that is mysterious, or mystical, or plain mad, it may be one way or other of practicing this attitude. When you find an Indian abstaining from meat, which many do, this should indicate a striving to be free from the tuggings of the physical. But the true Yogi (the skilled one) is free from both the emotion and any feeling *against* that emotion.

Relating this freedom to our subject, eating and cooking, it is the difference between a gourmet and a gourmand. The difference between a gourmet and a person who has gone past the need of food lies in this freedom. There is nothing wrong with the life of the Pandit of Ellora, inasmuch as he had lost all craving for food, good or bad. "He looks equally on day and night, and on grief and pleasure; free from blame and praise . . . the same in living and in dying. Whoso regardeth nothing of small account, yet pursueth nothing . . ." Without being free from

God (who represents the highest degree of any value) man can never know what God or any value or human being is.

This dynamic concept I found in the wandering recluse to whom the farmer had sent me for his wisdom in Indian music, and his culinary skill. I found the two talents not incompatible. The recluse was called a Muni or Sage (from the word Maunum; the Silent One; his wisdom cannot be expressed in words but experienced and shown in action and living).

On the day after the rains had lifted, he cooked for me and another friend food of miraculous taste. He took none; ate only fresh fruit or vegetables; he had simply outgrown the need for meat. We were not alone. Several villagers and a tramp were there for handouts.

Sometimes he cooked, and sometimes he sang. Most of his time was spent in meditation. His cooking was done neither for pleasure nor as a duty. It was a skill he had learned thirty years earlier, before he adopted this life of the Muni, and he used it when he could. Skill is a virtue. What is sacred is well done. What is badly executed, botched, or shoddily completed is profane.

The recipes that have preceded this explanation are the kind the Muni made.

These that follow are the Briani rice recipes. Here the principles for cooking meats and vegetables are combined with the style of rice cooking. The preparation is not difficult, nor is it unfamiliar. You will find in the Briani many methods used in the recipes you have been making.

LAMB BRIANI

2 pounds rice
5 tablespoons butter
4 onions
¾ tablespoon coriander
1 teaspoon turmeric
salt
¾ pint yoghurt
1 pound lamb
2 cardamons (seeds of)
¼ inch stick cinnamon
3 cloves
¼ teaspoon chili (P)
2 hard-boiled eggs
rose water

Steep the rice in cold water 35 minutes. Heat 2 tablespoons butter and fry till pale gold 2 onions, sliced. Mix the fried onions with the coriander, turmeric, salt and yoghurt. Rub this well into the lamb, cut in medium slices, and let stand 35 minutes. Take the remaining 2 onions and pound them with a mortar and pestle; combine them with the lamb mixture. Cook without adding butter till it begins to dry. Half-boil the rice (about 10 minutes).

In a heavy casserole arrange a layer of the meat and a thicker layer of rice. Another layer of meat, and the rest of the rice. Sprinkle the cardamon seeds, cinnamon and cloves with the chili powder. Now pour over the surface the remaining 3 tablespoons of melted butter. Splash with a few drops of water and hermetically close the lid. Cook it for 50 minutes, over very low heat or in the oven, making it as low as possible and turning off the heat after 45 minutes of cooking. Decorate with the eggs and sprinkle with a little rose water. Serves 10.

CHICKEN BRIANI

(*Dalliance in a Garden*)

2-pound chicken
1 tablespoon coriander
1 tablespoon chopped ginger
(⅜ teaspoon powdered)
salt
1 onion
4 pints yoghurt
¼ cup blanched almonds
rose water
9 tablespoons butter
1 teaspoon cummin
2 cloves
2 cardamons (seeds of)
1 inch stick cinnamon
½ teaspoon black pepper
2 pounds rice
2 teaspoons turmeric

Cut the chicken into 12 or 18 pieces. Pound the coriander with the ginger, salt and onion. Mix with the chicken and simmer in enough water to cover the chicken. Reserve chicken. Mix the chicken liquor with the yoghurt.

Pound half the almonds with enough rose water to moisten them. Add these to yoghurt and sauce. Fry the rest of the almonds in a little butter and reserve them.

Melt the rest of the butter, put in chicken with cummin, cloves, cardamon seeds, black pepper, cinnamon, crushed, and cook them together over gentle heat for 5 to 7 minutes. Mix the gravy with the chicken and remove from heat.

Half-cook the rice and put it over the chicken, adding the turmeric. Give the casserole a good shake. Close the lid hermetically and cook over medium heat for 5 minutes. Then place in a preheated (200°) oven for 35 minutes. Serves 10.

Cooking Rice with Fish

WHEN CHOOSING fresh or salt-water fish, see that it is firm textured, preferably non-oily. Keep the quality in mind, for the saying goes in India, "The flowers and fruits are better than the tree; better than curds is butter said to be, and better than oil cakes the oil that trickles free." It is rather important to select a good firm fish, for it is likely to crumble. If it oozes more oil than we ask for, in the Briani, we will be in the position of the Brahmin and his goat.

A Brahmin named Good-Feeling was returning home with his goat, a plump creature, on his shoulders. He was seen by three rascals, who were numb with the cold, their stomachs arching to their backbones with hunger.

Seeing the Brahmin with the plump goat, they rubbed their hands. "Come now! What is this we see! Oh, if we could put our teeth into that dainty creature."

The first of the knaves made a detour and crossed the path of the Brahmin. He said, looking incredulous, "O pious man, what is it that you're carrying? It's so unconventional and ridiculous to carry a dog on your shoulder. You must remember that the dog, the barnyard rooster, the camel, and the hangman with the ass defile a person. Don't touch them but pass along."

The Brahmin, indignant, shouted, "Are you blind that you see doghood in a goat?"

But a little farther on he met the second rogue, who stood aghast. "Holy sir, even if this dead calf was a pet, it is not seemly to carry it about."

The Brahmin was incensed and brushed off the man for calling his goat a calf. But a little further on he met the third of the rascals. "Ah! sir," that one said, "but this is most improper. Fancy carrying a donkey on your shoulder. You should know how unclean this animal is . . ." The Brahmin, overtaken by the cold, the dark and the suggestion, imagined he was carrying some horrible goblin, threw it on the ground, and ran. The three knaves met and feasted well.

I tried buying a fish, to make this Briani for a guest, some years ago in Paris. The fishmongers were putting up their shutters early, for this was a holiday. My fishmonger had gone, and the proprietor of one of the remaining shops in the market called me in. I asked for sole and it was brought to me, skinned and filleted. Didn't the fishmonger think, I asked, that I should have been shown the fish before he proceeded to scalp it? I looked in alarm at the fish, for it was no sole. The man insisted with great cordiality and amity that it was the best sole he ever caught. The neighboring fishmonger finished closing his shutters and ambled in. Ah, what a sole it was, he said. If only he had it for dinner. As I hedged and fidgeted, trying to retreat from the shop, another fishmonger strolled in, eyes rolling with proper appreciation. What a turbot, by the life of the Saints. If he had it he'd keep it for his wife.

The fish looked more like a skate than any sole. But since I had promised fish to my guest and the Briani was expected, I took the fish with misgivings. I never had a chance to find out what it tasted like. With the first heat and the frying, the fish broke into tiny portions. When the liquid was added, all there was left was a messy porridge that now swam in its true colors; it had been April Fool's Day which the French call *Poisson d'Avril* — April Fish.

So be careful in the choice of fish. As they say: Is any man uncheated by the diligence of new servants, the praise of guests, a woman's tears, and roguish eloquence?

Indifferent food cheats nobody. Here is our:

BRIANI MACHCHI

(*Briani Rice with Fish*)

2 pounds fish
3 tablespoons olive oil
flour, or split-pea flour (p. 000)
1 pint yoghurt
2 onions
¾ tablespoon turmeric
¼ pound butter
salt
2 tablespoons coriander
1 pound rice
4 cardamons (seeds of)
6 cloves
2 tablespoons anise seed
2 tomatoes
1 pimento (canned or fresh)

No matter how good your fish is, if you want your cooking to be not indifferent, treat the fish as follows: cut it in large pieces with a sharp knife that leaves no jagged ends. Wash it gently in several changes of water. Rub the oil well — but remember, gently — all over the fish. Let stand for 15 minutes. Then wash it again in water. Now rub the flour or split-pea flour and pounded anise with a gentle but firm hand over the fish. The flour absorbs much of the superfluous smells and oils. The anise imparts an indefinable flavor. Wash the fish again in water.

Boil the rice for 10 minutes. Then marinate the fish 35 minutes in ½ pint yoghurt well mixed with the onions, fried and pounded, also pounded cardamon seeds and cloves. Place these in a casserole, sprinkle on some of the turmeric, add half the butter and salt, half of the coriander; then put on top the half-cooked rice. Pour on the rest of the yoghurt, the rest of the butter, the coriander, rest of the turmeric, anise seeds, the tomatoes sliced in thin rounds, and pimentos in strips. Pour on the remaining 4 tablespoons butter and the salt.

Close the lid hermetically, give the casserole a little shake, and cook 4 minutes over brisk flame. Then place in the oven, heated to 200°, for 35 minutes. Serves 6.

Many briani differing from these recipes can be found. But it is not good to ask the cow for milk every passing hour.

We will regale our guests with the *Sweet Pellaos* of India. These are the *Zarda*, the *Meetha Pellao*, the *Chasneedarh Pellao*. The last is sweet-pungent. These are served as dessert. Most Indians would eat bread, not rice, for the main course, and keep the sweet rice for the dessert.

The most justly beloved of all sweet pellaos is the *Zarda*. The next is a recipe for the *Ekna Zarda*, to distinguish it from other variations called the *Dugna* (twice) *Zarda*, and the *Chugna* (four times) *Zarda*.

EKNA ZARDA

(Sweet Rice with Almonds, Pistachio Nuts, Raisins)

1 pound rice
9¾ cups water
salt
½ teaspoon saffron strands, or ¼ teaspoon powdered saffron
2 cups sugar
¾ pound butter
3 cardamons (seeds of)
5 cloves
½ lemon (juice of)
¼ cup light or dark raisins
¼ cup pistachio nuts, shelled, unsalted
¼ cup cashew nuts or Brazil nuts or filberts (shelled)
¼ cup blanched almonds
1 cup heavy cream, whipped and sweetened (optional)

Half-cook the rice in 6 cups boiling water with salt and saffron (using more if needed; it must color the rice rich gold). Drain and reserve rice. Boil the sugar in the remaining 3¾ cups water for 1 minute, stirring well to make a thin syrup.

Melt the butter in a heavy casserole, fry the cardamon seeds and cloves over very low heat for 10 minutes. Add syrup (saving ½ cup) to the butter. Boil 1 minute, then add rice to the casserole. Cook it gently (about 10 minutes), stirring gently also, till the butter has been absorbed.

Add the lemon juice, raisins and all the nuts. Cook for 5 minutes over brisk heat. Then on very low heat till rice is done. Stir once or so to prevent the rice from sticking. But remember that one of the causes of soggy rice is overstirring. For 8 to 10.

As this is cooked by the Little Water Method, use the ½ cup syrup, if required, to make rice tender. The exact amount of water, to reiterate, in this or any rice dish, depends upon the thickness of the casserole and the exact amount of heat.

Lastly, remove from the heat. Cover firmly for 5 minutes in a cool place. Serve with whipped cream if desired.

SIMPLE SWEET PELLAO

4 tablespoons butter
1 pound rice
3 cardamons (seeds of)
6 cloves
½ cup raisins
½ cup blanched almonds
1½ tablespoons sugar
2 blades mace
pinch of salt
4 inches stick cinnamon
strong pinch of saffron

Melt the butter and add the rice; brown it well without scorching it. After 5 minutes add the cardamon seeds, cloves, raisins, almonds, sugar, mace, the pinch of salt and saffron. And cover with water. Add the cinnamon and boil for 1 minute. Then lower to a mere whisper of a flame and cook till tender. If the

1¼ inches of water is not enough add more, a little at a time, till rice is done. Then cover for 5 minutes in a cool place.

If it is desired to make this sweet pellao by the steamed method, half-cook the rice and put it on top of the raisins browned in half the butter. Add the almonds to the rice, with the spices and sugar. Stir it well, but gently. Sprinkle the melted butter and the saffron on the surface, also a few drops of water. Then close the lid hermetically. Cook 2 minutes over medium flame, and put into the oven (200° or less) for 35 to 45 minutes.

This sweet rice is preferred dry by some and somewhat more soft by others. Increase the water a little according to your preference. Serves 6.

SWEET PELLAO FOR A POOR MAN

(*Meaning Pampered or Spoiled*)

- 3 tablespoons almonds (blanched)
- 2 tablespoons cashew nuts
- 2 tablespoons cucumber seeds (dried)
- 2 tablespoons squash seeds (dried)
- 1½ quarts milk
- 1 pound rice
- ¾ to 1 pound sugar
- ½ pound butter
- 6 cloves
- pinch of salt
- ½ lemon (juice of)
- 6 slices orange or grapefruit (soaked in sugar)
- 5 ripe mango slices (optional; if available)
- 6 tablespoons grapes (peeled)
- 2 tablespoons raisins (white preferably)
- 2 tablespoons rose water
- 2 cardamons (seeds of)

Dried cucumber and squash seeds, among many others, are used in India. The simplest way to prepare them is to wash them thoroughly and then dry in the sun or oven. Keep in airtight jars for use. They are wonderful for cooling the bodily system in summer heat. Also considered fine for brainwork, and are known as "Brains of five gourds."

Grind the almonds, cashew nuts, cucumber and squash seeds in a mortar and pestle. Add to 1½ quarts of milk. Mix well and reserve. Make a syrup of the sugar in 3 cups of water and reserve. Half-cook the rice and strain: reserve it.

Melt the butter in a heavy casserole and stir in the cardamon seeds, cloves ground fine, and salt. When their aroma assails you, add the milk and the syrup. Stir well and cook it on medium heat for 12 minutes. Put in the rice, squeeze the lemon juice. Close the lid tight and cook for 10 minutes over brisk heat. Then add the fruits, nuts and raisins. Give the casserole a good shake and place in oven or on the lowest heat you can imagine for 35 minutes. Serve with the rose water sprinkled over the rice. For eight to ten persons, who should be politely shown the door if they do not ask for another helping.

Steep a firm avocado pear in heavy warm syrup if mangoes are not available.

About the squash and cucumber seeds: these can be left out if you do not care to take the time to cure them. They do contribute to the original taste, but are not essential to this recipe.

This recipe for Sweet Pellao is not for everyday fare. It is best for holidays, feasts, anniversaries and good times when friends gather. Serves 6.

ANANAS PELLAO

(Pellao with Pineapple)

1 pound pineapple (fresh or canned)
2 pounds pork
2 tablespoons butter
¼ onion
salt
8 cloves
1¼ pounds sugar
1 cup lemon juice
¼ teaspoon ginger
2 pounds rice
5 cardamons (seeds of)
1 inch stick cinnamon
1½ tablespoons coriander

If using fresh pineapple, pare and cut into medium-thick slices. Reserve.

Slice the pork medium thick; brown well in the butter, with onion sliced thin, cloves, salt and coriander, for 12 minutes. Add 1½ cups of water, bring to a boil and simmer for 20 minutes. Strain the gravy, adding if necessary enough water to make 1 cup. Reserve meat and gravy.

For fresh pineapple, boil the sugar, lemon juice and ginger for 5 minutes to make a syrup.

Boil half the pineapple till soft, using just enough water to keep from sticking. Boil the other half in syrup till tender, using only enough to cook it. Both portions of pineapple should have the moisture dried out.

If canned pineapple is used, there is no need to cook half the quantity in water, for this pineapple is already softened. The other half of the pineapple is cooked in a syrup of lemon juice and sugar in proportions of 3 to 1. This syrup is not the normal chasnee, but the canned pineapple is presweetened, and more lemon juice is needed to give it the right sweet-pungent flavor. Fresh pineapple is recommended for a fresher, more delicate flavor.

Cook the rice, in plenty of water or by the Little Water Method (1½ inches of water to cover). Mash the pineapple cooked in water and add it to the rice. Arrange the mixture over the pork. Add the cardamon seeds, cinnamon, and sprinkle with a few drops of water. Place on top the pineapple slices cooked in syrup. Close the cover hermetically and cook in a preheated oven (about 200°) for 35 to 45 minutes until the moisture has dried out.

KELA-GELASS PELLAO CHASNEE

(Banana and Cherry Pellao with Pork)

2 pounds lean pork
¼ teaspoon ginger
5 cloves
1½ tablespoons coriander
salt
6 tablespoons butter
2 onions
5 cardamons (seeds of)
1¼ pounds sugar
1 cup lemon juice
2 pounds rice
12 bananas
½ pound cherries
(fresh or canned)

Slice the pork thin and cook in plain water, ginger, cloves, coriander, salt and 2 teaspoons butter till it is done. Use enough water to leave about 1½ cups liquid. Remove pork and fry with onions thin sliced in 3 tablespoons butter and cardamon seeds. Reserve the liquid.

Make a syrup of the sugar and lemon juice in 8 cups of water. In half the syrup mix the liquid reserved and boil the rice in this till done. In the other half, mix the pork and cook till the syrup has been absorbed and reduced by half. In this half of the syrup left, boil the bananas (quartered) and the cherries (canned cherries will need no cooking). Arrange the rice over the pork. On top put the bananas and the cherries. Dot over with the remainder of the butter. Close the lid hermetically. Heat the casserole for 6 minutes and then place in the oven, preheated to 200°, for another 20 minutes or so. Serves 12.

In the light of the experience you will have had with the different kinds of pellao, you will find it easy to adapt any of the Sweet Pellao recipes for plain salted Pellao. The chasnee is left out, and even the fruits can be dispensed with. Each adaptation will have to be individually thought out. It is important to make the changes according to the strict principles and fixed quantities of ingredients for all Pellao cooking.

There are numerous other sweet pellaos, but we have to go on to other things. Indians also believe 'tis best to stop where good sense dictates. "... Eat only what will gratify the hollow within, with good digestion ... Put not your health in question." There is enough in these recipes to satisfy both the mind and the appetite. But throwing caution to the wind, just one more recipe for a sweet pellao that is supposed to leave you breathless.

Duck is the sacrificial victim to the ingenuity of this pellao.

PELLAO WITH STUFFED DUCK CHASNEEDARH (*Breathing Breathless*)

1 small duckling
2 teaspoons cummin
4 anise seeds
4 cloves garlic
½ tablespoon green ginger (⅛ teaspoon powdered)
salt
½ pound butter
½ pound onions
¼ cup blanched almonds
¼ cup raisins
¼ cup sugar
¼ pound carrots
2 tablespoons heavy cream
½ pound yoghurt
1 quart milk
2 lemons (juice of)
2½ pounds rice
1 teaspoon coriander
¼ teaspoon saffron
8 cloves
1 inch stick cinnamon
5 cardamons
rose water or orange water
1 cup stock (or use 5 bouillon cubes)

Wash the duckling well and dry it. Then prick it all over with a sharp-tined fork. Rub with a mixture of pounded cummin, anise seeds, garlic and salt, made into paste with water. Let stand for 45 minutes.

In a heavy casserole, melt 3 tablespoons butter and fry the onions sliced thin. When well browned, mix them with half the almonds, slivered, the raisins, sugar, grated carrots and a little rose or orange water. Stuff this inside the duckling and roast it in the oven or cook it on the rotisserie. Baste with the following sauce.

Pound the rest of the almonds with cream; add to the yoghurt, ½ cup of milk, the juice of 2 lemons and 3 tablespoons butter. Baste the duckling with this while roasting or cooking the duckling on the spit.

Boil the rice in a mixture of coriander, salt, milk, and 1 cup concentrated stock.

In a heavy casserole arrange the duckling, a layer of half the rice colored with saffron, and the rest of the rice uncolored. Dribble the rest of the butter (melted) over the rice, and all the liquid left in the rice. Add the cloves, cinnamon and cardamon. Mix them in. Now, close the lid hermetically and cook 6 minutes over a medium fire. Then place in a preheated oven (175° to 200°) for 25 minutes. Then open, sprinkle with a little rose water or orange water, and serve in a cloud of aromatic steam from the pellao and its treasure of stuffed duckling. For 12 to 14.

Or the stuffing may be of cooked and slivered beets and carrots grated finely. The onions are left out. Sugar is reduced to 2 tablespoons. Add orange water or rose water, enough to give a positive aroma and light, sweet taste.

With this recipe we end this section on Indian rice cookery. There are many more recipes in India that could bear detailed elaboration, but the desire for more variety is not helped by additional recipes. Through sleeping sleep is not checked, through love not women, through wood not fire, through drinking not liquor . . .

It is the work of the wife and housewife to administer the household carefully and with exactitude. This is to be done in a manner that will elicit the admiration of others and bring her satisfaction at having performed something beautifully.

In many Indian households the lady of the house will eat last. Old Indian injunctions even advise that the household, guests and servants, shall all be fed before she feeds herself. This is not a cross that she bears, as many visitors to India might think, but a voluntary behavior that she likes and that we may say is her fulfillment.

This feeding of the servants before herself is not much practiced in modern India. Wherever this custom is found, it is likely to be in the poorer homes, which do carry on admirably some of the best disciplines in living.

Women like these are given much love and respect. In a rapidly changing society, where there is inevitably a certain amount of chaos, a rigid observance of this practice would seem artificial. But wherever the housewife does approximate the ideal, her influence over others is tremendous.

Accordingly, beauty is not recognized only in the young and ravishing, but in mothers, grandmothers, and even in women not in their youth favored with good looks. Seen thus, shorn of sentimentalization, the Indian housewife emerges as a powerful force in national education.

It is no mystery that, among other things, the Indian housewife is the best of cooks and that the best food is found in the Indian home. Indian women — practically all of them — view the restaurant with disdain. Their instincts are right, for it represents an invasion of her field — the home and hearth — which is still of vital importance to Indian life.

The dishes, with their recipes, in this book will seldom be found in an Indian restaurant. Those in the next section, for poultry, are all from Indian homes.

CHAPTER 7

Poultry and Game Birds

THE RECIPES in this section are mostly for chicken and duck, but may be adapted for game birds — the obtaining of which is a matter of opportunity and luck.

The poultry is the same in the United States and Europe as in India. Pullets are plump, young hens. Capons are male chickens castrated to improve the quality and flavor. The ordinary chicken is only less plump than the pullet, and has longer, bonier legs. The chicken is used for frying and for roasts. Broilers (young chickens) come in best for cooking on the spit, for grilling, and for cooking in a covered casserole. The youngest chickens — squab chicks — and squabs (baby pigeons) should be grilled, spitted, or cooked in a casserole as the following recipes show. Chicken should be skinned, except when roasted or grilled, because the skin becomes clammy and prevents absorption of flavors.

I suggest that the remarks on cooking of white meats, in the section on Rotisserie and Barbecue, be read. Skill in cooking fine poultry is not difficult to achieve. The few instructions given in that chapter are all that are required.

With a young chicken we have our first recipe.

SIMPLE CHICKEN CURRY

1 3-pound chicken
3 tablespoons butter
1 onion
¼ teaspoon chili
2 teaspoons turmeric
salt

Skin the chicken and cut into 12 to 18 pieces. Warm the butter, fry the onion, sliced thin, to a deep brown. Then put in the chicken and brown it on all sides. Add the chili, turmeric and salt. Pour in 6 cups of water and cook till chicken is tender — covered or uncovered. Always cook the chicken — after the initial browning — over low heat; uncovered for the last 5 or 10 minutes. The sauce in this recipe is thin, somewhat clear, and should be kept at the 6-cup level. It will taste as nice, or perhaps better than the chicken.

The success of this recipe, and all other chicken recipes in this book, depends on correctly frying the chicken, after the onion has browned. Cook on medium heat, and turn the chicken when necessary. It must brown *well*, but never scorch or stick to the casserole. Serves 4.

CHICKEN WITH CORIANDER

2 pounds chicken
3 onions
3 tablespoons butter
1 teaspoon turmeric
1¾ tablespoons coriander
¼ teaspoon chili (P)
pinch of black pepper
salt
squeeze of lemon juice

Have the chicken cut at the joints. Remove skin and set the chicken aside, scattering over it the onions, well chopped.

In a casserole heat the butter and add the turmeric, coriander, chili, black pepper and salt. Cook over very gentle heat, mixing them well, for 1 minute. Then add the chicken and onions.

Mix these well with the spices and brown them all for 12 minutes. Add now the chili powder and ½ cup water. Bring to a boil for a few seconds, then lower heat, clapping on the lid tight. When more water is required, sprinkle with 2 tablespoons water and again close the lid. Repeat as often as necessary till chicken is cooked. Squeeze a little lemon juice (¼ or ½ lemon) over it before serving.

The gravy in this recipe should be reduced to a few spoonfuls. If too much remains, reduce it by raising the heat and shaking the casserole, to keep the chicken from scorching. Or place chicken in 200° oven for ¼ hour. Serves 4.

This one is a more suave chicken; has more to say.

CHICKEN KORMA CURRY

1 2-pound chicken
4 cloves garlic
3 onions
salt
1 inch green ginger
 (⅛ teaspoon powdered)
1 pint yoghurt
4 tablespoons butter
1 tablespoon turmeric
½ tablespoon cummin
½ teaspoon mustard seeds
½ teaspoon poppy seeds
5 peppercorns
2 cardamons (seeds of)

Cut the chicken in 12 pieces, prick with a fork and soak in a marinade made of the following ingredients: garlic, pounded, 1 onion pounded, salt, ginger pounded (or if powdered, added to these), and yoghurt. Set aside from ½ to 1 hour.

Meanwhile heat the butter and brown lightly the remaining onions, sliced. Add the turmeric, cummin, and the mustard and poppy seeds well bruised in mortar and pestle. Fry these for 1 minute over very low heat and then put in the chicken and the marinade and cook over a low flame, on both sides, till the yoghurt is dried out. Then put in an extra tablespoon of butter, the peppercorns and cardamon seeds, crushed. Close the casserole and give it a bhogar (shake). Add a scant ½ cup of water. Close and simmer till water has dried out. Repeat once or twice till chicken is ready. Dry out remaining gravy. Serves 4.

In India "forest sesame, crow barley, and the barnyard hen" are accounted of little worth. They are like "frail wit, which causes all undertakings to come to a sticky end." So for this next recipe choose a plump, tender, tight-skinned pullet; one that has been nicely cosseted and not made to run about too much, developing sinewy muscles.

CHICKEN KHARE MASSALE-DARH

(Chicken with Happy Spices)

- 1 2-pound chicken
- 4 tablespoons butter
- 2 teaspoons turmeric
- ¼ teaspoon ginger (P)
- 4 onions
- 2 cloves garlic
- 4 cardamons (seeds of)
- 5 cloves
- ½ inch stick cinnamon
- strong pinch of chili (P)
- salt

As usual, wash the chicken well. Cut it at the joints into 8 or 12 pieces. Heat 3 tablespoons of the butter and lay in the chicken, skin downward. Sprinkle the turmeric and ginger over it. Shake it well and continue to fry chicken till well browned. Turn over and brown slightly the under side.

Sprinkle onion, chopped and garlic well crushed over the chicken, the cardamon seeds, cloves, cinnamon, chili and salt. Lastly sprinkle 1 tablespoon butter over it. Close the lid of the skillet or casserole and shake it once, after raising the heat to very high. Cook on high heat for ½ minute, then reduce to low. Cook covered (about ½ hour more) and then serve. Shake the casserole twice more during the preparation. Serves 4.

CHICKEN DOH-PEEAZAH

- 1 2-pound chicken
- 1½ teaspoons ginger (P)
- salt
- 2 pounds onions
- 5 tablespoons butter
- 1 clove garlic
- 1 cardamon (seeds of)
- 1 tablespoon turmeric
- ½ tablespoon cummin
- 1 tablespoon coriander
- ½ cup yoghurt
- 5 peppercorns

Disjoint, wash and dry the chicken. Prick it with a fork, rub the ginger and salt in well and set aside.

Fry half the onions dark brown in butter, adding the garlic, crushed. Remove the onions and reserve. Put in the cardamon seeds and cook for ½ minute. Set aside and reserve 2 tablespoons of this butter.

Place the chicken in remaining butter (there should be 3 tablespoons; add more if needed) with the turmeric, cummin, the fried cardamon seeds and yoghurt and cook over medium heat, occasionally raising to high for a few seconds.

When the yoghurt is dry, add the reserved butter in which the cardamon seeds were cooked. Pound the reserved fried onions and garlic and add with 1 cup of water. Boil till dry. Then add the remaining onions, sliced thin, the peppercorns, crushed, and an additional cup of water. Cover and cook over low heat until the chicken is tender. Serves 4.

For variations this recipe can be made with the chicken kept whole. For this, rub the ginger inside the cavity and outside. Fry the chicken whole, with extreme care, and turn it on all sides to brown it well, together with the onions reserved, the turmeric, cummin, coriander, cardamon seeds, black pepper and butter. When the whole chicken is nice and brown, spread with the yoghurt mixed with crushed garlic and salt. Close the lid tight and cook gently till the yoghurt is dry. Then add ¼ cup water. Shake the casserole and cook gently over low heat till the liquid is dry. The chicken should now be done. If it is not, repeat by sprinkling in no more than 2 tablespoons water at a time. Cover and cook till tender.

The recipes above have used the same ingredients. The taste of one is not necessarily better than the other; only different: it resolves itself into a problem of fancy and mood, which *should* count when cooking in the classic manner.

Now for an adaptation of a very elaborate dish which I have not been able to puzzle out to this day. The recipe, as given here, should please the most cuisine-weary gourmets.

CHICKEN MOTIA (*Chicken Jasmine*)

1 2½-pound pullet
¼ teaspoon black pepper
1½ teaspoons ginger (P)
½ pound butter (pale, unsalted, or use vegetable shortening)
1 pint yoghurt
salt
pinch of chili (P)

Prick the chicken; rub mixture of pepper and ginger on the surface and inside the cavity.

Heat the butter in a very heavy skillet and add yoghurt and salt. Mix them well and put in the chicken. Cook for a few seconds on high heat, then reduce to low. As the chicken is frying on one side, baste the upper side with the mixture of butter and yoghurt. After one side is somewhat cooked, turn it breast downward, meanwhile basting the other parts. After cooking the breast, rest the chicken first on one wing, and then on the other, and so cooking the whole chicken. By this time the whole chicken is well browned (though it has taken on not a brown, but a delicious jasmine-white color, pearly and opalescent). It will be almost ready, and the liquid in the skillet reduced.

Sprinkle a pinch of chili over the chicken, spoon the liquid over it and place in 275° oven for a few minutes. Test for doneness by pricking the leg with a sharp knife. Serves 4.

Essentially, this recipe calls for frying the whole chicken in a mixture of yoghurt and butter till it is done. This is one of the recipes where the chicken does taste as well as its fragrance.

It is vitally important to cook over low heat. Also to handle the chicken with great tenderness.

A variation of this is made by pounding ¼ cup blanched almonds and adding them to the cooking mixture about ¼ hour after cooking begins.

CHICKEN SUKH

(*Chicken for the Evening — You want to pamper yourself*)

1 2½-pound chicken
½ pound onions
¾ tablespoon green ginger
(¼ teaspoon powdered)
salt
½ pound dried chick peas
¼ pound butter
15 cloves
1 teaspoon cummin
2 tablespoons coriander
7 cardamons (seeds of)
1 teaspoon black pepper

Disjoint, wash and dry the chicken. Sprinkle half of the onions, thin sliced, over the chicken, with the ginger (green ginger chopped) and salt. Wash, soak and cook the chick peas, reserving the liquid.

Spread the chick peas over the chicken. Melt half the butter and gently cook the cloves in it for 1 minute. Add to the chick-pea water; then add all the spices, pepper the remaining onions, sliced thin. Simmer this liquid.

Put the chicken, with the chick peas, onions and ginger, into another casserole with the rest of the butter, melted. Fry the chicken for 10 minutes and add the liquid to it. Now cook them together covered till done. Uncover for the last 10 minutes and dry up any liquid, which should be a few spoonfuls only. Serves 4 to 6.

CHICKEN SUKH TURCARRI

This recipe can be made to have a lot of gravy. Begin by frying the chicken (see preceding recipe) and cooked chick peas in all of the butter. Add all spices (except cloves) and the onions, sliced thin. Fry for 10 to 12 minutes; then add chick-pea liquid (adding enough water to make 10 cups). Bring to a boil and then simmer covered till done. Uncover for last 5 minutes over very low heat; 15 minutes before chicken is finished, fry the cloves in 1½ teaspoons butter for 1 minute and add to the chicken.

CHICKEN IN A POT

1 2-pound chicken
½ teaspoon chili (P)
1 inch green ginger
(¼ teaspoon powdered)
¼ pound rice
3 tablespoons green pepper
2 tomatoes
¼ pound mushrooms
6 tablespoons butter
salt
4 mint leaves
4 onions
¾ tablespoon turmeric
2 tablespoons coriander
¼ tablespoon cummin

Wash the chicken well and dry it. Prick it all over with a fork and rub with the chili and pounded ginger.

Boil the rice. Mix with green pepper and tomatoes, chopped, halved mushrooms, I tablespoon butter, salt and bruised mint leaves. Stuff the chicken with this.

Heat the remaining butter, brown the onions, and add the turmeric, coriander and cummin, and fry the spices for 2 minutes over very low heat. Then put the chicken in and brown it well on all sides, mixing it well with the spices and onions.

Put the chicken in an earthenware casserole, with all the gravy. Sprinkle salt and a pinch of turmeric over the chicken and add ¾ cup water. Close the lid really tight and cook in a preheated oven (about 250°) till done. Add more liquid if necessary. Test the chicken for doneness. Uncover in oven for 5 minutes, raising the heat to high. Serves 4.

For persons of discrimination, who do not always look for the elaborate, this recipe will be great fun.

CHICKEN CURRY "SUPERLATIVE"

1 teaspoon sesame seeds
1 tablespoon turmeric
1 teaspoon poppy seeds
1 tablespoon coriander
1 teaspoon cummin
1¼ tablespoons chopped mint leaves
3 red peppers
¾ tablespoon green ginger (¼ teaspoon powdered)
salt
2½ tablespoons butter
3 small onions
1 2-pound chicken

Pound all the spices, seeds, the mint leaves, with ginger, pepper and salt in mortar and pestle. Now divide the resulting powder into 2 equal parts. Mix 1 part with just enough lemon juice (or water) to make into a paste. Rub into the chicken.

Melt the butter in a heavy casserole. Put in the onions, sliced thin. Brown them well and place with them the chicken rubbed with the spice paste. Fry the chicken on each side for 7 minutes and then add the other half of the pounded spices. Fry together for another 5 minutes. Then add enough water to cook. Cover and simmer till tender. Uncover for last 5 minutes. For 4.

INDIAN CHICKEN MOLEE

(*With Coconut Milk*)

½ pound potatoes
1 2-pound chicken
1 quart coconut milk
5 tablespoons cooking oil (olive or other)
3 small onions
1 tablespoon turmeric
½ tablespoon cummin
½ tablespoon sesame seeds
½ tablespoon coriander
1 teaspoon peppercorns
salt
1 teaspoon red pepper, chopped
5 cloves garlic
¼ cup lemon juice or vinegar

Wash and halve the potatoes. Reserve.

Wash the chicken and cut into 14 parts and simmer in fresh coconut milk (or make from coconut flakes, see p. 55) till half done. Then heat the oil and lightly brown the onions till transparent. Add the chicken with the spices, and sesame and coriander seeds, bruised; also the peppercorns pounded with salt and the red pepper. Add the drained chicken to the spices, then the garlic crushed in 1 tablespoon coconut milk and the ¼ cup lemon juice mixed with ½ cup coconut milk. Bring to a boil and then lower to a simmer. Close the lid tight and finish cooking, adding the raw potatoes ¼ hour before serving time. Serves 4.

This is a special way of boiling fowl. It boils without boiling the chicken.

INDIAN BOILED CHICKEN

dough
1 5-pound fowl
1 blade mace
¼ pound butter
1 tablespoon lemon rind (no membrane)
salt

Make a firm, thick, pliable sheet of dough, using flour and water. Set the dough aside for ½ hour after kneading. Stuff the fowl with the butter mixed with lemon rind, mace and salt. Sew it up so the butter does not run out. Truss the fowl so that legs are neatly tucked in. Place the chicken on the dough and fold the sheet of dough over it, pinching the seams. Care must be taken to fold the dough securely and not break the surface.

Now heat water in a big kettle and place the dough-enclosed fowl in the water. Boil till done. A 5-pound fowl will take about 4 hours to cook. Chicken or pullet can be used. As these are somewhat tenderer a 3-pound chicken will require about 1½ hours cooking time. Serves 8.

Uncase and serve the fowl with Liver Sauce (p. 29) and Chili Sauce (p. 30), passed separately. This will be unlike any other boiled chicken you have ever eaten.

Oysters or baby shrimps can be used to stuff the fowl; oysters to be used raw and shrimps half cooked.

TWO CHICKENS IN ONE

(Or One in Two)

1 3-pound chicken
2 onions
1 pound ground lamb
¾ tablespoon green ginger
 (¼ teaspoon powdered)
1 tablespoon cummin
½ cup boiled rice
2 tomatoes
4 tablespoons butter
Akni (p. 28)
6 mint leaves
1½ tablespoons turmeric
1¾ tablespoons coriander
½ teaspoon chili
salt
1 tablespoon mustard seeds

Wash and dry the chicken. Take off the skin very carefully in one piece without breaking it.

Pound the onions well and mix with ground meat, also pounded. Pound the green ginger, mix with the cummin. Combine these with the rice and tomatoes, sliced. Place them in the chicken skin and sew up, not too tight, as the meat expands during cooking. Fry the stuffed chicken skin, in 2 tablespoons butter, over low heat. When well browned and crisp, pour in enough Akni to cover. Cook till tender.

Meanwhile cut the chicken at the joints into 4 parts. Bruise the mint leaves and place in melted butter, adding the turmeric, coriander, chili and salt. Fry over very gentle heat for ½ minute and place the chicken in it. Cook over a medium heat for 12 minutes. Then close the lid tightly and cook for another ½ hour or so till done. Serve the chicken in pieces and the stuffed chicken skin together. Serves 8.

To Herald Springtime

THE northern Indian festival of Basant Panchami is the overture to spring. Winter has gone, and the first urgings of new life are everywhere. After the hard, near-freezing temperatures, cold but always sunny, one day spring runs out its flags. The sky, seen starkly through the webbing of leafless trees, is fainter behind frilly foliage. In the fields of the Punjab, one of the world's greatest agricultural and wheat-growing centers, mustard flowers over emerald stalks knock their heads together in the breezes. The sap has mounted to the top in a blaze of uncompromising yellow. In little tremors the burning gold runs over the horizon, lapping at the walls of the towns and cities.

In a halleluiah of saffron, the color of spring catches the imagination everywhere. For this Basant Panchami, turbans are mustard; women's shawls are canary. Vivid gold is in their head veils. Handkerchiefs and bandannas make gay spots of pristine yellow . . . In the bazaars tempting mounds, intricate pyramids and fragile domes of sweets are similarly colored.

The passion and the urge of the quick color has its inspiration in the fields, but the frenzy of its activity is in the skies. Flying kites, hundreds of thousands of them, run up the banners for spring, for new life. Every house is stocked with piles of kites of fragile paper and supple bamboo. They are hung on walls, placed on divans and spread on floors, for space may not be enough. For days before the festival, one or more rooms are set aside for the kites and the enormous globes of colored glossy string which in their tight windings are many miles in length.

The Basant kite flying can take on the same following as baseball in the United States but everyone here is the fan or the player. Early in the morning the rooftops erupt with sudden life as people abandon house interiors and streets. Kites are strung and floated with a bewildering complexity of techniques, and a variety of kite styles. The sumptuously colored balls of twine are coated with a mixture of starch and powdered glass that is not hard enough to rasp the hand, but strong enough for the kite battles that will take place.

The strings spin out and mesh in a pattern that holds the sky like fragments of a puzzle. Thousands, many thousands of kites fill the sky and seem to clot the distant horizon. The balls of twine, some of them 15 miles in length, spin out till the kites are invisible high above; the only sign of them is the unrelenting pull of the string. Evening may come over the struggle of two men in an evenly matched kite battle, and the string will have to be deliberately severed. All through the day, there are victories but the inevitable defeats also. With the severing of the string the heart sinks and the strength put forth by the arms spurts into the emptiness and the slackness. This is a pain that transcends the physical.

The string is some sort of umbilical cord to the birth of man, to his victories and understanding of the earth. It is a rite of the first man with his first life — controlled and so discovered. Out of the chaos of life unknown comes the sense of rhythm, and of the recurring cycles. It is re-enacted here with all the gusto of the first man's discovery.

On the roofs, kites are run up. Many persons perch precariously over dizzy drops to the street. Each defeat or victory is greeted by yells, catcalls and blasts on brass-throated trumpets. As the momentum of the battle mounts, children get pushed to one side, for this is a man's game. Physical strength is wanted as much as kite-skill. There are big kites, heavy enough to carry a child with them. Others, sharklike, all points and deadly fins, seem to harness all the force of a gale, and constantly tug a man's arms out of his sockets. These are the marauders of the spring skies and all other kites veer away. These special kites give dominance, but they are hard to control, wanting a constant juggling, a ceaseless watch, and a complete understanding.

The women of the house, who understand what it is all about but wisely keep silent, scan the shining threads, held in a great curving loop, or in an exciting tautness. The mirth of people soars. They grin at this buffeting with an unseen force in the eddies high above. Like the first woman of the first spring, the women watch and understand without any explanation of this joy. Woman's strength lies in understanding, not emulating what man can do much better. There are things, like husbanding the fruits and making them grow, that he would never have the knowledge and the care to do. Taking things that are her own, and leaving him what is his, she escapes being half-man and only half a woman. She becomes wholly woman.

This Basant Panchami is a festival of untrammeled fun; strong, clear, clean, and without contradictions.

For this season, the food has a positive touch of this quick-life color. The Chicken Basant is an appropriate accompaniment.

CHICKEN BASANT

- 1 2-pound chicken
- 1½ tablespoons coriander
- 1 tablespoon green ginger (½ teaspoon powdered)
- 1 onion
- 4 tablespoons butter
- 5 cardamons (seeds of)
- 3 cloves
- 1 teaspoon saffron (P)
- salt
- 1 pound yoghurt
- ¼ teaspoon black pepper
- 2 tablespoons chopped mint leaves
- ¼ pound mushrooms
- ¼ pound spinach

In India they use small sticks of bamboo placed on the bottom of the casserole. The sticks prevent the meat from scorching and yet pass on the heat. Some cooks use this device for all meat recipes. Here it is definitely needed. You may use any other wood, cleaned, boiled, and cut very thin — about the thickness of a nickel. Or you may use a trivet instead. Place a few strips of bamboo or wood in the bottom of the casserole.

Cut the chicken into 8 portions and place inside the casserole. Raise the heat and let the chicken draw till it has exuded some moisture. Now remove the chicken and carefully but thoroughly wipe away all moisture with an absorbent cloth.

In the casserole, put the coriander, ginger pounded, onion pounded also, with half the butter, the cardamon seeds, cloves, saffron and salt, mixed with just enough water to cook the chicken. Simmer, during this time, on a brisk flame.

When the chicken is tender, strain the yoghurt into it through a fine sieve or coarse cloth, adding the pepper, mint leaves and the remaining butter. Mix them; boil for a little while till the yoghurt is reduced by one third.

Fry mushrooms separately with a suspicion of saffron and arrange on the chicken. To complete the spring touch, cook ¼ pound of spinach and arrange it in shreds near the edge of the serving dish. Serves 6.

To "draw" the moisture from the chicken, the method of steaming on page 66 can be used. Keep the lid on the cloth stretched over the vessel (which should be heavy), and turn the heat on without adding any moisture to the pan.

CHICKEN RAINBOW

An enormous kettle is required; also a trivet or a stand, for the chicken is not to touch the liquid in the vessel.

4 quarts Akni (p. 28)
4 tablespoons turmeric
bunch of mint leaves
1 teaspoon rose water
salt
1 2-pound pullet
1 lemon (juice of)

Place the Akni in the vessel (depending on the size, more or less than 4 quarts may be required) and put in the trivet. See that the trivet's surface is above the liquid level. Heat the liquid and when it is simmering, add the turmeric, the mint leaves, the rose water and salt. Place the chicken on the trivet. Close the lid of the vessel hermetically. Keep cooking till the chicken is done. A guess will have to be hazarded, as the age of the chicken, the thickness of the vessel and the exact degree of heat determine the cooking time. Squeeze lemon juice over before serving.

It is very important to cook with the lowest heat. The idea is to steam the chicken slowly in the aroma of the spices. For 4.

The residue of the Akni water and spices may be made into a sauce by mixing 2 tablespoons rice flour (p. 33) to 1 pint of Akni. Stir thoroughly over a gentle heat, mixing with some tomatoes, and reducing the sauce to correct consistency. This is not an Indian sauce, but a suggestion. An Indian meal would serve the Chicken Rainbow with dabs of relishes and chutneys, and plain Indian bread.

DUCK VINDALOO

This recipe for duck is aromatic and hearty.

1 duck (fatty)
2 tablespoons coriander
1 teaspoon red chili
2 tablespoons turmeric
1 tablespoon cummin
2 tablespoons green ginger
(¾ teaspoon powdered)
8 cloves garlic
olive oil
4 onions
1½ to 2 cups vinegar
4 tablespoons butter
10 bay leaves
salt
1½ inches stick cinnamon

Carefully wash the duck, dry it, and cut into 8 to 12 pieces (remove some of the small bones from the duck if you care to). Now make a paste of all the spices (except the bay leaves and cinnamon), the ginger, garlic, chili and onions in a little olive oil. Rub this all over the duck which has been pricked with a sharp fork. Put in the vinegar, mixing it well with the spice paste and the duck, and leave the duck to marinate overnight for 18 to 24 hours.

To cook use a heavy casserole; heat the butter; put in the duck with all the marinade; add the bay leaves, salt, cinnamon and simmer covered, very gently, till done. No water or liquid except the vinegar is used in the Vindaloo. Serves 4 to 6.

BATAKH PISTA

(Duck with Pistachio Nuts)

1 duckling
1 cup pistachio nuts, shelled
2 teaspoons cummin
2 onions
3 egg yolks
½ cup yoghurt
4 tablespoons butter
2 tablespoons rose water
Akni (p. 28)
salt
10 peppercorns

Have the duckling boned and left whole. Make a stuffing of pistachio nuts, well bruised, cummin, pounded onions, egg yolks, yoghurt, butter and rose water. Stuff the duckling with this; shape it and tie it well. Roast the duckling for ¼ hour in the oven, then put it in a casserole with enough Akni to cover it. Add the salt and crushed pepper. Cook uncovered till liquid dries, and the duckling is ready for serving. Pour melted butter over it. Serves 4 to 6.

There is one for goose in the section on cooking for the barbecue and the rotisserie. The next recipe calls for quail, but partridges, squab chicks (young and milk-fed) or squab pigeon may also be used.

QUAIL "IRON AND GOLD"

8 quail (or squab chicks or other selection 4 pounds)
flour, or split-pea flour (p. 33)
¼ pound butter
5 onions
4 tablespoons green ginger (1½ teaspoons powdered)
1 pint stock (or bouillon infusion)
6 cloves garlic
2 teaspoons black pepper
4 cloves
saffron (P)
1 lemon (juice of)
salt

Split the birds down the back. Wash well and prick all over with a sharp fork. Rub the flour or split-pea flour into the birds. Wash them again.

Heat the butter, brown the onions, thin-sliced, and pounded ginger. Add the birds, close the lid and give them one bhogar (shake).

Cook 1 pint of stock (or bouillon infusion: 4 cubes to a pint of water) with 1 tablespoon butter, the pounded garlic, the pepper and cloves, give it a bhogar (shake) also.

When the birds have been well browned, pour in the above

stock and cook till all liquid is almost dry. Mix the saffron with the lemon juice and salt and add to the casserole, frying and drying it over medium heat. When the birds begin to glaze, serve them piping hot. For four to six.

Quail in India is tiny, eaten bones and all. Four to six of those suffice for one serving. Serves 8.

This recipe can be finished off in another manner. In addition to the ingredients in this recipe, take 1 tablespoon blanched almonds and 1½ tablespoons heavy cream for every pound of meat. Also use 1 tablespoon coriander for 4 pounds of meat, and the juice of ½ lemon more.

When the stock is only three fourths dry, add the saffron, with lemon juice and the cream mixed with pounded almonds. Mix them well, and simmer over the lowest heat for ¼ hour.

CHICKEN RAINCLOUD

1 2-pound chicken
Akni (p. 28)
6 onions
6 tablespoons butter
1 teaspoon turmeric
1 teaspoon cummin
6 cloves
4 cardamons (seeds of)
1 teaspoon black pepper
1 tablespoon coriander
4 blades mace
salt

Disjoint, wash and prick the chicken. Reserve for the moment.

Boil 4 quarts of Akni with 3 onions kept whole. When liquor is reduced by one third, strain it through a coarse cloth and reserve.

Take half the butter and brown the remaining 3 onions, shredded fine. Remove the onions and fry the chicken with turmeric well on both sides. As the butter dries, add 4 tablespoons of the liquor reserved; add the cummin, cloves, cardamon seeds, black pepper, coriander, mace and salt. When this liquid dries, add the rest of the butter. Close the lid of the casserole, and give the whole one good bhogar (shake).

Then uncover and add as much liquid as required to cook the chicken. Serves 4.

The recipe can be made both dry (dried of all liquid) or it can be made *turri-darh*. In this case add all the Akni liquor and cook covered till done. Uncover for the last 10 minutes over very low heat.

Here is a recipe for the oven. It is quite a connoisseur's dish.

MURGHI KABAB

1 2-pound pullet
4 tablespoons coriander
1 tablespoon black pepper
2 tablespoons green ginger
 (¾ teaspoon powdered)
½ pound onions
½ tablespoon turmeric
2 cardamons (seeds of)
4 tablespoons butter
½ cup yoghurt
½ cup heavy cream
salt

Wash and dry the chicken. Prick it all over with a fork. Pound the coriander with the pepper and ginger and rub it well into the chicken.

Pound the onions (save 2) with the turmeric, cardamon seeds and butter. The blender can be used. Mix these with the yoghurt, cream and salt.

Roast the chicken for some minutes. When it begins to color, start to baste with the cream sauce. Serve with onion rings, placed on the chicken with the last of the basting sauce about 10 minutes before serving.

Some almonds, blanched and slivered, can be mixed with the basting sauce at the time the cream and yoghurt are mixed.

Another alternative is to mix some good raisins, previously soaked in lemon juice or vinegar for some hours to soften and acidulate them. In each case, add 2 tablespoons of either the almonds or the raisins to the basting sauce. Almonds and raisins to be coarsely slivered or chopped.

CHICKEN "WRAP AND TAKE AWAY" (*With Potato Casing*)

2 pounds chicken (boned or leftover)
butter, oil or fat
2 onions
1½ teaspoons turmeric
salt
1 teaspoon chili
12 cardamons, 1 teaspoon caraway seeds, 6 mustard seeds, 5 cloves, ¼ inch stick cinnamon, ground together
8 potatoes
3 eggs
½ cup bread crumbs
2 tablespoons parsley
1 tablespoon lemon juice

Grind the chicken. Brown it in butter with onions, chopped, turmeric, salt, chili and the pounded spice mixture. Add 1 cup of water and cook till tender. Dry off all liquid. Reserve for the moment.

Boil the potatoes, cool, and mash them thoroughly till smooth (use an electric mixer if possible). Shape a little of this potato "pastry" in the hollow of your hand and place some chicken in each. Fold it over, ball it, and then flatten into cakes. Dip in well-beaten egg, then in bread crumbs. Fry on a griddle or in a skillet over low heat with a little fat, oil or butter. Serve with chopped parsley and a squeeze of lemon juice when the potato cakes are well browned.

The ground chicken may be mixed with a few green peas kept whole and cooked just enough to make them edible.

MURGHI SEEKH KABAB

(*Roast Chicken*)

¼ pound onions
4 cloves garlic
¾ teaspoon ginger (P)
½ teaspoon black pepper
6 cloves
salt
¼ pound butter
1 2-pound roasting chicken

Make a paste of the onions, garlic, ginger, black pepper, cloves and salt with the butter. Prick the whole chicken and rub this paste over it. Then roast it in the usual way, basting it with the juice in the pan.

Before serving, sprinkle with 1 tablespoon melted butter. For 4.

MURGHI KEEMA KABAB

(*Ground Chicken Croquettes*)

2-pound chicken, boned and ground
1 pint yoghurt
1½ tablespoons turmeric
1 tablespoon coriander
½ teaspoon chili (P)
salt
1 onion
2 egg yolks
butter

Mix the chicken with 2 tablespoons yoghurt and all the spices, salt, and onion chopped fine. Bind them with egg yolks. Make small meat balls from the ground chicken. Fry very gently in butter. When browned on all sides, pour in the yoghurt. Dry the liquid on a medium flame. Serve when all moisture is gone. Serves 2.

MURGHI BHOGAR

(*Chicken Bhogar Technique*)

1 3-pound pullet
¾ tablespoon green ginger
(¼ teaspoon powdered)
2 cardamons (seeds of)
1 tablespoon chopped mint leaves
2½ tablespoons coriander
salt
½ pint milk
¼ pound butter
½ pint buttermilk
2 lemons (juice of)
½ inch stick cinnamon
pinch of cayenne
½ cup heavy cream
½ cup white stock

Wash, cut the chicken in 12 pieces and dry it. Pound in a mortar and pestle the ginger and cardamon seeds with half the mint leaves, all the coriander and a pinch of salt. Mix this with the milk.

Fry the chicken for 2 minutes in half the butter and add the milk with its spices. Cook together for 10 minutes. Now strain the milk, mix with buttermilk, add the lemon juice and reserve.

Melt the rest of the butter, add the cinnamon and again put in the chicken. Give it two successive bhogars (shakes) in 5 minutes. Open the cover and put in the stock. Cook on high heat and dry up the stock. Add the buttermilk mixture with the cayenne. Cook again over high heat and dry it off.

Add the remaining mint leaves, pounded, and the spice, milk, and lemon-juice liquor reserved. Add the cream and salt. Cover and cook till done. Then serve with the gravy that remains. For 6.

Correctly prepared, this recipe has hidden and not too obvious flavor.

Some of these recipes came to me from the Himalaya. The great mountain range which the Indians think of as *one* mountain, and never as the Himalayas (plural), is the lodestar for the Indian imagination, just as Mecca is for all Moslems and the Holy Land is for Christians. Not only the rain that fills the parched land with life, but the many rivers that nurture infinite water for perennial use, are in the Himalaya. The idea of one land mass, the longest and the highest in the world, straddling the country from one end to another, is enough to have touched the Indian with a magical vision which has never left him.

Down in the plains, where people live who will never see the Himalaya, the Magic Mountain, the Pillar of the Universe, finds itself echoed in little facsimiles — the carved temples boldly perpetuate the Abode Of Snow. Plans in architecture, motifs in art, patterns in craft, metaphor in literature draw the mind to Himalaya.

In Himalaya, the basis of the first "inspiration," the primary "revelations" that have projected the Indian character, was defined. Today, there are Ashrams — schools for meditational study — and the groves where some of the world's crankiest and noblest men may live uninterrupted lives, where the meanings they seek can become plain.

There is the spectacle of the pilgrimages, which become awesome if you see what happens to the life of the individual pilgrim over a hazardous journey from which he may not return.

There are remains of ancient kingdoms from which came wonderful schools of painting and which yet conserve customs that have died out elsewhere. There are medieval cities; lost temples among the pines and cedars, lifting their spires to bleak skies, over forgotten valleys. Uplands where human foot has never passed; a completely independent domain where all sense of the world can escape you, can run out as water through the fingers.

Then there are the gales, and the storms, and the store of incalculable energy that the ancient Indians were quick to recognize and correlate to the rest of life. Overriding this is its spell more than can be explained.

As in the story, the Himalayan Prince was defeated and forced to pay tribute to the King, his overlord in the plains. Each time he returned to his Himalayan fastness he rebelled, and stood defiant. Twice he was defeated and brought captive before his overlord. Twice he was penitent in the court of his enemy. By the code of Indian ethics, the victorious King could not punish the Himalayan Prince, since he was submissive in the court. Puzzled and wanting a way out of this impasse, the King asked his wisest minister the reason for this alternative submissiveness and open defiance. The minister, a wise man, said: "It must be the Himalayan soil, and his mountains. It breeds an amazing loyalty and independence of spirit." So here, in court, the Prince was truly submissive and meant it sincerely.

Before the arrival of the captive Himalayan Prince, the King had soil from the Himalaya strewn over the court chambers. When the captive stepped on the Himalayan earth, his docility changed to open defiance. He drew his sword and broke away from his guards. The King's men, waiting for their chance, with consciences mollified, threw themselves on him and cut him to pieces.

Some years ago, in August, an English girl, a Scot and myself were trekking down the high Himalaya to the plains of the Punjab in northern India. We had stopped for lunch at a little clearing in the last valley before the foothills. Over the camp table we were silent. Our thoughts were with ourselves, for it is always a little sad to leave the Himalaya.

The hillsides around us were alive with iridescent butterflies over miles of rhododendrons. In our small clearing, against a bank of silver birches and Himalayan oak, the wide lawn of fine turf offered room for endless leisure. The familiar high peaks now seemed far and alien in their world of haze and sun-clouds. I must have said so much to her: unwisely. At this her face grew sad; eyes turned dark with misery. Finally, putting her arms on the camp table, the girl buried her face and wept. After a while she raised her face, "I know that I shall never be coming back," she said with a sigh, "There will always be the 'once more' feeling . . . this will be lost, lost forever . . ."

CHAPTER 8

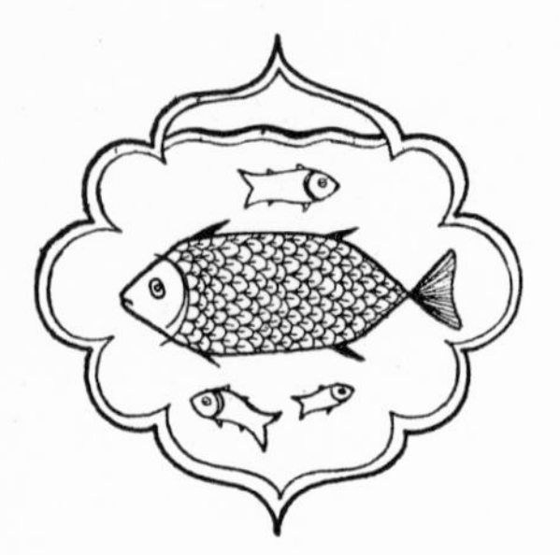

Fish and Sea Food

MORE THAN two thousand distinct species of fish are found in India; both sea-water and fresh-water fish. Some, like the Mahaseer, a river fish, can weigh up to seventy pounds, and capable, at that weight, of carrying hook, line, sinker and the fisherman with it. Some of the fish cannot be found outside India. A few are really revelations in eating pleasure. However, most of the fish is like the variety found in the United States and in Europe.

To cook fish, use the same styles of preparation as for meats: frying, boiling, poaching, braising, steaming, broiling or grilling over the open fire with revolving spits or on grids and baking.

For frying, use small fish, and not overlarge or thick pieces of fish, or you will run the risk of overcooking the exterior and getting an unpleasantly raw interior. Fried fish must be properly drained before serving.

Deep fried fish must be cooked in smoking-hot medium, and for a short period. Long cooking in fat makes the fish soggy and unpalatably greasy.

Boiling is done in salted water. The process of cooking must be gentle. It is best to bring the water to a boil, and (as some of the pellaos were cooked) leave the fish covered near the heat.

When using Akni or water, place whole fish in boiling liquid and reduce the heat. With fish cut in pieces, immerse in cold or warm water and gradually bring to a boil.

Poached fish is best cooked by covering with the Akni or water and letting remain in a slow or moderate oven till it is done. It then can be drained, finished in the desired manner and served with the appropriate accompaniment.

Braising is best for whole fish, cooked in a fish kettle that is shaped to hold it, and also involves the least use of any liquid for cooking. Too much liquid causes the fish to stew, not braise. In the braising of fish, the lid should not be overtight, for some steam must escape to allow the liquid to dry. The fish is placed on a trivet or bamboo strips placed in the kettle (see p. 145).

Fish is steamed in India in the usual manner. Or the method of steaming recommended on page 66 can be used, with or without cover placed over the cheesecloth. Yet another manner of steaming fish in India is to take certain kinds of grass, firm and upright (like delicate reeds). The grass is tied in a bunch and then placed in the cooking vessel. The fish is laid over the grass (which covers the bottom of the vessel) and steamed by the vapor coming through the grass stalks. Some aromatic kinds of grass used impart a very gentle fragrance to the fish.

For broiling or grilling the fish, best results are obtained by making incisions on both sides of the fish, or fish pieces.

Baking is like the technique called au gratin for the oven, with all the care and requirements for this style.

It is best to cook with more oil or butter than you think necessary, as this will prevent the drop in temperature which is responsible for most of the bad fish cookery we encounter.

The medium for cooking fish in India, even in regions where butter is used exclusively for other cooking, is mostly oil. Mustard oil, if of the best quality, imparts a certain new taste and crispness to the fish. Oil is in general considered better for fish cookery (in French cuisine too) because it has a much higher burning point. Butter burns at 248°, but oil can withstand at least 555°. Moreover, oil is best for thin pieces of fish that must brown and cook simultaneously. Fish cooked in butter, however, is lighter in taste.

Indian cuisine lays great stress on the washing and cooking of fish. The process of rubbing the fish with split-pea flour (use ordinary flour in a pinch) is designed to rid the fish of superfluous oils, muddy taste and exudations, the removal of which makes an appreciable difference in the taste. The technique is to rub the fish with split-pea or white flour and then wash it off. Repeat twice or more. Or the fish can be rubbed with the flour, let stand half an hour and then washed.

FRIED FISH PIQUANT

2 pounds fish
¾ pound split-pea flour (p. 33)
1½ cups yoghurt
2 teaspoons coriander
salt
¼ teaspoon black pepper
2 cloves
¼ pound butter

Cut the fish, if it is a large one, into slices thin enough for frying. Wash and dry as recommended above.

Make a mixture of the yoghurt with coriander, salt, pepper and cloves ground together. Rub this over the fish. Heat the butter or oil and fry the fish on both sides. Serves 4.

TALI MACHCHI (*Deep-Fried Fish*)

2 pounds fish
3 tablespoons lemon juice
1 teaspoon chili (P)
salt
7 tablespoons split-pea flour (p. 33)
1 tablespoon turmeric
2 tablespoons chopped parsley
1 tablespoon crushed mint leaves
oil for deep frying

Wash and dry the fish; cut into portions. Lightly rub the lemon juice over all the surfaces; sprinkle with the chili and salt. Reserve.

Make a batter with the split-pea flour and ½ or ¾ cup warm water, adding the water gradually and mixing it well. Add the turmeric, parsley, mint leaves, salt. Whip the batter well. Coat the fish thickly and fry in a deep fryer. Turn the fish once or twice and as soon as it is nicely brown, remove and serve hot. For 4.

MACHCHI ZEERA BHOGAR

(Fish with Cummin Bhogar)

2 pounds fish
1 cup split-pea flour (p. 33)
1 tablespoon turmeric
½ cup oil
2 teaspoons cummin
6 anise seeds
salt
1 tablespoon chopped green ginger (⅜ teaspoon powdered)
2 cardamons (seeds of)
5 tablespoons butter
1 pound onions
¾ pound yoghurt
4 tablespoons lemon juice

Wash and clean the fish. Dry it well and prick it with a very sharp knife point. Cut into pieces. Rub half the split-pea flour over the fish.

Mix the turmeric in the oil and put the fish into it. Let stand for 1 to 1½ hours. Then rub the rest of the flour into the fish. Rub the cummin, anise seeds and salt, pounded and made into a paste with a little water, into the fish. Pound the ginger, cardamon seeds, and sprinkle over the fish.

Melt the butter, put the onions, thin sliced, into the casserole and brown them medium. Add the fish and brown lightly. Close the lid and give it two bhogars (shakes) in 5 minutes. Then uncover and add the yoghurt. Cook very gently till the yoghurt is dried off. Then add the lemon juice (or tamarind fruit juice if available) and cook on very low heat till done. Serves 4.

COCONUT-MILK FISH CURRY

- 2 pounds fish
- 1¼ pounds rice
- 1 teaspoon mustard seeds
- 2¼ cups coconut milk
- 1½ teaspoons turmeric
- 2 onions
- 3 cloves garlic
- 1 green pepper
- 1 tablespoon lemon juice
- 2 tablespoons butter
- salt
- ½ teaspoon chili (P)

Wash, dry and cut the fish into small pieces. Pound the raw rice and the mustard seeds; mix them with the coconut milk. Strain through coarse sieve into a casserole. Add the turmeric and stir. Slice the onions, pound the garlic, chop the green pepper and add it to the coconut milk.

Heat the casserole and start cooking the coconut milk. When it thickens a little, add the fish and cook below the boiling point till done. Drain any liquid left. Add the lemon juice. Cook till this is dry. Then sprinkle the butter, salt and chili on the fish to serve.

This recipe can be made without the coconut milk. Fish fumêt, or Akni (p. 28) is a good substitute. The recipe is finished as in the preceding recipe. Serves 4.

SALT-WATER CURRY WITH TOMATOES

- 2 pounds sea bass, or other salt-water fish
- 1 tablespoon turmeric
- 8 tablespoons yoghurt
- 3 tablespoons butter
- 1 onion
- 2 cloves garlic
- ¾ tablespoon chopped green ginger (¼ teaspoon powdered)
- salt
- 8 tomatoes
- 1 tablespoon lemon juice
- ½ tablespoon mint leaves

Wash and dry the fish. Cut in medium portions, rub in the turmeric and the yoghurt.

Melt the butter and brown the onion sliced. Put the fish in

and brown over gentle heat for 10 minutes. Pound the garlic and the ginger with the salt in ¼ cup water. Sprinkle this over the fish. Cook fish for another 2 minutes. Then, 4 to 6 minutes before serving, cover the fish with rounds of tomatoes. Cook covered. Open the cover and sprinkle the lemon juice over it. Add the mint leaves last and cook no more than 1 minute longer. Serves 6.

KORMA MAHI (*Fish Korma Curry*)

2 pounds fish
1 cup chick-pea or split-pea flour (p. 33)
1 cup oil
salt
1½ teaspoons turmeric
½ pint yoghurt
¾ cup vinegar
2 teaspoons anise seeds or fennel
1 teaspoon cummin
½ inch stick cinnamon
¾ tablespoon green ginger (¼ teaspoon powdered)
5 tablespoons butter
3 onions
1 tablespoon coriander
¼ cup capers in 3 tablespoons lemon juice

Clean, dry and cut the fish in medium-sized pieces. Prick the fish all over with a sharp fork. Wash (meaning to rub the fish pieces gently) with half the split-pea flour. Then rub with the oil, salt, and turmeric. Let the fish stand 1 hour.

Wash the fish in cold running water. Rub it again with split-pea flour and half the yoghurt. Then wash this off with the vinegar. Rub with ginger, wash again. Now rub into the fish the anise seed (or fennel) and cummin ground in water with the cinnamon.

Heat the butter in a heavy casserole and brown the onions, sliced, raising the heat very high for an instant. Place the fish in a casserole and lower the heat. After 6 minutes of cooking, sprinkle the coriander, ground fine, over the fish. Pour over the capers with lemon juice. Cover tight and cook gently till done.

Shake it frequently to prevent sticking. During the preparations, handle the fish with care in order not to break it. Serves 4.

Spinach and pimentos can be used for stuffing the fish pieces. Split the pieces down the middle and insert ¼ pound of spinach, cooked in ½ cup of yoghurt, with salt, sprinklings of water and 3 tablespoons of mixed pimentos chopped well. Close the fish by skewering with a cocktail stick. Cook exactly as in the above recipe.

The Law of the Fish

In India, the law of instinctive life has been called "Matsya Nyaya," the Law of the Fish . . . where the big ones eat the smaller ones and are eaten in their turn. This is the Law of the Deep and it must be avoided at any cost. To avoid it, the Law of the Fish must be squarely faced. Perspicacity helps everyone; even the fish . . .

There was once a heron, in a place on the edge of a lake. With old age, laziness had set in. He sought an easy way to catch his fish. So, one day, he lingered about the edge of the lake with an irresolute air, not bothering to catch the fish that were obviously within his grasp. Among the fish was a crab. Swimming to the surface, he approached the heron. "Uncle, why do you neglect today your food and amusement?" The heron replied, "A great disaster is overshadowing all our lives. As I am old, this is going to end my life and pleasures. For this reason I am depressed."

The crab enquired the nature of this impending calamity. The heron continued. "Today I overheard some fishermen talking. 'This is a good lake,' they said as they passed. 'Today we'll fish in the lake near the city, and then return here within a few days; clean off all the fish.' They are armed with dreadful nets. You are lost, and so am I."

When the water-dwellers heard this they were thunderstruck.

Imploring the heron, they cried, "Uncle! Father! Brother! Friend! Thinker! As you have informed us of the calamity, you must have the remedy. Save us!"

Then the heron said, "I am a mere bird and cannot contend with humans. This, however, I can do: transfer you from this to another lake, a bottomless one." He went on artfully to outline his plan. "Take *me* first, help *me* first," the fish shouted.

The old rascal shook with noiseless laughter and hummed joyfully to himself. Having made a show of thinking this through, he agreed. Lifting some fish, he carried them to a great stone and ate them there. Days passed in great delight and satisfaction. He kept their confidence with new artfulness.

The crab, one day, asked for his turn. The heron, quite tiring of the diet of fish, reflected that crabmeat would be good, for a change. He was different, thought the heron. Picking up the crab, he flew off with him.

The crab saw no signs of water and, his eyes widening at the sight, in the distance, of the great rock with hundreds of fish skeletons, said, "Uncle, where is the bottomless lake?" The heron chuckled and told the crab, "It is there on the rock."

The crab, who was brought up on the principle of fearing fearful things when they threatened, and of meeting them by striking back, resolved that as the heron dropped him he would grip his neck. And just so, the crab nipped off the heron's head, painfully dragged it back to the lake, and told the water-dwellers the story . . .

The heron, however, was no more rapacious than the fish toward each other, nor humans to humans, especially in politics. The Matsya Nyaya, or Law of the Fish, became known to scholars in Europe a few decades ago. It is best indicated in the work known as the *Kautilya Arthashastra* (the Science of Power and Wealth). This scholarly and sophisticated work deals with the attainment and the control of power. The treatment is shorn of sentiment. On the human level, a cynical, needle-sharp intellect emulates the Law of the Ocean.

Unlike Machiavelli's work, *The Prince*, the *Arthashastra* is without patriotism. When the scholars first read the Indian document they were aghast, as no doubt the Indian Chancellor would have been at the Italian work. To the European, the cold-bloodedness of Machiavelli's work is saved by his aim: patriotic good. The Indian recoils from giving such sanctity to evil. To excuse ice-cold cynicism for love of country or God is tantamount to accepting it. It passes evil off as good. Insidiously, secretly, it corrupts human life.

Like fish that swim in water and about which one cannot say whether they drink or do not, so it is impossible to detect a *little* corruption in a man; one cannot help tasting the honey on one's tongue, so one cannot refrain from stealing a little in government, and rationalization does not make the stealing any less.

There we have, in one way, the distinction between the Indian attitude and the Western. However, there is more room for agreement in food than in politics and government. Keeping in mind the old Indian proverb: "Sweet and placid waters smile, but beware the crocodile," we turn from this troubled sphere to:

MACHCHI KABAB HIMALAYA

(*Fish in the Kabab Style*)

Kababs may be flaked fish made into croquettes, whole fish, or fish steaks, as here.

2 pounds fish
½ pound flour, or split-pea flour (p. 33)
vinegar
¾ tablespoon green ginger (¼ teaspoon powdered)
½ pint yoghurt
1¼ tablespoons coriander
2 onions
3 cloves
2 or 3 egg whites
¼ teaspoon cayenne
salt
4 cardamons (seeds of)
5 tablespoons butter

Wash the fish with flour or split-pea flour (see p. 158), and cut fish in medium portions. Wash again by rubbing with a little vinegar. Dry the fish. Pound the ginger, mix with yoghurt and pour this over the fish.

Heat 4 tablespoons butter, brown the onions, sliced, and give the fish two bhogars (shakes). Then uncover and cook till yoghurt is dry. Sprinkle the coriander and cloves, well crushed, over the fish with just enough water to make it moist. Repeat this till the fish is almost done. Shake it occasionally to keep it from sticking.

Remove the fish. To whatever butter remains, add the remaining butter, the whites of eggs, cayenne, salt and crushed cardamon seeds. Mix well, and with the hand rub this mixture over the fish. Then fry it again in additional butter or oil. For 4.

MACHCHI KABAB ACHKAAN

(*Fish in a Jerkin*)

2 pounds fish
½ pound split-pea flour (p. 33)
3 tablespoons split peas
(roasted in skillet or griddle)
1½ teaspoons anise seeds
(roasted in skillet or griddle)
1 tablespoon coriander
1½ teaspoons ginger (P)
1 egg
1 teaspoon black pepper
salt
3 tablespoons yoghurt
¼ pound butter
4 onions

Wash the fish and dry it well. Make a dough, using three quarters of the split-pea flour and water, and encase the fish in a medium-thick sheet. Bake the fish in the oven (325°) till the pastry is a good brown. Then remove casing (and flake the fish).

Mix the flaked fish with the remaining quarter of split-pea flour. Combine this with the roasted split-peas, the anise seeds, coriander, ginger, egg, black pepper, salt and yoghurt.

Pat the mixture into shapes of fish the size of a large sardine.

Steam these over the cheesecloth arranged tight over the top of a big vessel (p. 66).

The fish can be served as it is now, or fried in the butter with the onions sliced very thin (or omit the onions).

The steamed fish is ready when it is firm on both sides. Turn once, to steam both sides. Serves 4.

The Monsoon

THIS is the season of the monsoon. The parched land is showered with rain for a few months. Life begins again. Every day that it rains is a "fine day": children play truant from school. On the verandas the housewife concocts special treats for the family coming home. The poets are happy with the introspective melancholy that precedes creative work. Lovers grow amorous. Peacocks dance under racing white clouds; in the fields the farmers smile, and women stop their work to dance. Under the first pearl-drops of rains from skies soft or thunderous, the mynah birds talk their hearts out about all they know of men and the world. The sap mounts in everything alive, and voices tauten with fresh life . . . Over long terraced fields in the Himalaya skirted women work, singing in rhythm as their sickles and scythes swing in the cool air. One, a young woman, supple waisted and standing straight as a lance, raises her head as a male voice from a far-off field floats over; "O! little blossom of Chamba, what is it that you seek?" As she bends to work, the women sing in unison, "O! bee that sips the honey in the blossom, it is you I seek . . ." And the wind carries the words back to the men; air and clear sunny rain, and "cloud messengers" carry contentment everywhere.

KORMA MACHCHI MONSOON

(Fish "Rainy Season")

2 pounds fish
¼ pound rice
1 inch green ginger
(⅜ teaspoon powdered)
7 cardamons (seeds of)
4 tablespoons butter
2 onions
1 tablespoon turmeric
salt
2 to 3 tablespoons lime juice

Wash and dry the fish. Then wash with lemon juice or vinegar. Rub flour over the fish. Wash again and dry it. Prick it with a sharp knife.

Pound the onions, turmeric, ginger and salt into a paste. Rub it over the fish and fry it gently in butter, on both sides. Keep shaking gently to prevent sticking.

Now pound the rice (use the electric blender or mortar and pestle), mix with 1 cup water and cardamon seeds. Pour over the fish. Cook till almost done. Add the lemon juice. Simmer for a minute and serve carefully, without breaking fish. Serves 4.

MACHCHI BADAM-MALAI

(Fish with Almonds and Cream)

2 pounds fish
½ pint yoghurt
½ pound blanched almonds
1 teaspoon turmeric
salt
5 tablespoons butter
1 inch stick cinnamon
½ pint cream
¾ teaspoon black pepper
3 onions
1 cup milk

Wash and soak fish 1 hour in water, cut into medium pieces.

Melt half the butter and fry the onions, with cinnamon. When brown, place the fish over them. Sprinkle with turmeric, black pepper, salt and 1 cup milk. Shake the casserole and simmer till fish is almost done. Dry up all the liquid, and fry the fish, adding the rest of the butter. Pound the almonds, mix with yoghurt and cream. Simmer together till reduced by half. Then pour it over the fish. Keep covered for ¼ hour, over low heat, or in an expiring oven. Shake 4 or 5 times (very gently) during this period. Serves 4.

FISH MOLEE

½ cup coconut flakes (unsweetened)
4 tablespoons butter
2 onions
2 cloves garlic
10 cloves
8 bay leaves
1 teaspoon chili (P)
2 teaspoons lemon juice
4 tablespoons heavy cream
pinch of saffron
salt
1 teaspoon tarragon
2 pounds fish
pickled beets
gherkins
green and red chili peppers

Soak the coconut overnight in 1 cup water. When ready to use, simmer very lightly, covered, for 1 hour. Strain, and reserve the coconut milk (kept at 1-cup level).

Heat the butter and fry the onions, cut in rings, and the garlic chopped fine. Fry the cloves and bay leaves. After 5 minutes add the chili, lemon juice and coconut milk (1 cup) and salt. Simmer gently for ½ hour. Strain again and combine with the cream, and the saffron dissolved in ¾ cup of boiling salted water and tarragon.

Fry the fish plain, and pour this sauce over it. Bake in a slow oven, or cook over low heat till done. Serve, garnishing the fish with pickled beets, gherkins, and green and red chili peppers preserved in vinegar. Serves 4.

FISH CURRY FRAGRANT

2 pounds fish
2 tablespoons butter
2 onions
Akni (p. 28)
salt
bunch of celery tops (leaves)
pinch of cayenne
1 teaspoon capers
1 tablespoon lemon juice
pinch of saffron (optional)

Wash, clean and dry the fish. Melt the butter in a heavy casserole. Fry the onions, sliced thin, a dark brown. Add the fish and fry for 7 to 10 minutes on both sides. Then sprinkle with a few tablespoons of Akni. Shake the casserole. Add salt, place the celery leaves on top of the fish and add cayenne. Cook covered till done. If more moisture is required, sprinkle over top of celery leaves and close the lid again, so the fish can braise gently.

Before serving, add the capers with lemon juice to the fish under the celery leaves. Raise the heat and reduce all liquid to a glaze. Sprinkle with a little saffron powder, if desired.

The celery leaves give the fish a delicate aroma, but because most greens or vegetables will not yield enough moisture, water or Akni will be required to cook the fish. Do not use more than a handful of celery leaves, or you run the risk of overflavoring. The celery leaves, which most people mistakenly throw away, can make good eating. Serves 4.

Since grilled fish is done in much the same way as in American and French cuisine I give no specific recipe here. I remember one of the tastiest of all fish I ever ate. It was while camping. Snow trout, fleshy and silvery, lay on the grassy bank. Our cook, who had trekked to the next village to get some provisions for our next move, was missing at eventime. Unable to wait any longer for dinner, the two men who were in the camp with me started a fire in the improvised grate of stones the cook had set up for his work. Help came to hand (for in those days I had never cooked) in the shape of the ponyman whose pack ponies we were using for the trip. Grilled over the wood fire, the trout were done to perfection. Our surprise at his culinary skill was doubled when we found in the stomach of the biggest of the snow trout another fish, a tiny one of its own kind. There is a saying in India that:

> Some eat the countries; these are kings;
> The doctors those whom sickness stings;
> The merchants, those who buy their things;
> And learned men the fools.
>
> The married are the clergy's meat;
> The thieves devour the indiscreet;
> The flirts their eager lovers eat;
> And Labor eats us all.
>
> They keep deceitful snares in play;
> They lie in wait by night and day;
> And when occasion offers, prey
> Like fish on lesser fish.

FISH IN "HOT WATER"

- 2 pounds fish
- 1 teaspoon turmeric
- ¼ teaspoon black pepper
- 1 quart buttermilk
- 1 teaspoon lemon juice
- 1½ teaspoons cummin
- 2 tablespoons chopped green peppers
- 3 tablespoons butter
- salt

Clean, wash and pat the fish dry with paper toweling. Gently rub in turmeric and black pepper. Let stand for a few minutes, and then poach it in buttermilk (see poaching at beginning of this chapter). As soon as the fish is half cooked, remove it. Reserve the liquor also. Keep fish warm.

Add lemon juice to the liquor and simmer, reducing it to slightly less than one half. Replace the fish and add the cummin and green peppers. Reduce the liquid to a few spoonfuls.

Add the butter, melted and slightly browned, and salt. Close the casserole and give the fish one bhogar (shake). Open cover and with high heat reduce the liquid to a glaze. Turn the fish over, if you can without breaking it. Serves 4.

The process of adding very hot, slightly browned butter (clarified butter is much preferred) at this stage of cooking is a favorite technique with Indian cooks — especially in the Punjab. It is excellent for vegetables too, as we shall see later. This technique, called *Tarka,* can be practiced with shredded onions browned dark in the butter, or perhaps with garlic; or even with a spice to give it a different flavor.

'Tis said that:

> Remember that a single grab
> Suffices for fish or crab.

Oysters are different. Let us see how we can induce them to appear with the help of this recipe.

KASTURA TURCARRI (*Oyster Curry*)

4 tablespoons butter
2 onions
2 tablespoons sesame seeds
2 teaspoons turmeric
salt
½ cup coconut (desiccated, unsweetened)
1 cup clear stock
3 bay leaves
3 dozen oysters (fresh or frozen)
½ cup coconut milk

Melt the butter, brown the onions, chopped, and for the last minute, the sesame seeds slightly bruised. Then add the turmeric and the coconut. Fry for 1 minute together, and add the stock. Add bay leaves and simmer over very low heat for ½ hour.

Now add the coconut milk and boil furiously for 5 minutes. Then add the shelled oysters and their liquor, and salt. Simmer for a few seconds only, till the oysters curl and cook. Serve hot. For 4.

FISH FRIED "NONCHALANT"

The nonchalant refers not to the fish but to the recipe, being a kind of self-modesty that really amounts to patting his own back . . . whoever thought of this recipe.

- 4 pounds fish
- 6 tablespoons oil
- ¼ pound split-pea flour (p. 33)
- 3 tablespoons lemon juice
- milk
- 8 cloves
- 5 cardamons (seeds of)
- 4 onions
- ¼ teaspoon saffron
- 2½ tablespoons coriander
- 1 tablespoon anise seeds
- 1½ tablespoons green ginger (½ teaspoon powdered)
- ½ teaspoon chili (P)
- 2 or 3 eggs
- 1 pint yoghurt
- ¼ pound butter
- 1 inch stick cinnamon

Cut the fish in big slices. Wash it 4 times in running water. Rub the oil over the pieces and let remain for ¼ to ½ hour. Then wash off oil with water. Rub the split-pea flour on the fish, and rub it off again. Boil the lemon juice in enough milk to wash the fish. Wash it with this.

Tie the fish in double-folded cheesecloth (better still, good muslin). Simmer in water with cloves, cardamon seeds and onions till cooked but firm.

Mix the saffron, coriander, ground anise seeds, pounded green ginger, chili powder and make into a paste with eggs and yoghurt.

Coat the fish with this. Meanwhile melt the butter, fry the cinnamon and cardamon seeds for 3 minutes over very low heat. Add salt. Then fry the fish. Serves 6 to 8.

There are more recipes for fish in the Rotisserie and Barbecue section.

SHRIMP DELICATE

2 pounds shrimp
3 tablespoons yoghurt
2 teaspoons coriander
pinch of cayenne
2½ tablespoons butter
½ teaspoon turmeric
1 onion
salt

Wash, shell and dry the shrimp thoroughly. In a casserole melt the butter and fry the onion, pale gold. Add the shrimp, with turmeric and coriander and fry in the butter for 7 to 10 minutes. Fry well on all sides.

Now add the yoghurt, salt, cayenne and mix well. Bring to a boil and immediately add ½ cup water. Lower heat. Cover and cook till done. Before serving, dry the liquid, so that only a few spoonfuls of gravy remain. Serves 4.

SHRIMP MALAI

2 pounds shrimps or prawns
3 tablespoons butter
2 tablespoons coconut
3 tablespoons blanched and slivered almonds
pinch of saffron
4 tablespoons raisins
3 bay leaves
salt
1 cup milk

Wash, clean and dry the shrimps thoroughly. Fry pale gold in the butter. Remove shrimps and reserve, keeping it warm.

Put the coconut in the butter (adding more butter if required); fry for a few minutes with the almonds; put back the shrimps. Mix well, adding the saffron, raisins, bay leaves and salt. Pour in the milk and boil up once. Then lower to a simmer; cook covered till done. Serves 4.

SHRIMP DOH-PEEAZAH

2 pounds shrimp
3 tablespoons coriander
2½ pounds onions
6 tablespoons butter
½ tablespoon turmeric
¼ teaspoon cayenne
3 cloves garlic
salt
½ green pepper

Clean, wash and reserve the shrimps. Boil enough water to just cover the shrimps with the coriander, and half-cook the shrimps. (Shrimps should not be overboiled. They can be cooked longer with butter, though.) Remove, and reserve the liquor. Take ½ pound of onions and pound them. Quarter the rest of the onions without cutting them right through, slightly separating the skins.

Fry the quartered onions with care, and set aside. In the butter mix the turmeric, cayenne and garlic, pounded, and salt. Fry over low heat for 1 minute and add the shrimps. Mix and fry for 5 minutes, adding also the pounded onions and green pepper, chopped. Now add the quartered onions and the reserved liquor. Bring to boil and cook till done. Two minutes before serving, raise heat and dry off any moisture. Glaze the shrimps somewhat and serve. Serves 6.

SPECIAL BROILED SHRIMPS

2 pounds shrimps
1 cup oil
1 tablespoon turmeric
¼ teaspoon black pepper
3 cloves garlic
1 tablespoon basil
1 tablespoon chopped mint leaves
salt
1½ teaspoons chili (P) mixed with 1 tablespoon vinegar

Wash, shell and dry the shrimps thoroughly. Make a marinade of the oil, spices, crushed garlic, herbs and salt. Mix well and leave to marinate overnight.

Place in a broiling pan. Under a high flame, broil the shrimps for 6 to 10 minutes (depending on their size). Turn them once while broiling, and serve with as much of the marinade as you fancy. Serves 3 to 4.

EK-AUR CHINGRA KORMA

(*Korma Shrimp Curry*)

2 pounds shrimps
6 tablespoons oil
1 teaspoon black pepper
4 cardamons (seeds of)
½ to 1 cup yoghurt
5 tablespoons blanched almonds
salt
1 tablespoon pistachio nuts
6 cloves
1 tablespoon coriander

Clean, wash and dry the shrimps. Gash each with a sharp knife. Soak them in oil for ½ hour. Then remove from oil and reserve.

Heat 5 tablespoons of oil. Put in the black pepper, and after 15 seconds the shrimps and cardamon seeds. Fry till they are red on all sides.

Mix the yoghurt with almonds, pounded, salt and pistachio nuts. Cook covered till done. In the remaining 1 tablespoon of oil, fry the cloves and coriander over low heat for 4 minutes. Then mix this with the shrimps. Cover tight. Place over high flame for a few seconds; then keep warm for 10 minutes before serving. For 4.

SHRIMP "DECREED"

(*Meaning, You Must Have It*)

2 pounds shrimps
1 pound breast of chicken
Akni (p. 28)
salt
1 tablespoon coriander
½ tablespoon chopped mint leaves
pinch of cayenne
3 egg whites
¾ cup buttermilk
¼ pound butter
¼ teaspoon saffron

Wash, shell and dry the shrimps.

Cook the chicken breasts (have them boned by your butcher, if possible) in Akni till tender but not too soft. Pound the meat (or use an electric blender) with the coriander, mint leaves, cayenne and whites of eggs.

Cook the shrimps in the Akni, and the buttermilk adding salt to taste, till almost done. Then drain, dry and coat thinly with the chicken mixture. Melt the butter and fry shrimps till done. Use very low heat.

Before serving, sprinkle with powdered saffron, to speckle the shrimps. For 6.

There are shrimps in India (on the west coast) that are the biggest in the world. They run four to a pound in contrast to the biggest from the Gulf of Mexico, which run about eight to a pound. The Indian shrimps often come *one* to a pound. They have a wonderful nutlike flavor and a complete absence of the iodine taste of most big shrimps. The size of the Indian shrimps makes them ideal for braising, baking, broiling and for cooking on the spit.

Now to the lobster pots!

LOBSTER CURRY

- 3½-pound lobster
- 3 tablespoons butter
- 2 onions
- 1½ teaspoons turmeric
- 5 mint leaves
- ¼ teaspoon black pepper
- ½ pint stock
- salt
- 1 tablespoon lemon juice
- 4 tablespoons boiled rice

Boil the lobster so that the meat is still a little underdone. Pick all the meat from the shell. Melt the butter, fry the onions, sliced, pale brown, adding the lobster meat, turmeric, mint leaves, bruised, and black pepper. Fry these for 5 minutes over low heat. Add the stock, salt to taste and simmer the lobster till done. Before serving squeeze in some lemon juice and add the boiled rice. Serves 3.

LOBSTER KORMA

- 1 3-pound lobster
- 4 tablespoons butter
- 1½ cloves garlic
- 1 onion
- 1½ teaspoons turmeric
- 1½ teaspoons cummin
- 2 cloves
- 3 pints yoghurt
- pinch of cayenne
- salt

Half-boil the lobster and remove the meat from the shell. Melt 3 tablespoons of the butter in a heavy casserole and add the garlic pounded with the onion and turmeric. Cook very gently for 2 minutes. Add the lobster and the cummin. Stir well and cook over slow flame for 3 minutes more.

Melt the other 1 tablespoon butter and cook the cloves, crushed, gently for 1 minute. Add to the lobster, close cover and give it one bhogar (shake). Open the casserole and add the yoghurt, with a strong pinch of cayenne, salt to taste. Cook over brisk flame till the yoghurt is two thirds reduced. Then remove from fire, cover and let stand for 5 minutes before serving. For 2.

LOBSTER IN THE SHELL

1 3½-pound lobster
¾ tablespoon green ginger (¼ teaspoon powdered)
8 mint leaves
butter
pinch of chili (P)
salt
3 eggs
rice flour (p. 33) or bread crumbs
½ green pepper
3 onions

Cook the lobster, and cool it. Take the meat from the shell. Keep the shell intact.

With the lobster meat mix the ginger and mint leaves pounded coarsely. Fry them in very little butter for a few minutes; enough to color the meat. Remove from heat and sprinkle chili and salt over it. Fill the shell and top with the following mixture: Combine well-beaten eggs with rice flour or bread crumbs, dip the pepper, sliced into strips, and onions cut into broad crescents in the egg mixture. Arrange them over the lobster in its shell. Pour the rest of the egg mixture over the lobster and bake in the oven till done. Serves 3.

LOBSTER WITH PEPPER AND SAFFRON

1 3-pound lobster
8 tablespoons butter
salt
1 tablespoon chopped ginger (⅜ teaspoon powdered)
1 cup buttermilk
½ cup cream
5 onions
5 cardamons (seeds of)
¼ teaspoon saffron
2 teaspoons black pepper
1½ tablespoons coriander
3 tablespoons lemon juice

Cut open a live (or parboiled) lobster. Divide the tail in sections and split the shell. Crack the claws.

Heat 3 tablespoons of the butter and begin to cook the lobster over a brisk flame. If alive, fry till the pieces are reddened and the meat somewhat cooked.

Pound the salt with ginger and 2 tablespoons water. Add the buttermilk and cream to this. Strain the whole through a coarse sieve over the lobster. Cover and simmer ¼ hour.

Then heat the rest of the butter and brown the onions with the cardamon seeds; remove the lobster, drain the liquor, reserving it, and add to the onions. Close the lid and give the lobster one bhogar (shake). Open and add the saffron, black pepper, coriander, and 2 tablespoons of lemon juice. Cover. Give one more bhogar. Meanwhile, simmer the rest of the buttermilk liquor with 1 tablespoon lemon juice. When this is reduced to half its quantity, add the lobster, and finish cooking another 5 to 8 minutes, over low heat, uncovered. Served in its shell. For 3.

INDIAN BROILED LOBSTER

3-pound lobster
butter
1 lemon
salt
Akni (p. 28)
½ teaspoon black pepper
2 teaspoons mustard seeds
20 bay leaves

The lobster may be cooked raw or first boiled in Akni for ½ to ¾ of the required cooking time. Crush the mustard seeds, mix with pepper and enough butter to spread on the lobster. As it is being broiled, let the bay leaves come near enough to the flame so that they burn and smoke. This aroma of burnt bay leaves is undefinable, but contributes definitely to the taste. Serve lobster with a squeeze of lemon juice if desired. For 3.

LOBSTER KOFTA (*Lobster Croquettes*)

3 pounds lobster meat (cooked)
¼ teaspoon thyme
4 mint leaves
salt
½ teaspoon black pepper
2 to 4 eggs
1 tablespoon coriander
2 cloves garlic (optional)
2 tablespoons butter
8 bay leaves

Pound the lobster meat well, adding any coral, thyme, mint leaves, salt, pepper, and enough egg to ensure binding.

Pound the legs of the lobster (or use the blender) with the coriander and garlic (if used). Fry this pounded mixture in butter, adding bay leaves. Then strain it through a cloth. Mix the juice with the lobster meat. Shape into croquettes and fry in butter, or broil. Serves 6.

Another way of serving this recipe: Slightly crack the lobster legs. Fry them with pounded garlic and coriander. Add ½ cup water after 5 minutes, and reduce the liquid to an almost dry state. Then serve the lobster croquettes garnished with the legs which will be full of juice. The lobster legs are of course eaten with the hands, crushed with the teeth and sucked. In any country that is the only way to eat the tiny legs, and if well cooked they are succulent.

INDIAN CRAB IN SHELL

3 pounds crabs
2 onions
1 tablespoon green ginger
(⅛ teaspoon powdered)
6 peppercorns
1¼ teaspoons turmeric
salt
½ teaspoon lovage seeds
1 tablespoon lemon juice
3 tablespoons butter
Akni (p. 28)
split-pea flour (p. 33)

Clean, wash and boil the crabs. Remove the meat and reserve any coral. Chop the crabmeat fine with onions, peppercorns, ginger, pounded turmeric and salt and mixed with 1 tablespoon water and strained into the crabmeat. Pound the lovage seeds and mix with the crabmeat, adding lemon juice. Fry this in 2 tablespoons of butter till meat is somewhat cooked. Then mix reserved coral, well bruised, with enough Akni to cook it. Simmer to thicken and add to crabmeat. Then put crabmeat in the shells. About 6½ crabs to 5 shells. Strew a little split-pea flour mixed with the butter over the crabs. Place it in the oven and bake for 5 to 8 minutes. Serves 3.

SHRIMP KOFTAS (*Shrimp Croquettes*)

- 2 pounds raw shrimps
- 2 tablespoons parsley and dill (mixed)
- salt
- 1 egg
- butter
- 1 tablespoon cummin
- 4 cardamons (seeds of)
- 4 bay leaves
- stock
- 1 tablespoon grated lemon rind

Clean, wash in salt and water and shell raw shrimps. Then pound them in mortar and pestle (or use blender). Mix the pounded green herbs and salt. Make the shrimp into koftas (croquettes), enclosing lemon rind in each, using the egg as a binder.

Melt the butter and, very gently, fry the croquettes on both sides. When these are partly cooked and firm, place in stock boiled for 5 minutes with cummin and cardamon seeds. Strain it over the koftas, and cook with a pinch of salt and bay leaves till done. The liquid will be reduced to a light gravy. Only a few spoonfuls should remain. Serves 3.

CHAPTER 9

Rotisserie, Barbecue and Grill

A BRIGHT NEW LIFE must have opened up one day, long ago, when our ancestor discovered food cooked over the naked fire. Glumly resigned to eating clammy, raw food, he was perhaps vouchsafed his first taste of cooked food through an accident. A forest fire, perhaps, or even the eruption of one of the numerous volcanoes that once covered the earth, left him with an abundance of game and birds already roasted and cured by the fire. Of these some were charred, some scorched unevenly, and quite a few cooked well and nicely.

It was centuries, or even millenniums, before man learned how to tame and use fire. But the taste, once acquired, and never forgotten, of fire-grilled foods was his first joy and will remain his greatest in food. There is no savor finer than perfectly cooked meats and vegetables revolved on the spit over the naked fire, or today on the gas stove or electric rotisserie.

There are many reasons for this. But before we go on to these, the cardinal point to remember is that barbecuing or cooking with a revolving spit is not merely a matter of lighting a charcoal fire, or turning the spit and letting the meat cook. Nor is the whole matter complicated. It does behoove the amateur cook and gourmet to keep a canny eye on the techniques of roasting or grilling, the differences in the cooking of red and white meats, whether braised, roasted or grilled; their basting, regulation of fire and heat.

A careful attention to those simple matters (they soon become a habit) will ensure your fire-cooked foods being superlative. Those who have invested in some excellent equipment and laid it away unused can turn their hand to this cookery again.

There are important differences in the cooking of red and white meats. Both kinds can be harmed by overcooking — the meat rendered tough, rubbery, flavorless and drained of all its juices — but young tender white meats will suffer most.

Red meat and white each require their own kind of heat. Most failures with fire-cooked foods arise from ignorance of this point. Red meats, while cooking, demand (this is imperative) a searing and crisping to seal the surface and so conserve the juices and flavor inside the meat. During the cooking of red meats, the outward thrust of the juices, from the center, increases with the heat and length of cooking time. Thus red meat with surfaces that have not been seared and sealed, or that have been bruised or pierced after searing, will lose all its juices and become flavorless and tough.

The crisped surface, in red meats, also saves the meat from uneven cooking. There we have one of the most important reasons for cooking meats on the revolving spit. The revolving motion keeps the juices within the meat as it turns. The juices have little chance of dripping away. Revolving, the meat (red or white) receives its own drippings, juices and the basting sauce. This effect cannot be obtained in the oven. Moreover, in the oven, a fair amount of moisture is always present. This can mar the flavor of some delicate meats. Where an oven is used, take all possible precautions to keep the oven dry.

Open-fire (or open heat) cooking is *dry* cooking. To obtain the best results, it is essential to sear and crisp the meat at the beginning of the cooking period. Then the heat or temperature should be lowered as the meat, according to its weight and thickness, finishes cooking. If the charring or searing of red meats is continued too long, the hard, horny crust that forms will prevent all the heat from reaching the center. This will leave the interior undercooked. As soon as the surface is sealed with high heat, lower the temperature to normal. Keeping these points in mind, you should obtain meat so cooked that it is a real treat.

However, with a small or thin piece of red meat, the temperature or heat need not be reduced after crisping, as the piece will not require much more time to finish cooking. But I maintain that there is little reason to choose thin, small pieces and cuts for fire cookery. The bigger the joint (within reasonable limits) the better the transformation of the raw meat into an indescribable, savory, aromatic delight.

Red meats require basting. Use butter, or as in India, the clarified butter they call *ghee*. This prevents the drying of the meat surface and cracking and drying of the seared crust. And so, it becomes obligatory never to break the seared crust. If the surface is damaged, the long work of cooking will be ruined. Handle the meat as you would a baby or a bottle of rare cognac. Use special tongs for this purpose. It would be a shame to ruin the meat by maladroit handling at this point.

White meats do not require any searing or crisping. Owing to the formation of the tissue, the white meats have less concentration of juices. Their gelatinous cell structure gives them their own special texture and demands a different sort of handling than do the red meats. Veal, chicken and lamb belong to this class of meats. Because of the lack of concentrated juices, these demand a constant basting. Fish, too, except the very oiliest, requires a basting of butter to begin the cooking, and some more when it is three fourths done. This is the reason that small game and chicken are often larded. In a good chicken, or any other fowl, the meat on the breasts cooks differently from the meat on the leg. The structure and fat contents are different, and they do not "come together" at the same time.

While I do not believe in the hit-or-miss school of cookery, the time and temperature experts (with their thermometers) forget the imponderables: cut, quality and age of meat. There is no substitute for experience and judgment. Nevertheless, the thermometer is valuable. To believe in theories and fail to make the best use of technique, personal judgment and accurate equipment seems to be nobody's loss but the gourmet's.

The aim is to make a fire that is just right for the type of meat. A small fire can be augmented and stoked, while a big dramatic blaze is harder to maintain within required limits. The fire after being started should be left scrupulously alone until it is fit to receive the meat. The coal fire engenders a much greater heat than is supposed. So make a fire a little smaller than you would think necessary. A coal fire is set when the blaze has died and the coals present an ashy, gray appearance. They are glowing, but this is not apparent except when seen in complete darkness. Coals should be added only when the fire is slackening. Before attempting this, shake the brazier, or the equipment. This will give new life to the coals.

Of equal importance are the arrangements for keeping the surplus drippings from falling on the fire, with resulting smoke which can spoil good fire-foods. This can be done by building the fire slightly to the rear of the coals and placing a drip pan near the front where the drippings are likely to fall. A valuable hint may be borrowed from India. There, sand is the medium for receiving the drippings. Arranged near the coals where the drippings fall, the sand absorbs them, and also furnishes good heat. Sand once heated generates an amazing amount; when soiled, it can be washed and used again. Indians use sand on mammoth griddles for roasting popcorn and for drying fruits. It is the cleanest method. The sand cooks and sterilizes without burning. The other method of cooking food on the spit (besides the open-fire grill and the revolving spit) is the *tandur*, or clay oven. Often five or six feet high, it is made of baked clay. The narrow mouth conserves the heat from the wood or coal fire. The big, wide base contains the banked fire. A small plug blocks the hole, which is used also for fanning or bellowsing the heat if required. The chicken (or other meat) is put on a greased iron spit (called *seekhs*, hence the Seekh Kabab and many others made in this style) and lowered into the oven — the kind with which Big Brother Dilla performed his magic. Chicken is removed to be quickly basted, and lowered again. The soft ashes receive the drippings without burning or smoking. The chicken farthest down is the first done. It is slid off the seekh, and the next one, almost done, is lowered to take its place. A spit or seekh can hold four to eight chicken. Many spits can be used in the same oven, or only one. Small tandurs can be made to accommodate the small family or the bachelor.

The northern Indian, specially the Sikh, is much addicted to the tandur, for meats, and specially for his bread. I remember my parents, traveling yearly, during the exodus to the Himalaya resorts, with a tiny tandur made out of a galvanized tin bucket. This was coated inside with the clay and shaped to do service as a tandur. This special adaptation seems to have been the happy thought of my mother. In those days, as a child, it always gave me a tremendous thrill to see the look of incredulity and pleasure on the face of a Punjabi when the tandur-baked bread or delicacy was served. We had to wait a while, for the small tandur, portable and very efficient, could only accommodate so much. But waiting becomes a pleasure when you eat with nostalgia and surprise the best kind of cooking available to anyone.

If my hawklike but quiet waiting for the delighted reaction of friends was one thing, the constant and never diminishing wonderment of the cook was the same. He could never get over the diminutive tandur. I believe he looked forward to the times he handled it, as a new and curious toy. I had the feeling it made him, handling the tandur with ease, mastering it with comfort, feel twice the man he was.

Whether in that tiny tandur, a big one, revolving spits on an open fire or the electric rotisserie (also the barbecue on a stationary grill), remember that the thickness of the meat and its distance from the heat, plus its weight in pounds are all factors to be considered before cooking. A temperature of about 300° is best. Too high a heat will burn the meat. Lower than 250° may harden the meat and overcook it at the same time. But poultry can take much lower temperatures than can red meat.

If we consider the different ways red and white meats react to heat, the heat appropriate for both, the timing and the handling of the fire, there is no reason that a new field of cookery should not open up for those who like good food.

SIMPLE KABAB

¾ tablespoon green ginger
(¼ teaspoon powdered)
2 tablespoons coriander
2 onions
1 cup yoghurt
1 teaspoon black pepper
8 tablespoons butter
salt
2 pounds lamb (free from fat, skin and fell)

Pound all the ingredients well, making a thick sauce, and coat the lamb (shoulder, leg, or fillet) with it. Let stand for ¼ hour. Then skewer neatly. Cook on the revolving spit or on an open fire. For the latter, turn often. Baste with the sauce used above. If more basting is required, use butter. Salt and serve hot. For 4.

BARRA KABAB

2 pounds lamb
1 pint yoghurt
6 tablespoons lemon juice
3 tablespoons fresh ginger (1 teaspoon powdered)
6 onions
salt

Have the meat cut in medium-sized pieces. Rub the yoghurt and lemon juice into the meat. Now skewer 1 piece of lamb, 1 slice of ginger and 1 thin slice of onion dipped in yoghurt. Cook over the open fire or in rotisserie. Salt to taste. Baste with the remains of the yoghurt and lemon juice. If more is needed, use just enough butter to baste so the meat does not dry or burn. For 4.

KALEJEE KABAB (*Liver Kabab*)

2 pounds liver (lamb preferably)
lemon juice
1 tablespoon chili (P)
butter
salt

Wash, clean and dry the liver; cut in small pieces about 1 inch each. Marinate them in lemon juice, chili and salt. The juice of about ½ lemon will do for every ½ pound of liver. After ½ hour, remove from lemon juice and string the meat on sharp, thin skewers. Then dust them with chili and baste with a little butter and cook on the revolving spit, or open fire. Salt, and serve hot. Serves 4.

SEEKH KABAB KHATAEE

(*"Made Piquant"*)

2 pounds beef, veal or lamb (boned)
½ teaspoon ginger (P)
1 teaspoon turmeric
2 cloves garlic
2 onions
1 tablespoon green pepper, chopped
1 cup yoghurt
1 lemon (juice of)
salt
butter

Lay the meat on the table and make deep incisions lengthwise and crosswise, so the incised squares are about 2¼ inches each. Do not cut the meat all the way through.

Grind or pound all the spices with the garlic, onions and peppers. Mix with the yoghurt, lemon juice and salt. Rub the mixture vigorously on the meat. The meat may be then cut through where incised and left aside for 1½ hours.

Place on skewers and cook either on the revolving spit or the open fire. Baste with as much butter as required to keep the meat from drying and scorching. Serves 4.

GROUND-MEAT KABAB

2 pounds beef or lamb (lean)
½ teaspoon turmeric
¼ teaspoon black pepper
¼ tablespoon green ginger (⅛ teaspoon powdered)
¼ teaspoon mustard seeds
¼ teaspoon chili (P)
½ tablespoon cummin
¼ onion
salt
2 tablespoons yoghurt
2 egg whites
butter

Chop and pound the meat, rejecting all nerves or sinews. Mix the meat thoroughly with the spices well pounded and mixed with the onion, chopped, salt and the yoghurt. Bind with egg whites well beaten to make kofta (meat balls). Gently flatten them. Skewer them wrapped up in a banana leaf (if none are available, any smooth, thick fruit or vegetable leaf. Aluminum foil may be used). Cook it on the revolving spit or the open fire, basting with butter.

The purpose of the banana leaves is to prevent the kabab from crumbling, and also to enable it to bake through the leaves. Serves 4.

KABAB "TASTY"

2 pounds meat
1 onion
4 tablespoons green gooseberries (or ripe mango)
1 teaspoon black pepper
¾ tablespoon green ginger (¼ teaspoon powdered)
¼ cup shelled pistachio nuts
1 inch stick cinnamon
3 cloves
salt
¾ cup yoghurt
2 tablespoons flour
¼ pound butter

Cut the meat into 1½ inch squares. Pound the onion and gooseberries (or better: unripe mangoes) and black pepper, and pounded ginger. Rub this over the meat, and fix the pieces on the skewers. Cook over open fire, in rotisserie or under a broiler till done, basting with the following sauce:

Make a basting sauce of the pistachio nuts, pounded, cinnamon, cloves, salt and yoghurt, mixed with the flour. Fry in the butter. Serves 4.

CLASSIC SEEKH KABAB

2 pounds lean ground lamb or beef
1 onion
2 teaspoons green pepper, chopped
1½ teaspoons equal parts of pounded cardamon seeds, cloves, cinnamon, mustard seeds, poppy seeds
1 tablespoon chopped spinach, parsley or other greens
½ teaspoon chili (P)
salt

Pound the meat well, and mix it with the onion, pepper, greens, all pounded, chili, salt and the pounded spices and seeds.

Grease the skewer and with the hand, shape the meat around the skewer with a firm touch. Handle the skewer with care, and put on as many kababs, each about 3½ inches, as it will hold. Then cook it over the open fire or on the revolving spit. Serves 4.

SEEKH KABAB DIL-PASANDH

(*"Tease-Heart"*)

2 pounds lamb
2 tablespoons lemon juice
2 cardamons (seeds of)
¼ pound butter
½ teaspoon black pepper
pinch of coriander
1 quart yoghurt
1 onion
strong pinch of saffron
½ cup cream
1 clove
1½ tablespoons green ginger (½ teaspoon powdered)

Take a well-washed and well-dried piece of lamb kept whole. With a sharp knife score it heavily, cutting it halfway through. Make a paste of the lemon juice, crushed cardamon seeds, clove, black pepper, coriander and the yoghurt. Rub this well and with vigor into the meat. Let stand for 1 hour.

Brown the onion, crushed, in butter. Rub the butter, onion and ginger into the meat. Put the meat on the spit and begin to cook. Baste first with whatever is left of the butter, then with saffron and cream mixed. Serves 4.

PARCHA KABAB CLASSIC

3½ pounds boned leg or shoulder of lamb
¾ pound onions
8 cloves garlic
5 peppercorns
1½ tablespoons cummin
salt
4 red peppers
½ green pepper
butter

Wash the lamb, dry it perfectly. Pound to a paste the onions, garlic, spices, salt and green and red peppers. Place these in the center of the lamb. Roll it and tie, not too tightly, with a strong string to prevent the stuffing or juices from running out. A too tight string is to be avoided as the meat swells with cooking.

Put the lamb on the spit and cook. Baste with butter only. Served sliced. For 6 to 8.

SHRIMPS ON THE SPIT

3 pounds shelled raw shrimps
1 cup oil
½ cup yoghurt
½ teaspoon thyme
1 teaspoon black pepper
salt

Wash, clean and dry the shrimps. Mix the oil, yoghurt, thyme and pepper and marinate the shrimps in this for 3 hours.

Then put the shrimps on the spit, between grid clamps, if the spit is equipped with them. Cook, basting with the mixture of oil and yoghurt. A few minutes before they are ready, salt them. Sprinkle with pepper before serving. For 6.

MURGHI SEEKH KABAB

(*Chicken on the Spit*)

1 3-pound chicken
3 onions
4 peppercorns
3 cloves garlic
1 teaspoon cummin
salt
8 tablespoons butter

Wash the chicken, dry it well. Pound the onions with the peppercorns, garlic, cummin and salt. Rub this over the chicken. Let stand for 10 minutes and then put on the skewer.

Cook and baste with butter. Serves 4.

SEEKH KABAB BADAM MALAI

(*With Almonds and Cream*)

1 2-pound chicken
1 pint yoghurt
3 onions
salt
12 cloves garlic
3 tablespoons coriander
7 tablespoons lemon juice
strong pinch of saffron
1 pint cream
1 pound (cup) blanched almonds
¼ pound butter
½ pound Paneer cheese (optional, see p. 229)

Disjoint the chicken. Put the yoghurt in a cloth and squeeze out all the water you can. Reserve. Rub the chicken pieces with onions, pounded, salt, garlic, coriander mixed with lime or lemon juice and saffron.

Mix the yoghurt with the cream, the blanched almonds, well bruised, and the butter. Apply some of this to the chicken and put the chicken pieces on the spit (between grid clamps if you have them).

If you are using the cheese, bracket each piece of chicken

with the cheese, when basting with the cream mixture. Cook the chicken, basting as much as necessary.

Salt to taste after three quarters of cooking has been completed. Serves 4.

KOOKARH SEEKH KABAB

(Fine Prize Male Capon)

¾ pound ground lamb
¼ pound butter
¼ pound onions
salt
2 tablespoons coriander
1 4-pound capon
2 teaspoons black pepper
6 cardamons (seeds of)
2 tablespoons mint leaves (optional)
1½ teaspoons turmeric
¼ pound yoghurt
1½ teaspoons chili (P)

Have the meat ground very fine. Heat the butter and brown the onion, fine-shredded, with salt and coriander. Add meat and a little water and cook till done and the water is dried out.

Wash and dry the capon. Prick it all over and rub it well with black pepper, pounded cardamon seeds, mint leaves (if used) and turmeric.

Stuff the capon with ground meat; truss it well. Then put it on the spit and start to cook. Baste when necessary with the yoghurt mixed with chili and a little more butter over a slow fire. Serves 6.

PLAIN MURGHI SEEKH KABAB

Use about ½ cup of lemon juice to rub over the chicken. Let it stand for ½ to 1 hour. Then lightly rub with butter and put the chicken on the spit. Baste with butter and salt just before cooking is finished.

BATAKH SEEKH KABAB

(Duckling on the Spit)

This recipe asks for powdered sandalwood which is hard to get outside of India. Use a concentrated rose water as substitute.

- 1 5-pound duckling
- 9 tablespoons coriander
- 8 tablespoons split-pea flour (p. 33)
- 5 tablespoons rose water
- 1 onion
- 1 teaspoon anise seeds
- 4 cardamons (seeds of)
- 1½ pounds figs
- ¼ pound butter
- 1½ inches stick cinnamon
- 6 cloves
- salt
- ½ pound blanched almonds
- 1 quart yoghurt

Wash the duckling well. Then dip for a few moments in near boiling water (reserve water); remove and prick it over with a sharp fork. Mix 7 tablespoons coriander with water and steep the duck 3 to 4 hours in it. Then rub split-pea flour into it, and wash it all off.

Rub the duckling with 4 tablespoons rose water; soak it again in water with another tablespoon rose water for 2 hours. Wash the duckling again.

Pound the onion, the anise and cardamon seeds. Rub them over the duckling. Meanwhile give the figs, pounded, one bhogar (shake) with the butter and pounded cinnamon and cloves. Add rest of coriander and salt to it. Dry out the liquid and stuff the duckling. Truss it well.

Boil for 15 minutes. Reserve the liquid. Put it on the spit and begin to cook. Use some of the boiled water, mixed with pounded roasted almonds and yoghurt, for basting. Serves 4 to 6.

This technique is also successful with goose — that difficult bird.

The washing procedure is aimed at removing the high, greasy smell of the duck and goose, the smell from exuded fat.

MACHCHI SIKHANKHI

(*Fish on the Spit from the Sikh Country*)

2 pounds fish (firm fleshed)
½ cup split-pea flour (p. 33)
1 tablespoon pepper
salt
2 onions
8 tablespoons butter
4 tablespoons lemon juice
2½ tablespoons coriander
1 pint yoghurt
8 tablespoons cream
coriander or fennel leaves

Prick the fish and wash it in running water. Dry it and rub the split-pea flour over and inside the fish. Wash again and dry.

Pound the pepper and salt with a few drops of water and rub the fish gently with it. Pound the onion, fry in the butter and rub into the fish. Add the lemon juice, three fourths of the coriander, and the yoghurt and cream strained through a cloth. Rub this also on the fish. Arrange the fish on the rotisserie, with or without a clamp, sprinkle with remaining coriander and cook on both sides.

Lay the fish on a bed of dry coriander or fennel leaves. Before serving set the leaves on fire, and bring the fish on a flaming bed of leaves. These quickly burn and leave a fragrance and a nice char on the fish. Serves 4.

MACHCHI TIKKA KABAB

(*Fish Steaks on the Spit*)

2 pounds fish
1 pint yoghurt
1 teaspoon anise seed
4 cloves
split-pea flour (p. 33)
¼ pound butter
6 large onions
1 teaspoon black pepper
½ cup oil
1 teaspoon ginger (P)
salt

Cut the fish in slices about ¾ inch thick. Rub the fish with oil and wash it. Let stand ¼ hour; rub with split-pea flour. Let stand again for ¼ hour and wash well. Dry thoroughly. Make a paste of the pounded ginger, salt and little water. Rub this over the fish. Then rub the yoghurt mixed with coriander and cloves.

Cut the onions the same thickness as the fish. To cook, skewer each slice of fish with one of onion and baste using the yoghurt left over, with the butter and some sprinklings of milk.

Serve with little flecks of butter on the fish. For 4.

EGGPLANT ON THE SPIT

This recipe can be made with any other gourd type of vegetable.

2 pounds eggplant
¼ pound ground meat
6 tablespoons butter
3 onions
2 teaspoons cummin
salt
1 teaspoon black pepper
1 pint yoghurt
2 teaspoons turmeric

Cut a small portion or cap from the top of the eggplant(s) and scoop out the interior. Chop this and mix with the ground meat. Melt a little of the butter, fry the onions till soft and add the meat and eggplant mixture, the cummin, salt and pepper, mixing well. When three fourths done stuff inside the eggplant. Replace the cap, fastening it with a few toothpicks.

Arrange the eggplant on the spit, and cook. Baste with the yoghurt, remaining butter and turmeric. Last stage, baste only with butter. Serve sliced. For 4.

EGGPLANT WITH TURMERIC

For this, quarter an eggplant, about 1 pound, from the top but not quite to the bottom. Rub the inside with butter, 1 teaspoon turmeric, ½ teaspoon chili (P) and a little salt. Close the eggplant. Rub the skin with turmeric, and baste it with butter mixed with turmeric and chili. Salt before serving.

The Blessing of Food

Fire-cooked foods were the first love and will perhaps remain the final choice in eating pleasure. If we go past the present forms of our literature, poetry, music and dancing, we begin to see how their origins lay partly in the first use of fire by our ancestors. Manner, habit, ethics, many guiding principles were given their direction, and activated through the early hearth and man's approach to fire.

Life is interrelated, and poetic origins we invent for the greatest of man's inspirational works have had their origins from the simplest things.

For long, in India, there has been an elaborate philosophy of food that ties it not merely to the stomach pangs, but to the whole secret of human nature and of happiness. Food is regarded with reverence. It is the firstborn of this universe. An old teaching says: "From the Supreme Self was ether and space born. From space was born air. From air and wind was born fire. From fire was born water. From water was born earth. From earth arose herbs. From herbs was born food. From this came the generative powers. From this was born Man." So, man is food, being born from it. He grows by food and becomes food again when he dies. God too is food, for he projected all this from his own substance.

Here is a remarkable passage . . .

"In the beginning was the Supreme Self alone; he meditated: How can I propagate myself? So he travailed and practiced Tapa [complete creative introspective thought process: a part of Yoga]: then he begat Agni or Fire from his mouth [Indians relate heat to speech-sound as firstborn]; because he begat him out of his mouth, therefore is Agni food-devourer.

"The Supreme Self reflected: As food-devourer have I created this Agni out of myself; *but there existeth here nothing else besides myself* that he may devour, for at that time the earth was quite barren; neither herbs or trees were there; and this thought was heavy upon him. *Then turned upon him Agni with gaping maw;* Thus spake unto him his own greatness: *Sacrifice!* Then knew the Supreme Self: this my own greatness hath spoken to myself and he sacrificed . . . Because he sacrificed himself in this wise, he propagated himself, and because death in the form of Agni would have devoured him, he also saved himself from death."

This education is one that teaches the man the sacrifice of his most valuable possession (mind and his nature and then his actions).

Man's birth and that of the whole earth was created out of hunger or desire, and the satisfaction of this desire or hunger. Because the Supreme Self yearned to multiply himself and give *his* life so others may have life, this hunger is called life. Hunger is also death, as we have seen. Reality must include both recognitions and not only one. "From Abundance is scooped Abundance and yet Abundance remains," is the nature of this self or "food."

This detailed teaching shows that man has his link with divinity. He is not fallen, nor has he sinned. He is ignorant of real facts. This ignorance was necessary for life to grow, and dispelling this ignorance is also necessary to life. If Godhead, which Indians call Brahman or Parmatman, could dismember itself and make itself man's victim, man has to tread the same path. He can do no less in life. The truth is that if he does not duplicate this action, which is the law of his own life, he can spend millenniums finding the incorruptible happiness that all men seek. ". . . When a person dies he goes into his mind, his mind goes into his breath — the vital air — his breath into heat or formless energy that fashions all things and that into the highest divinity . . . the finest Essence. That is what man has for his own self. That is reality. That thou art thyself, O Man."

Again, man is told that everything begins with the intellect and ends with the elements. All that exists is food. From food life begins, from food it arises and grows, and as food it ends. Life is the essence of food. Mind is the essence of life. Understanding is the essence of mind. Complete bliss is the essence of understanding. He who knows this becomes possessed of food, life, mind, understanding, bliss — that indestructible joy with which all effort must end. Food it is that is worshipful. It is the physician. . . . Food is:

> I am the first-born of the divine essence,
> Before the gods sprang into existence, I was.
> I am the navel [the center and source] of immortality.
> Whosoever bestows me on others — thereby keeps me
> to himself.
> I am food. I feed on food and on its feeder.

This eternal eating and devouring is the mask and the means of the revelation of the significant. Human life is all related and the basic fact may never be forgotten.

The Indian conception of hospitality is founded on reverence for food. In an Indian household the guest is a god, and the host or hostess is playing, with all the perfection at their disposal, an archetypal role; duplicating the act of the Creator who dismembered himself to give life to his own children. This act is carried through first by an inward act and then by an outward. The two must coincide . . . So it is said that the man who, when food has been prepared, gives it to another gets it first too. When the food is given second, he also receives it second. When the food is bestowed last, it is the donor who receives it last.

Human relations can be the means to spirituality. "He lives," says another scripture, "ever sacrificing the function of the senses, using the mind as the ladle of the offering, pouring the ghee [clarified butter] of merit and demerit. This is the path of Yoga . . . The taste of this Food is redemption."

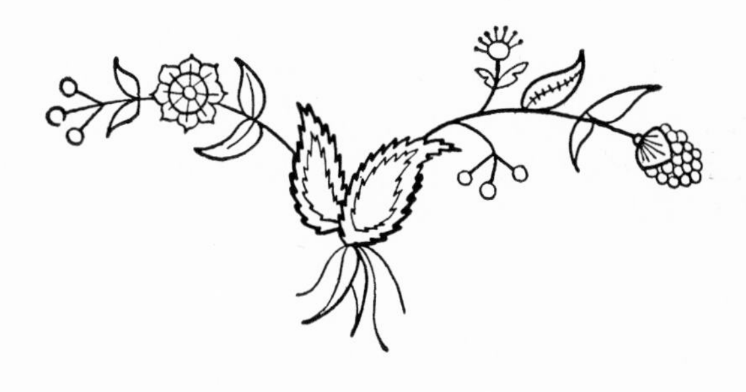

CHAPTER 10

Vegetables

INDIAN VEGETABLES are multitudinous. Most of the varieties found in the United States and in Europe are also to be had in India. No recipes for indigenous Indian vegetables have been included unless available substitutes can be used.

The common spud makes delicious food when seasoned with spices and prepared according to Indian cooking styles.

ALU TURCARRI (*Potato Curry*)

2 pounds potatoes
2½ tablespoons butter
1¾ teaspoons turmeric
½ teaspoon chili (P)
salt
3 tablespoons parsley or dill

Peel, wash and quarter the potatoes. Melt the butter and put in the turmeric with the potatoes. Fry them for 5 to 7 minutes; then add enough water to cover them. Bring to a boil, add the chili and salt and cook over slow or medium heat. When the potatoes are done, serve with finely chopped parsley, or dill sprinkled over the curry.

This is a liquid curry. If less liquid is desired add only enough to cook the potatoes. Serves 4.

SUKHE ALU (*Dry Sautéed Potatoes*)

2 pounds potatoes
4 tablespoons butter
2 onions
1 teaspoon turmeric
¾ tablespoon coriander
½ teaspoon cummin
salt
strong pinch of cayenne

Wash, peel and dry the potatoes. Halve or quarter them. Heat the butter and fry the onions to a pale gold. Add the turmeric, coriander, cummin and the potatoes. Mix well and fry for 10 minutes. Then lower heat and stir occasionally, cooking uncovered till the potatoes are done.

Add salt and cayenne 10 minutes before they are cooked. Serves 4.

The potatoes may also be cooked tightly covered. As all vegetables have much moisture, they will steam in good time.

A variation of this recipe is made by sprinkling the potatoes with the amalgam of spices called Garam Masala (p. 264).

ALU DUMN (*Potatoes Suffocated*)

2 pounds potatoes
¾ tablespoon turmeric
¾ tablespoon Garam Masala (optional, see p. 264)
1 pint yoghurt
6 tablespoons butter
6 bay leaves
3 red peppers
pinch of sugar
salt

Peel the potatoes and boil until half or three quarters done. Rub them over with a paste made of the turmeric, Garam

Masala (if used) and yoghurt. Heat the butter, fry the bay leaves and put in the potatoes. Add salt, the peppers, bruised, and a tiny pinch of sugar. Cover and simmer. Serve when all the yoghurt is dry. For 4.

ALU-MATTAR TURCARRI

(*Potato and Peas Curry*)

4 tablespoons butter
3 onions
¼ teaspoon ginger (P)
½ teaspoon black pepper
1½ pounds potatoes
2 teaspoons turmeric
4 tomatoes
1 pound green peas
salt
2 tablespoons lemon juice
chopped dill, parsley or other green herb

Heat the butter and fry the onions, sliced thin, with the ginger and pepper. Then add the potatoes, well washed, peeled, halved or quartered and turmeric. Stir them for 2 minutes and add the tomatoes. Cook on medium heat for 10 minutes. Then add the peas and the water (3 cups). Cook till the potatoes are tender. Add salt and lemon juice. Serve with chopped herbs sprinkled over the curry.

If using frozen peas, add 10 to 12 minutes before potatoes are ready. Serves 6.

ALU SAGH (*Potatoes with Spinach*)

2 pounds potatoes
2 tablespoons butter
2 onions
1½ teaspoons turmeric
¼ clove garlic
¾ pound spinach
salt
pinch of cayenne
¼ teaspoon ginger (P)

Peel the potatoes. Heat the butter and fry the onion pale gold. Add the prepared potatoes, turmeric and garlic, pounded. Close the lid and cook the potatoes on slow heat for 20 minutes. Then add chopped spinach, washed and thoroughly drained, to the potatoes. Add the ginger, salt and cayenne, stir well and cook uncovered till done. Serves 4.

GREEN PEAS CURRY

- 3 tablespoons butter
- 1 onion
- 1 teaspoon turmeric
- ¼ teaspoon chili (P)
- 8 mint leaves
- 1 pound peas
- salt
- ½ tablespoon lemon juice

Heat the butter and fry the onion, sliced, with the turmeric, chili and pounded mint leaves. When the onion becomes transparent, add the peas. Stir and fry for 5 minutes. Now add 1 cup water. Bring to a brief boil. Salt, add lemon juice, lower to simmer and cook till peas are tender. Serves 2.

MATTAR-PANEER (*Peas with Cheese*)

- 4 cups Paneer (p. 229) or cottage cheese
- 6 tablespoons butter
- 4 onions
- 2 pounds green peas
- 2½ tablespoons turmeric
- 3 mint leaves (optional)
- ½ teaspoon chili (P)
- salt

Make the cheese. Heat the butter, cut onions in thick slices. Fry them for 2 minutes; then add the peas, drained and dried. Mix them well with the turmeric and mint leaves. After 7 minutes add the cheese, chili and salt. Stir well and cook, open or covered, over low heat, till peas are done. Serves 6.

MIXED VEGETABLE CURRY

¾ pound carrots
1 pound green peas
1⅓ potatoes
1 pound string beans
1 clove garlic
¾ tablespoon green ginger
(¼ teaspoon powdered)
4 tablespoons butter
3 onions
2 teaspoons chopped mint leaves
½ cup yoghurt
¾ tablespoon cummin
1½ tablespoons tomato paste
½ teaspoon black pepper
salt

Shell and wash peas; dice the carrots; peel and halve the potatoes, add beans. Mix them together and put into a casserole or saucepan of boiling water. Cover, remove from heat and reserve.

Pound the garlic and ginger and mix with ¾ cup water. Heat the butter and fry the onions, sliced thin. When well browned, add the bruised mint leaves. Fry for 1 minute more, then add the yoghurt and the cummin. Cook very gently for 5 minutes. Then add the vegetables, drained. Cook these for another 10 minutes. Then add the ginger-garlic water, with tomato paste, pepper and salt. Cook till the liquid is dry. Now add 2 cups of the water from the vegetables. Cook covered (adding more water if necessary) till done. Serves 8.

MUSHROOM SAUTÉ

1½ pounds mushrooms
3 tablespoons butter
1¾ teaspoons turmeric
pinch of cayenne
salt

Wash the mushrooms and dry well. If small-sized, halve them. Quarter the big ones. Leave the button-sized whole.

Melt the butter and put in the mushrooms, with the turmeric and cayenne. Mix well and cook over a medium flame. They will be ready in a few minutes. Salt just before serving. For 4.

MUSHROOMS WITH TOMATOES

4 tablespoons butter
2 pounds mushrooms
¼ teaspoon ginger (P)
¾ pound tomatoes
salt

Melt the butter and put in the mushrooms, prepared and sliced. Fry for 2 minutes with ginger, then add the tomatoes, chopped. Mix and fry. Add a little sprinkling of water. Cook covered till done. Then open cover and on a high flame dry off any moisture; add salt and glaze the mushrooms somewhat. For 6.

BRAISED CAULIFLOWER

1 large cauliflower
1½ tablespoons green ginger (½ teaspoon powdered)
2 tablespoons butter
1 onion
¼ to ½ tablespoon turmeric
1 teaspoon dry mustard
½ teaspoon cummin
salt
½ teaspoon black pepper

Wash the cauliflower; break into flowerets of equal size and dry well. Slice the ginger and fry in melted butter for 1 minute. Slice and add the onion. When this is brown, put in the cauliflower, with the turmeric, mustard and cummin. Stir well so that the spices coat all the pieces. Fry for 7 minutes and then sprinkle with salt and 3 tablespoons water. Close the lid hermetically and cook. Sprinkle on more water (never more than 2 tablespoons at a time). When the cauliflower is tender, add the pepper and raise the heat high. Turn the cauliflower once or so without breaking it. Serves 4.

About 3 or 4 potatoes to a head of cauliflower may be added. Cut the potatoes ½ the size of the cauliflower flowerets, to enable them to cook at the same time.

SPINACH

2 pounds green spinach
water or Akni (p. 28)
salt
2 onions
2 tablespoons butter
1 tablespoon green ginger
(½ teaspoon powdered)

Wash the spinach and chop it very fine. Boil some water or Akni (p. 28), and cook the spinach till tender, using as little liquid as possible. Slice the onions and fry in butter. Ten minutes before serving the spinach, add the onions and butter, ginger and salt. Cook till all liquid is dried off. Glaze for a few seconds over a high flame. Serves 4.

Another way to cook spinach is to melt the butter and brown the onions, then fry the chopped spinach with the ginger for 3 minutes. Add just enough water to cook the spinach. Salt a few minutes before serving.

A third variation: Cook the spinach in water till perfectly tender. Remove from heat and strain coarsely or mash thoroughly with a heavy fork. In a skillet, melt the butter, brown the onions, raise the flame high and add the spinach with the ginger and salt. Stir and cook in butter for 5 to 10 minutes.

This recipe and method of cooking can be tried with most greens.

SPINACH WITH TURNIPS

3 tablespoons butter
1 onion
¾ tablespoon coriander
1 teaspoon turmeric
strong pinch of cayenne
salt
¼ cup yoghurt
1¼ pounds baby white turnips
2 pounds spinach
2 cloves garlic
1 tomato, chopped

Melt the butter and brown the onion, sliced. Add the coriander, turmeric, cayenne, salt and yoghurt. Cook very gently for 7 minutes, stirring a few times. Add the turnips, split but not cut through, and the spinach, well chopped. Mix well and cook for 12 to 15 minutes.

Pound the garlic to a paste with 1 cup of water. Splash this into the casserole, with the tomato, chopped, and cook covered. When the liquid dries, add water and repeat process, if necessary, till both turnips and spinach are done. The recipe will be ready in about 20 minutes (slow cooking, covered) after the garlic-water has been added. Serves 6.

SCORCHED TOMATOES

2 pounds tomatoes
1⅛ tablespoons green ginger
  (½ teaspoon powdered)
1 teaspoon coriander
1 teaspoon cummin
4 mint leaves
1 teaspoon black pepper
salt
2 tablespoons butter
2 tablespoons lemon juice

Bake the tomatoes in a hot oven till they scorch and begin to crack and burst. Then put in a casserole and thoroughly mash with a heavy fork, mixing in the spices, salt, pepper and butter. Heat and begin to cook a little so as to smooth the mixture. Before serving, add the lemon juice and stir over high flame. Serves 4.

STUFFED GREEN PEPPERS

2 pounds potatoes
6 tablespoons butter
2 onions
1 teaspoon chili (P)
salt
3 tablespoons chopped parsley
4 green peppers
½ tablespoon cummin

Boil the potatoes till soft. Then peel them and mash or strain through a sieve. Melt 2 tablespoons butter and lightly brown the onions chopped fine. Mix in the potatoes with cummin, chili, salt and parsley. Fry for a few minutes. Reserve.

Cut off the tops of the peppers, or halve them. Remove seeds and stuff with the potato mixture. Melt the butter in a skillet and fry the peppers, turning them so each pepper is browned on all sides. Serves 4.

The same recipe can be made with a stuffing of rice. Boil the rice, using enough turmeric to make it deep yellow. Mix 2 chopped tomatoes with rice, salt and some green herbs. Stuff the pepper, rub it with butter and bake in the oven till peppers are tender. Salt before serving.

PEPPERS STUFFED WITH GROUND MEAT

3 tablespoons butter
1 onion
1 pound ground meat
2 teaspoons turmeric
½ pint yoghurt
salt
4 green peppers

Melt the butter and brown the onion, chopped fine. Add the meat, with turmeric, and fry it 5 minutes. Add the yoghurt and cook the meat covered till tender. Dry off any liquid. Salt the meat, and reserve.

Stuff the peppers with meat and bake in the oven till peppers are tender. Serves 4.

GREEN BEANS WITH AKNI

2 pounds green beans
Akni (p. 28)
3 tablespoons lemon juice
3 tablespoons butter

Simmer (not boil) the beans in strong Akni. Use only enough to cover the beans. Drain off any moisture. Then mix lemon juice with the butter and roll the beans in it. Serves 4.

The beans, for this type of cooking, may also be simmered in water, 3 tablespoons coriander and 6 mint leaves. Then roll the beans in butter, or fry them for 5 minutes, before serving.

TURNIPS KORMA CURRY

2 pounds white turnips
5 tablespoons butter
3 onions
1½ teaspoons turmeric
1 tablespoon coriander
1 teaspoon cummin
1 pint yoghurt
salt
¼ teaspoon ginger (P)

Halve the turnips, or if small enough, keep whole. Melt the butter and brown the onions, thick-sliced. Add the turmeric, coriander and cummin. Fry gently with onions for 1 minute and then add the turnips. Fry the turnips well for 10 minutes. Add a little yoghurt (about ¼ cup) with salt and ginger. Cook covered till yoghurt dries. Then add a little more. Repeat the process till turnips are ready. A little water may be added if there is not enough yoghurt to cook the turnips. Before serving dry off any liquid and with a high flame glaze the turnips, remembering to turn them with great care, so as not to break them. For 4.

MIXED VEGETABLE CURRY PIQUANTE

½ pound beets
¼ pound carrots
½ pound red cabbage
½ pound white cabbage
½ pound pumpkin
½ pound peas
6 tomatoes
6 tablespoons lemon juice
4 onions
1 clove garlic
4 red peppers
1 tablespoon coriander
6 tablespoons butter
salt
1 teaspoon turmeric
3 tablespoons capers

Clean vegetables: Slice beets; dice carrots; halve or quarter cabbage according to size and tenderness; cut pumpkin in thick slices; shell peas; halve tomatoes; cut onions in thick slices; crush the garlic and peppers. Boil the water with the coriander, garlic and peppers. Put in the vegetables and cook till tender. These vegetables have different cooking times, so place them in the saucepan according to the length of cooking time for each.

Crush the capers and soak in lemon juice for 1 hour. When vegetables are done, drain them and add the lemon juice with capers. Leave them to cook, well covered, over gentle heat. Meanwhile warm the butter and brown the onions. When medium brown add the vegetables with salt and turmeric. Handle with care, turning and frying the vegetables till done. Serves 6.

COCONUT CURRY

1 fresh coconut and its milk
1 teaspoon lemon juice
3 tablespoons butter
2 tablespoons ground onion
1 teaspoon turmeric
1 teaspoon coriander
1 teaspoon chili (P)
4 onions, thin-sliced
salt
5 eggs, hard-boiled

Grate the coconut and mix with lemon juice. Heat the butter and fry the ground onion with the turmeric, coriander and chili for 1 minute. Add the coconut and cook well for a few minutes. As it begins to cook, add the coconut milk and the sliced onions. Simmer till done. Add salt. A few minutes before serving, pour the coconut on rounds of eggs. Leave covered for 10 minutes and serve. For 4.

VEGETABLES RAINBOW

- Akni (p. 28)
- 3 tablespoons turmeric
- 2 baby cabbages
- 1 small squash
- 3 zucchini
- 2 cucumbers
- salt
- ½ tablespoon lemon juice
- lettuce leaves

Fill a huge vessel with Akni, adding turmeric. Bring the liquid to a boil and place a trivet in the vessel. Now halve the cabbage. Cut the squash in thick long slices. Split the zucchini and cucumbers lengthwise. Now lower the heat to a mere suspicion; sprinkle some salt and lemon juice over the vegetables. Cover them with one or two large lettuce leaves and hermetically seal the lid. Steam till done.

Vegetables Rainbow are served with chutney, or with melted butter sprinkled over them just before serving.

They can also be served with cream, chopped parsley and a few caraway seeds. The cream is served separately and the vegetables may be dipped into it. Serves 6.

SQUASH CURRY

1 medium squash
2 tablespoons butter
1 onion
1 teaspoon turmeric
salt
½ teaspoon black pepper
3 tomatoes
¼ cup yoghurt
2 tablespoons chopped tarragon

Wash and scrape the squash. Cut it into medium-sized squares. Steep in salt water for ¼ hour. Drain.

Melt the butter, slice the onion and fry dark brown. Add the turmeric and the squash pieces. Stir and fry for 7 to 10 minutes. Then add the salt and pepper. Stir and add the tomatoes. Cook till the vegetables are going dry. Add the yoghurt and simmer. Add a sprinkling of water, if necessary, but cooking covered and over low flame. Before serving, dry off any liquid, over a high flame, glazing the squash somewhat.

Serve mixed with tarragon chopped and bruised. For 2.

CABBAGE CURRY

2 pounds cabbage
2½ tablespoons butter
2 teaspoons cummin
¼ cup buttermilk
salt
¼ teaspoon cayenne
½ tablespoon lemon juice
6 mint leaves
¼ teaspoon saffron (P)

Shred the cabbage and steep in salt water ¼ hour. Drain well. Melt the butter and add the cabbage, cooking it for 10 minutes with the cummin. Add the buttermilk, salt, cayenne, lemon juice and mint leaves, bruised. Stir and cook uncovered. When the liquid is almost dry, add the saffron, powdered. Mix well once or so, and serve steaming hot. Serves 4 to 6.

For eggplant one recipe is to be found in the chapter on rotisserie cooking. This one is really new in taste.

SCORCHED EGGPLANT

2 pounds eggplant
3 tablespoons butter
2 onions
strong pinch of turmeric
¾ teaspoon Garam Masal (p. 264)
salt

Place the eggplant over a naked high flame, or under electric broiler. Let the skin scorch, burn and crisp. Turn it so it is scorched all over. By this time the skin will be softened. With a blunt knife, scrape off the scorched skin. If small bits adhere to the vegetable, leave them.

Melt the butter; slice and fry the onions pale brown. Then add the eggplant, cut and mashed with a heavy fork. Sprinkle with turmeric, and cook for 20 minutes. Then add the Garam Masala and cook for a little while. Salt to taste.

The eggplant made in this style has a fine smoked flavor that will keep your guests guessing. Take care, before cooking, to reject any overripe or dried out, hard bits.

EGGPLANT CURRY

2 pounds eggplant
4 tablespoons butter
½ teaspoon turmeric
¾ tablespoon green ginger (¼ teaspoon powdered)
¼ teaspoon chili (P)
2 onions
2 cloves garlic
salt
2 tablespoons chopped sweet peppers
4 tomatoes

Wash and cut the eggplant into pieces 2½ inches each. Melt the butter and add the eggplant, with the turmeric and ginger and chili. Mix them and fry well for 10 minutes.

Pound the onions and garlic in 1 cup water. Add the peppers to the eggplant and sprinkle in the garlic-onion water. Raise the heat and cook till this is dry. Then add salt, and tomatoes sliced fine. Mix and stir. Cover tight and cook over very gentle heat till done. Shake the casserole a few times during this time. For 6.

EGGPLANT SAUTÉ

½ cup oil
2 pounds eggplant
1 tablespoon turmeric
2 teaspoons chili (P)
salt

Warm the oil, cut the eggplant in ¾ inch slices. Add the turmeric and chili to the butter and cook over low heat for 15 seconds; then add the eggplant and fry it on both sides till done. Serves 4.

STUFFED SQUASH OR ZUCCHINI

2 pounds squash or zucchini
1 onion
strong pinch of saffron
4 tablespoons butter
¼ cup yoghurt
1 cardamon (seeds of)
½ pint cream
5 tablespoons almonds blanched
½ tablespoon lemon juice
salt
1½ teaspoons coriander
¼ teaspoon black pepper

Split the squash or zucchini lengthwise. Remove the interior, leaving enough so that the shell will not be too thin.

Chop the extracted vegetable; mix with onion, chopped, and saffron. Melt the butter and fry these for 5 minutes. Then add the yoghurt and the cardamon seeds, crushed. Cook till the yoghurt is dry. Then add the cream mixed with the almonds, pounded. Add the lemon juice and salt, and cook. Before the mixture dries out, place it in the zucchini shells. Speck them with small bits of butter and sprinkle with coriander and pepper. Bake in a moderate oven till nicely browned. Serves 4.

PURÉE OF ARTICHOKES AND POTATOES

6 artichoke hearts (bottoms)	3 tablespoons butter
1 teaspoon cummin	1 tablespoon mustard seeds
1 pound potatoes	¼ teaspoon cayenne
2 tablespoons chopped green herbs	1 tablespoon lemon juice

Cook the hearts (bottoms) of young artichokes till tender with the cummin. Then sieve them and mix with the potatoes, cooked and mashed.

Mix the green herbs in the butter and heat it. Fry the mustard seeds till they snap and crackle. Then add the purée of artichokes. Stir and cook well in the butter. Mix the cayenne, lemon juice and ½ cup yoghurt. Cook till all liquid has dried. Raise the flame high and glaze the purée a little. Serves 4.

RED CABBAGE IN LEMON JUICE

2 small red cabbages	1 tablespoon coriander
8 tomatoes	2 teaspoons cummin
salt	3 tablespoons butter
¼ cup yoghurt	1 teaspoon black pepper

½ cup lemon juice

Separate the cabbage leaves without breaking the cabbage. Quarter the tomatoes, mix with salt, yoghurt and half the coriander and cummin. Stuff the cabbages with the mixture, removing some leaves if necessary. Tie the cabbages at the top.

Heat the butter and roll the cabbages in it for 10 minutes, adding the remaining coriander and cummin. Then cover and cook. When it dries, sprinkle the pepper, more salt and lemon juice over the cabbages. Then cover tight and braise. Repeat till done. No water is to be used. Serves 4.

FRIED CUCUMBERS

2 pounds cucumbers
salt
2 cups split-pea flour (p. 33)
¾ cup yoghurt
2 cloves
3 cardamons (seeds of)
1 tablespoon coriander
¼ teaspoon chili (P)
strong pinch of saffron
¼ teaspoon black pepper
8 tablespoons butter

Peel the cucumbers and cut into long slices. Salt them well and reserve. Make a paste of the flour and the yoghurt, pounded cloves, cardamon seeds, coriander, chili, saffron and pepper.

Heat the butter. Dip the slices of cucumber in the flour paste and fry. Brown on both sides over a medium flame. Serves 4.

FOOGATH

5 tablespoons grated coconut
1¼ pounds radishes
½ a sweet green pepper
1 tablespoon parsley
2½ tablespoons butter
1½ teaspoons mustard seeds
2 tablespoons kidney beans, soaked and drained
1 tablespoon lime or lemon juice
salt

Grate the radishes, cut the pepper fine, bruise the parsley, and put aside with the grated coconut.

Melt the butter and fry the mustard seeds, the kidney beans and green pepper, chopped, for 4 minutes over low heat. Add the radishes and cook over very low heat till almost done. Then add the coconut with lime or lemon juice and the parsley. Salt to taste; mix and cook till coconut is done. Salt before serving. For 4.

BHINDI (*Okra*)

2 pounds okra
butter
1½ teaspoons ginger (P)
½ teaspoon chili (P)
salt

Wash and dry the okra. Heat the butter or oil and fry the okra, stirring well with the ginger powder and chili sprinkled over it. Salt before serving. For 4.

An appetizing way to prepare okra is to slit the center and stuff them with dried pomegranate seeds, salt and a pinch of turmeric. Then fry them and cook covered till done.

BRAISED OKRA

2 pounds okra
3 tablespoons butter
4 onions
¼ teaspoon chili (P)
salt
½ tablespoon mint leaves
lettuce leaves
¾ tablespoon turmeric

Wash the okra, decap it and dry it well. Melt the butter, and fry the onions to pale gold cut in thick (¾ inch) slices, adding okra, turmeric and chili for 7 minutes. Then add salt, mint leaves and cover with a few large lettuce leaves (washed). Cover the vessel and cook till the okra is tender. Shake a few times during this stage of preparation. Serves 4.

VEGETABLE KORMA MALAI

(*Lima Beans and Mushrooms*)

4 tablespoons butter
2 onions
1½ pounds lima beans
2 teaspoons coriander
1 clove garlic
¾ tablespoon green ginger
(¼ teaspoon powdered)
½ teaspoon black pepper
2 teaspoons turmeric
1 pint yoghurt
2 tablespoons boiled rice
6 tablespoons blanched almonds
½ pound firm mushrooms
2 cloves
3 cardamons (seeds of)
salt

Melt 2 tablespoons butter. Slice the onions and fry pale gold. Add the beans, shelled and washed. Mix with coriander and fry gently for 10 minutes.

Meanwhile pound the garlic with the ginger, pepper and turmeric. Mix this with half the yoghurt and ½ cup of water. Simmer this mixture gently for 4 minutes.

Then add this mixture to the beans. Cook gently, covered. Pound the rice with the almonds. Melt the other 2 tablespoons butter and put in the halved or quartered mushrooms. Stir and add the almonds and rice. Mix in the cloves and cardamon seeds. Fry for 5 minutes; add the rest of the yoghurt. Put this in with the beans. Mix well, salt to taste and cook together till done. Then open the cover and over a high flame dry off any moisture and glaze the vegetables somewhat. Serves 4.

Lentils, Beans and Other Legumes

THERE are more than sixty varieties of lentil in India. Lentils are known as the "poor man's meat," owing to their great protein value. Most Indian meals, especially in the North, are served with lentils. There are many different ways of preparing them, but as Indian lentils are not available outside India, I will give a few recipes for the lentils available in the United States and in Europe. The best lentils are found in the Punjab, where the best cooking is. Among these lentils, one kind, the best to my mind, is white and grows to half an inch. It is cooked so that it emerges, after preparation, separate like rice. Others can be made into a purée. Lentils may be black, gray-and-black, gray, red and also dark green.

There are three widely-known ways of cooking lentils. (1) They may be fried with the spices and other ingredients, then finished with enough water to make them tender; (2) lentils may be simmered (not boiled) in plain water or Akni, and then joined to spices and butter; (3) they can also be cooked in water and spices and then joined to plain butter and green herbs. Slow cooking is a prerequisite for lentils. It gives them the extra flavor, creaminess and unctuousness.

The lentil in a Punjabi household, especially in the farmlands, may be cooked for nine to twelve hours in hot ashes over the merest breath of charcoal fire, set on a clay-baked grate that at once radiates and conserves its heat.

Since lentils and most dried legumes are often tenderized before packing, follow directions on the packages for soaking and cooking.

LENTILS

1 pound lentils
3 tablespoons butter
2 onions
¾ tablespoon green ginger
  (¼ teaspoon powdered)
1 teaspoon turmeric
½ teaspoon chili (P)
salt
squeeze of lemon juice

Soak the lentils according to directions on the package. Melt the butter. Chop the onions, slice the ginger, and fry together. Add the lentils washed and drained. Mix in the turmeric and chili. Fry lentils over slow fire till they have absorbed the butter. Then add the salt and about 1 quart of water. Bring to a boil and lower to a simmer. Cover and cook till done. Replenish with as much water as necessary. Dry off as much liquid as required with a squeeze of lemon juice before serving. This is a matter of personal preference. Serves 4 to 6.

SPLIT PEAS

1 pound yellow split peas
Akni (optional, p. 28)
3 tablespoons butter
¾ tablespoon mustard seeds
1 onion
1 teaspoon turmeric
½ teaspoon cummin
pinch cayenne
½ teaspoon black pepper
salt
green herbs

Cook the split peas in Akni (or water) till very tender. Then remove and drain.

Melt the butter and put in the mustard seeds. Fry till they begin to crackle and snap. Add the onion, finely sliced, and fry to a dark brown. Then put in the peas with turmeric, cummin, cayenne, pepper and salt. Mix and cook till the spices and butter have been absorbed. Mash the peas with a heavy fork and add more Akni or water, to reduce to a thick purée. Cook covered. When serving, sprinkle with chopped green herbs. For 4 to 6.

INDIAN CHICK PEAS

- 1 pound chick peas
- 4 tablespoons butter
- 2 onions
- 1½ teaspoons turmeric
- ¾ tablespoon green ginger (¼ teaspoon powdered)
- 6 mint leaves
- ½ teaspoon chili (P)
- 2 tomatoes
- salt

It is best to soak the chick peas (like most lentils) overnight, or at least for a few hours. Wash them in several changes of water before soaking.

Bring the chick peas to a boil in 2 quarts of water. Then simmer till tender. Drain and reserve the stock also.

Melt the butter; slice the onions and fry. Mix in the turmeric, ginger, mint leaves, pounded, chick peas. Add also the chili and tomatoes. Fry this well for 10 to 12 minutes; then add the chili and salt. This is ready to serve, if you like the chick peas gravyless. To make them more liquid, add enough stock to cover the chick peas. Simmer till spices and stock are mixed. Then add the juice of a lemon and sprinkle over some finely chopped herbs. Serves 4 to 6.

DRIED BEANS

(*Limas and Other Legumes*)

- 1 pound dried beans
- ½ pound bones (ham, lamb or other)
- 3 tablespoons butter
- ½ pound onions
- 2 cloves garlic
- ¼ teaspoon ginger (P)
- 2 tablespoons chopped green pepper
- 1¼ teaspoons turmeric
- 1 teaspoon coriander
- 1 tomato
- salt
- ½ teaspoon black pepper
- 1 tablespoon lemon juice
- 1 tablespoon chopped green herbs

Soak the beans overnight. Then boil with the meat bones. Collect any scum that rises. Then drain stock through a fine cloth. Reserve this and the beans.

In a heavy casserole or skillet, melt the butter and fry the onions, medium sliced, with pounded garlic, ginger, green pepper, turmeric and coriander. Put in the beans and cook them for 10 to 12 minutes. Then add the tomato, sliced, salt, pepper and cook these for another few minutes. Add the stock, as much as is required to bring the liquid to the desired quantity, and simmer for ¼ hour. (Chick peas, because they do not disintegrate readily, can be cooked much longer than the above ¼ hour after frying.) Lemon juice may be added before serving. Chopped herbs to be sprinkled over just before serving. For 4 to 6.

BLACK-EYED PEAS

These can be cooked in the same style as the chick peas.

1 pound black-eyed peas (dried)
water or Akni (p. 28)
squeeze of lemon juice
1½ teaspoons coriander
salt
black pepper
yoghurt (optional)

Soak the peas for several hours. Wash and cook in water or Akni with the coriander and salt till tender. Then strain. Add chili and serve with a squeeze of lemon juice and a little black pepper. These can be mixed with whipped yoghurt and eaten chilled. Serves 4 to 6.

For variation (this part of the recipe is not an Indian recipe) try mixing the cooked black-eyed peas with French dressing; the classic one of good wine vinegar, olive oil, salt and *nothing* more.

DRIED PEA CAKES

Cook a mixture of black-eyed and yellow split peas in water till very tender. Then mash them, mix with green herbs (1 tablespoon to a pound), crushed caraway seeds and chopped onions. Bind with white of egg and fry in a skillet.

BHALLE

1 pound yellow split peas	1 quart yoghurt
pinch of caraway seeds	strong pinch of black pepper
salt	chopped mint leaves
butter	strong pinch of chili (P)

Soak the washed peas overnight. Then pound them or use an electric blender until frothy and smooth. Use a little moisture to work the blender, but do not make the mixture thin. Season with the caraway seeds and salt.

Shape them into balls. Press gently, to squeeze out the water, and flatten them into croquettes. Steam over boiling water.

Heat some butter and fry them over low heat. Turn once. These are crisp and can be eaten as they are. More frequently in India they are soaked in lukewarm water for 5 minutes.

Then whip the well-chilled yoghurt. Place the lentil cakes in this. On top sprinkle the black pepper, chili, caraway seeds and mint leaves. Chill before serving. For 4.

CHAPTER 11

Eggs, Cheese and Milk

EGGS ARE USED in much the same way as in other cuisines. There are a few Indian recipes, and one intriguing preparation with eggs that I give here.

KHAGINA (*Indian Omelet*)

6 eggs
4¼ tablespoons split-pea flour (p. 33)
strong pinch of black pepper
1½ medium-sized onions
5 cardamons (seeds of)
strong pinch of coriander (P)
5 tablespoons butter
½ cup yoghurt
salt

Break the eggs. Mix them with the flour, pepper and onion, sliced thin. Pound the cardamon seeds and mix with coriander. Combine with eggs, stirring till smooth.

In a heavy skillet, melt the butter, stir in the yoghurt, salt, and add the egg mixture. Cook till somewhat set. Then fold over once only. Turn once. To serve, slice it crosswise. For 4.

The Khagina can be made by mixing the yoghurt with eggs and flour. Melt the butter and put in the egg mixture. Cook as above. Serve sliced crosswise.

ANOTHER INDIAN OMELET

6 eggs
1¼ teaspoons turmeric
1½ tablespoons onion juice
1 tablespoon green herbs
salt
2½ tablespoons butter

Mix the eggs well with turmeric, onion juice, green herbs and salt. Melt the butter; put in the eggs. Cook as an ordinary omelet. Serves 4.

OMELET CURRY

4 tablespoons butter
6 eggs
2 onions
1 tomato
¼ tablespoon lemon juice
2 teaspoons turmeric
1 teaspoon coriander
¼ teaspoon black pepper
salt
Akni (optional, p. 28), milk or stock
¼ cup yoghurt

In a skillet, melt the butter and fry the eggs, well-beaten, but do not fold the omelet. Cook till half done. Then set aside and keep warm.

Slice the onions and tomato; mix with turmeric, coriander, pepper and salt. Simmer 12 minutes in Akni, milk or stock. Reserve stock and place the onions and tomatoes on the eggs. Fold the omelet over firmly and finish cooking till it is set. Then, keeping omelet warm, pour the yoghurt, and lemon juice and some of the stock into the skillet. Simmer for 7 minutes and reduce the stock so it is thick. Serves 4.

Egg Curries

Egg curries are made by hard-boiling the eggs. Then prepare any one of the mixture of spices in the meat or vegetable chapter. In place of other material, add the eggs cut in half. Cover with the liquid and cook for 10 minutes.

Potatoes and ground meat may be added to egg curry, but this kind of curry is frowned upon by Indian purists.

This one is original and as good as it sounds. There is more in it than the eye can see.

ANDA KABAB (*Egg Kababs*)

6 eggs
⅜ tablespoon green ginger
(⅛ teaspoon powdered)
1½ onions
1¼ tablespoons coriander
¾ tablespoon turmeric
dough
6 tablespoons butter
½ pint yoghurt
3 cardamons (seeds of)
¼ teaspoon black pepper
salt
½ cup almonds blanched
pinch of cayenne

With a sharp knife, make a small hole at the top of each egg. Pour out the eggs into a bowl. Chop the ginger, chop the onions, mix with coriander and half the turmeric. Mix this with the eggs and beat them well.

Fill the shells with the egg mixture (about 5 eggs will fill 6 shells) and close the hole with whole-wheat or flour dough. The dough has to be well kneaded. It should be firm and sticky.

Boil the eggs till they are hard. Then cool them. Shelling, you *can* serve them as they are, but this recipe is finished as follows. Prick gently but firmly, with a very sharp-tined fork, all the eggs. Rub them with the remaining turmeric and cook them on a skewer over the open fire. Or broil them gently. They can also be baked in the oven.

Use a basting sauce of the butter and yoghurt well mixed together, with salt, turmeric, crushed cardamon seeds, pepper, salt and pounded almonds. Serve hot with a pinch of cayenne to each egg. For 3.

The stuffing of the egg can be made with tiny strips of boiled shrimp, small pieces of ham, chopped oysters, or other choices you may fancy.

Here are some preparations from milk, including cheese and yoghurt. This delicious Indian cheese does not run or melt; it keeps its shape and has the consistency of shellfish.

PANEER (*Indian Cheese*)

Bring a quart of milk to a boil, and remove from heat. Stir into it 1 teaspoon alum (powdered; available in any drugstore). Mix well and stir over a slow fire till it curdles and the liquid is quite separate. Then drain it, pressing the cheese in a muslin bag. Squeeze out all the liquid and place the cheese under a heavy weight for 5 to 8 hours. The cheese will set. It can be cut in squares, and simply fired with a touch of turmeric. This cheese has the texture of sea food.

CRUMBLY PANEER (*Soft Cheese*)

1 quart milk
1 teaspoon alum

Bring the milk to a boil and then reduce to a simmer. Put in the alum and stir, until the milk is curdled and the liquid is separated. Drain and place the curds in a cheesecloth or sieve.

Keep for ¼ hour. Then it is ready for use. This cheese can be mixed with vegetables too.

Both these recipes can be made with lemon juice instead of alum: 2 tablespoons for each quart of milk. Alum makes a better precipitation than lemon juice, or yoghurt which can also be used.

RAITA (*Indian Yoghurt Punch*)

1 quart yoghurt
1 cup boiled potatoes
salt
½ teaspoon chili
1 teaspoon Garam Masala (p. 264)
1½ tablespoons chopped green herbs
1 teaspoon caraway seeds

Whip the yoghurt well. Put in small slices of potatoes boiled in salted water. Mix well with salt and sprinkle with the chili, Garam Masala, the green herbs and the caraway seeds and chill before serving. For 8.

This punch can be made with raw onions and 4 tablespoons of chopped mint leaves. Quantities same as above. Chill.

Another variation is with thin-sliced, salted and drained cucumber. Herbs and spices same as in parent recipe. Chill.

Squash can be used in place of cucumber. Spices, herbs and quantities same as in parent recipe for Raita. Chill.

Make Raita out of eggplant. Broil, without basting, under the broiler. Then cut up in 1½ inch pieces. Peel the scorched skin carefully before mixing with yoghurt. Chill.

CHAPTER 12

Indian Breads

THESE ARE mostly of whole-wheat flour. The North Indian Punjabis are about the greatest wheat eaters in the world. This area, before its division between India and Pakistan, was one of the world's great wheat-growing regions.

Refined flour is not much used, except when making the European type of leavened bread. Whole-wheat bread is enormously nourishing, and the mainstay (with butter, milk and green vegetables) of the tough, sturdy Punjabis. All bread, save for an exception or two, is unleavened. It is made when required and always eaten smoking hot.

CHAPATIS

(*Whole-Wheat Pancakes on the Griddle*)

3¾ cups whole-wheat flour
1 teaspoon salt
2 cups water (approximate)

Sift the flour, mix the salt, and gradually add the water, smoothing out any lumps. Knead it well; the better, the lighter will be the bread. Then cover it with a double-folded cheesecloth and leave aside for 1 to 1½ hours.

Before baking, knead it once or so. Then make small cakes; flatten and roll them the size of pancakes or a little larger. They should be paper-thin. Heat an ungreased griddle. Cook the pancakes on both sides, pressing firmly to increase the rate of cooking. Turn once, and then finish on a hot tin plate over the gas fire (the bottom of the oven, just above the heat, will do), and the bread will rise like *Pomme Soufflé*.

Serve it hot, plain or with a dab of butter in the center.

To keep, place one chapati on top of another, in a thick, treble-folded napkin. These can be placed for a few minutes in an expiring oven. However, to remain puffed, the bread should be served when ready.

The next bread has many uses. It is made from whole wheat and baked on a greased or buttered griddle.

PARATHAS (*Whole-Wheat Buttered Bread*)

3¾ cups whole-wheat flour
¾ tablespoon salt
2 cups water (approximate)
4½ tablespoons butter

Prepare and knead the flour into dough as for Chapatis (p. 231). Cover it with wet cheesecloth and let stand for 1 to 1½ hours.

Make small balls out of the dough. Roll them out thin and even. Then with the back of a tablespoon rub the pancakes with melted butter. Fold once, and rub with more butter. Repeat once, or better still, twice. Then roll them out again in triangle shapes. Heat the griddle and butter it slightly. Cook on both sides, turning once. When finished, the bread is of a mild honey color.

These parathas are crisp. To make them even crisper, substitute 2 to 4 tablespoons milk for that amount of water, while forming the dough.

Stuffed Parathas are a gourmet's and a gourmand's favorite.

STUFFED PARATHAS

3 medium-sized potatoes
4¼ tablespoons butter
2 onions
1½ tablespoons green herbs
¼ teaspoon ginger (P)
salt
2 tablespoons lemon juice (optional)
½ teaspoon chili (P)
3¾ cups whole-wheat flour
½ teaspoon salt
2 cups water

Boil the potatoes; peel and mash. Heat a little butter and fry the onions, finely chopped, with green herbs and ginger, adding salt, lemon juice (if used) and chili. Set aside.

Make dough as for Parathas (p. 232). Make a ball, flatten and roll it out. Rub it with butter and place on it a tablespoon of the potato paste. Fold it round and roll it out again. Cook on a heavy, buttered griddle on both sides till crisp and evenly golden.

PARATHAS WITH GREEN PEAS

Use 1½ cups green peas, with 8 bruised and broken mint leaves, a sprig of parsley, salt, ½ teaspoon chili and a squeeze of lemon juice. Cook them in a little butter till soft. Then form the bread as preceding recipes. Stuff with the peas as you did the potatoes and cook in exactly the same style.

PARATHAS WITH CAULIFLOWER

Mix 1½ to 1¾ cups of finely chopped cauliflower, using only the tender flowerets, with ½ teaspoon ginger (P), ¾ teaspoon chili, a pinch of black pepper and a few shreds of tomato (about 1 tablespoon).

Fry these in a little butter. Stuff the bread with peas or potatoes (as on page 233). Cook in precisely the same style.

PARATHAS STUFFED WITH RADISHES

Mix 1¾ cups radishes (red or horseradish) with 1⅛ tablespoons green ginger, slivered (⅛ teaspoon powdered), salt, ½ teaspoon chili powder, 1 finely chopped onion and 1 tablespoon lemon juice. Cook a little, and then stuff bread as on page 233. Cook in the same manner.

MAKKI KI ROTI (*Maize Bread*)

- 1 pound water-ground corn meal
- 1½ teaspoons salt
- 1½ cups water (approximate)
- 1 tablespoon butter

Sift the meal. Mix salt, and taking enough meal for one loaf, mix with water and knead into a hard dough. Keep adding as much water as necessary. Shape it into a round loaf (about 8 inches in diameter and ¼ to ½ inch thick). Cook on a heavy hot buttered griddle. While it cooks, press it down without breaking it. Also turn it around a bit while it cooks. Cook till done on both sides.

The corn meal can be mixed with 2 tablespoons chopped spinach — to be incorporated while kneading the dough.

PURI (*Indian Deep-Fried Bread*)

3¾ cups whole-wheat flour	1 teaspoon salt
¾ tablespoon butter	1 cup warm water

Sift the flour, melt the butter, and add to the flour. Add the salt also, and rub with the hands, making it into a hard dough. Add the water gradually. Knead well and let stand for ½ hour.

Use a deep-fryer, and have the fat smoking hot. Put in the bread, rolled out in small pancakes (4 inches diameter and paper-thin). Cook over medium heat, pressing down to make them swell. Cook on both sides, and when light gold, serve. The pancakes should have puffed out. Drain on paper toweling for an instant before serving. These can be kept in an expiring oven, before serving, but the soufflé effect will not last long.

Puri can be made tastier and crisper by kneading with 2 cups yoghurt in place of the water. Also rub butter (¼ to ½ pound for 2 pounds flour) into the flour.

Lacking a deep-fryer, you can make them in a deep skillet, using enough fat or shortening to make the bread float.

Here are a few delicacies and savories. The first make excellent snacks or cocktail savories.

SAMOSAS (*Stuffed Pastry Cones*)

2 cups white refined flour	1 teaspoon salt
2 tablespoons butter	5 tablespoons yoghurt

Sift the flour, melt the butter, and mix with flour and salt. With the yoghurt, added bit by bit, knead the flour into a stiff dough.

Make a small ball of the dough, roll out perfectly round and very thin (diameter about 4 to 6 inches). Cut this pancake in half. Shape each half into a cone. Put in stuffing (see below), pinching in the edges and the peak and folding over the mouth of the cone. Use a touch of water if necessary. Fry in deep-fryer till crisp and medium brown. Remove and drain. Serve hot.

The stuffing may be made of potatoes, diced the size of a pea, mixed with chopped onions, mint leaves or other green herbs, salt and a pinch of chili. A little lemon juice added to the potatoes before stuffing adds a zest.

Green peas, with chopped onion, green herbs, salt, chili, lemon juice and a touch of caraway may be used to stuff the samosas.

A mixture of green peas and mashed potatoes with onion, salt, chili, green herbs, a touch of powdered coriander, lemon juice and black pepper is also good for stuffing the samosas.

SAMOSAS WITH GROUND MEAT

Make a Samosa pastry dough as in preceding recipe. Stuff with the following mixture:

1 tablespoon butter
1 onion
1 tomato
½ pound ground meat (lean)
¼ teaspoon turmeric
1 tablespoon green herbs
½ tablespoon lemon juice

Melt the butter, fry the onion and tomato, sliced; add the meat with turmeric, herbs and lemon juice. Mix and fry for 10 minutes, using enough water to cook. Then dry out perfectly.

PAKORA (*Batter-Fried Vegetables*)

2 cups split-pea flour (p. 33)
1¼ cups water
2¼ teaspoons salt
¾ teaspoon turmeric
1 to 1½ teaspoons coriander
¼ teaspoon chili (P)

Sift the flour and gradually mix with the water, making a thick batter. Then beat or whip well. Leave aside for ½ hour. Then add the salt, turmeric, coriander, chili and beat again before using.

Now take an assortment of vegetables; boiled potatoes, rounds of onions, diced peas, diced eggplant, cauliflower flowerets, green peppers, sliced, or shredded spinach. Dip your choice of vegetables in the batter, coating it heavily. Then deep-fry them till brown on both sides. Cook carefully and do not crowd the pan. Then drain and serve hot or cold.

These can be cooked about three quarters, then dipped into the deep-fryer again just before they are required.

CHAPTER 13

Sweets and Desserts

INDIANS are a sweet-toothed people. Unlike most foods, which are best made in the home, the Indian sweetmeats sold in the bazaar are better. The main reason is the time and complicated preparations that prevent the Indian housewife, no matter how much domestic help she has, from trying them all at home.

The recipes given here are those that may be easily prepared in the kitchen. Both sweetmeats and desserts are given together, though the recipes for dessert are distinguished with the letter (D) in parentheses. However, the sweetmeats can be also served for a dessert, when a mouth-sweetener is desired.

HALWA GAJJAR (*D*)

This is a new, quite exciting dessert. It is full of vitamins, and the children will love it.

1½ pounds carrots
2 quarts milk
strong pinch of saffron
4 to 5 tablespoons butter
2 cardamons (seeds of)
1½ cups sugar
2 tablespoons raisins
2 tablespoons honey (optional)
½ inch stick cinnamon
2 tablespoons blanched almonds

Use an electric blender (if possible) for this one. Dice the carrots and coarsely blend with enough milk to moisten them and make the blades work. Repeat till all the carrots are chopped. Otherwise grate them.

Scald the milk and then add the carrots. Stir and cook over a simmer burner or very low heat. Stir frequently. In fact the more stirring there is the better will be the dessert. When the milk has almost dried, add the saffron, honey, cinnamon and cardamon seeds, butter, sugar and raisins. Mix and stir, and let it cook till all liquid is dry. Then put in another tablespoon butter and fry over medium heat. It will gradually turn a deep red color. Sprinkle with the almonds and serve hot, preferably. It can also be served cold, will keep well about a week in the refrigerator and can be reheated.

The consistency can be made crisp by continuing the frying, or placing under the broiler (low heat) for a while. For 6 to 8.

HALWA "FOR A STRONG MAN" (*D*)

- 4 pounds carrots
- 2 cups sugar
- ¼ to ½ teaspoon saffron
- ¼ pound butter
- 2 pounds blanched almonds
- ½ teaspoon nutmeg

The blender can be used for this, to chop the carrots fine. Otherwise grate and boil the carrots in water till soft and the water has evaporated. Reserve.

Make a syrup of the sugar and ½ cup of water, boiling till it threads. Clear any scum. Add the carrots with saffron. Cook till the sugar is absorbed and the liquid is dry. Then add the butter, with slivered or pounded (use electric blender) almonds. Mix well. Sprinkle with nutmeg, mixing well. Serves 10 to 12.

SPECIAL HALWA BADAM

(*Almonds, D*)

2 pounds blanched almonds
2 cups flour
butter
1 cup sugar
rose water

Mix the almonds with the flour and fry them with a little butter. Remove when brown. Separate the almonds from the flour. Then blend, or pound them in a mortar and pestle, till the result is a fine flour. Put the sugar into ¼ cup of water and boil it till the syrup threads. Clear any scum that rises to the top. Then put in the almond flour and 1 tablespoon of butter. Mix well and cook till it thickens. Add enough rose water to flavor. Serves 8 to 10.

HALWA "FOR A VISITING DIPLOMAT" (*D*)

1 pound semolina
¾ pound butter
½ cup rice water (from cooked rice)
5 tablespoons blanched almonds
1½ to 2 cups sugar
rose water

Soak the semolina in 1 cup water (or just enough to cover). Leave overnight. Then add 2 cups boiling water. Stir, mix and knead well.

Strain out, and reserve, all the liquid from the semolina, rejecting the semolina. Heat the butter till it bubbles, then add the semolina milk and rice water. Stir and cook till the mixture becomes clear. Add the sugar, stirring well for 5 minutes. Add the almonds, slivered, and cook the mixture till transparent. It is ready when a knife put into it comes away clean. Flavor with rose water. Serves 6.

HALWA KELA WITH BANANAS (*D*)

4 tablespoons butter
6 bananas
1½ cups water
¾ cup sugar
rose water or other flavoring
1¼ teaspoons cardamon seeds
2 tablespoons blanched almonds
saffron (P)

Melt the butter in a heavy skillet. Peel and cut bananas into 1-inch pieces. Fry in the butter for 5 to 7 minutes on medium heat. Stir often and mash them when they have been frying 5 minutes. Then add ½ cup water. Simmer with care on low heat for 3 minutes, stirring all the while. Stir the sugar into 1 cup water and add to bananas. Then boil gently for ¼ hour. Stir often to prevent scorching and to thicken mixture.

Add the rose water, orange water or your choice of flavoring agent. Remove and pour into a shallow pan. Sprinkle with the cardamon seeds, bruised, almonds, slivered, and enough saffron to color the whole a pleasant gold. Now drain any butter, if left, and serve hot or slightly chilled. For 4.

HALWA PETHA (*Pumpkin or Squash, D*)

1 pound pumpkin
¾ cup brown sugar (about)
5 tablespoons butter
½ cup milk
1½ tablespoons blanched almonds
1 teaspoon cardamon seeds
½ teaspoon grated nutmeg

Remove seeds, scrape and grate the pumpkin, then weigh it. Place in a heavy casserole and let it simmer in its own moisture. When all the moisture is dry, add enough brown sugar to equal the weight of the pumpkin before preparing. Cook together till the mixture is thick. Do not burn. Before it browns, add the butter and milk. When the mixture shrinks from the pan it is ready for the almonds, slivered, and cardamon seeds and grated nutmeg. Then press into a buttered dish. Place in the oven for a few minutes before serving. For 4 to 6.

HALWA PETHA II (*D*)

1 cup milk
1 pound pumpkin
1 pound brown sugar
1 tablespoon raisins
1¼ tablespoons grated coconut
2½ tablespoons blanched almonds
¼ inch stick cinnamon
½ teaspoon cardamon seeds
5 tablespoons butter

Bring the milk to a boil and put in the pumpkin which has been peeled, scraped, seeded and grated. Boil 10 minutes, stirring constantly. Then thoroughly break up the pumpkin with a heavy fork. Dry off any moisture. Add the brown sugar and simmer briskly for another 10 minutes. Add the raisins, grated coconut, almonds, slivered, cinnamon, crushed, and butter. Mix and stir for another 6 minutes. Pour into a well-buttered dish, sprinkling the cardamon seeds, bruised, over it. Serve hot. For 4 to 6.

HALWA ANDA (*Egg Halwa, D*)

6 eggs
¼ pound butter
¾ cup sugar
2 tablespoons slivered almonds or pistachio nuts
2 tablespoons raisins
½ inch stick cinnamon
1 tablespoon grated coconut (optional)
1 cup milk

Beat the eggs well. Melt the butter in a heavy skillet and pour in the eggs. Stir and cook over gentle heat (about 5 minutes). Mix the sugar with the milk, raisins, cinnamon, and boil gently for 2 minutes. Add this syrup to eggs. Simmer them over low heat for another 10 minutes, stirring often. When the mixture is thickened add the grated coconut and nuts, slivered, and serve hot. For 3 to 4.

SEVIAN (*Vermicelli, D*)

1¼ tablespoons honey
¼ cup sugar
1 cup water
6 tablespoons butter
1¾ cups vermicelli
½ teaspoon grated nutmeg

Make a syrup of the honey, sugar and water. Boil for 3 to 4 minutes. In a heavy skillet melt the butter and fry the vermicelli, broken in small bits, till it is a rich brown. Add the syrup and boil together for 3 minutes. Lower the heat and cook till all the moisture is dry.

Before serving, add the nutmeg. Mix and place 5 minutes in a medium oven. Serve hot. For 4.

KHEER OR SHEER (*Indian Milk-Rice, D*)

1 quart milk
¾ cup rice
¾ cup sugar
1¼ tablespoons raisins
6 tablespoons blanched almonds
½ tablespoon cardamon seeds
1 clove
1½ tablespoons rose water

Boil the milk; add the rice washed and drained. Stir and boil gently. When the milk has been absorbed somewhat (about 1 hour of cooking), stir in the sugar with the raisins, almonds, cardamon seeds, bruised, and clove. Cook, stirring often, till it is thickened. To serve hot, place in oven for ¼ hour. It can also be served chilled.

Mix in rose water before serving hot, or if serving chilled, before cooling. For 6.

NAREAL PITTA (*Steamed Coconut Cookies*)

½ pound grated coconut
¼ pound brown sugar
6 cardamons (seeds of)
pastry dough (flour or rice flour)

Brown the grated coconut in a heavy skillet with the brown sugar and cardamon seeds, bruised. Prepare some light pastry dough. Take up a little (about 3 tablespoons) and make a hollow in the center. Fill with the browned coconut. Fold over and steam gently on cheesecloth tied over a kettle of boiling water, till thoroughly cooked. Then serve as they are, or cold, or brown in the oven before serving. They can also be fried lightly in a greased skillet or griddle.

BARFI (*Flaky Milk Cookies*)
HARLEQUIN PATTERN

1 pound powdered milk
½ cup sugar
rose water
2 teaspoons cardamon seeds, bruised
¼ cup pistachio nuts

Sift the powdered milk. Boil the sugar with about 1½ cups of water, to make a heavy syrup. When this threads very thickly, add the powdered milk, gradually, stirring all the time. Add rose water and cook over gentle heat to a heavy batter consistency. Then pour into a buttered pan or pans to a depth of 2 inches. Let the sweet and nuts stand for 8 hours. Then press into it the cardamon seeds, bruised. Cut into lozenges or diamonds with a sharp knife.

Barfi is also made in India from heavily condensed milk. This milk is condensed at home by stirring milk over the gentlest fire till it is reduced to a paste, all the moisture having evaporated.

Making condensed milk is laborious, and powdered milk does very well.

INDIAN CHEESE CAKE

2 cups milk
½ tablespoon lemon juice
2 egg yolks
1½ tablespoons butter
½ cup ground almonds
pastry dough
¾ cup sugar

Boil milk and add the lemon juice. Place in a cloth bag and drain off the liquid. With the resulting cheese, mix the egg yolks, butter and almonds to a perfect smoothness.

Make a little pastry dough and line some baking cups or bigger molds with it. Fill with the cheese. Sprinkle with sugar and bake in a moderate oven till done. Serves 4.

INDIAN BANANA CHEESE

12 bananas (ripe)
¾ cup Cream of Wheat
¾ cup sugar
1½ tablespoons butter
¼ teaspoon cinnamon (P)

Peel and thoroughly pound the bananas (or use electric blender) with the Cream of Wheat. Mix in the sugar and butter. Place in a double boiler and cook very gently, with cinnamon, for 3 to 3½ hours. Then cool and chill. Cut into pieces before serving. For 6 to 8.

BOLE COMADARE (*Coconut Cake*)

1 cup sugar syrup
½ pound rice flour
¾ pound grated coconut
3 eggs
½ pound brown sugar
½ tablespoon anise seeds
1 cup coconut milk

Make the syrup. Mix with the rice flour, well sifted, and reserve.

In a skillet, brown the grated coconut with whisked egg yolks, brown sugar and the anise seeds, stirring constantly. Then add the syrup and the coconut milk. Mix well again. Pour into a buttered dish and bake in a very low oven till nicely browned and cooked. Serves 4 to 6.

COCONUT COOKIES

1¼ cups grated coconut
1¾ cups milk
rose water
1 cup sugar
1½ teaspoons cardamon seeds
2 tablespoons cashew nuts (unsalted)

Mix the coconut (save 2 tablespoons), finely pounded or worked through a blender with the milk, and boil for ½ hour. As the liquid thickens, add the sugar and continue to cook for ¼ hour. Stir all the while at this stage. Dry off all moisture. Add the cardamon seeds and nuts, crushed. Pour in a buttered dish and leave till almost cool. Sprinkle with rose water and cut into any shape you like.

INDIAN LEMON DESSERT

½ pound butter
12 eggs
2 cups sugar
4½ tablespoons bread crumbs
½ to ¾ cup lemon or lime juice (depending on egg size)

Mix the butter with egg yolks and sugar till smooth; add bread crumbs and lemon or lime juice. Beat the egg whites stiff; fold into the mixture. Pour into a well buttered dish and bake in a moderate oven till done. Serves 6 to 8.

JALEBI (*Indian Crullers*)

1 package dry or compressed yeast
¼ cup warm water
2⅔ cups sifted all-purpose flour
1 teaspoon saffron strands
¼ cup hot water
fat for frying
2 cups light syrup (corn syrup or other)

Soften the yeast in the warm water. Combine the flour with 1½ cups water and the yeast, in a mixing bowl. Beat hard with wooden spoon till mixture is very smooth. Stir in the saffron, soaked in hot water.

Melt enough cooking fat in a skillet to make a depth of 2 inches. Heat to 350°. Put the batter into a funnel with a very small spout. Moving it in circles over the skillet, drop as many spiraled crullers as possible without crowding the pan. Cook on each side till golden. Then remove and drain.

Keep the syrup warm in a double boiler. Dip the crullers in this for a few seconds, and then drain again. They may be eaten hot or cold. It is best not to keep them too long. For 6 to 8.

The next two will delight the sweet-toothed.

RASGULLAS

2½ cups milk
4 tablespoons lemon juice
1¾ tablespoons pounded semolina
lump sugar
blanched almonds
2¼ cups sugar
4¾ cups water
2 tablespoons rose water

Heat the milk, stirring all the while. When it comes to a boil, mix in the lemon juice (lukewarm). Boil till the milk has separated well. Then place in a cloth and strain well, squeezing out all the liquid. This is important. Use a weight if necessary to rid the resulting cheese of moisture.

Mix the semolina with the cheese and knead it well. Shape into small balls the size of a big plum, shaping it over a lump of sugar and a sliver of almond.

Make some thin syrup of the sugar and water. Boil and place the rasgullas in it. Lower heat immediately to a simmer. Thin the syrup when necessary to keep at proper consistency. Cook them together for 1 to 1½ hours. Then remove. After 5 minutes sprinkle with rose water. They may be eaten hot or cold or chilled.

Raisins rolled in sugar or honey can be placed in the center before shaping the rasgullas. Soak them in a mixture of heavy and light cream and chill.

SANDESH

6 cups milk
4¼ tablespoons lemon juice
¾ cup sugar
6 tablespoons pistachio nuts
1½ teaspoons cardamon seeds
pinch of grated nutmeg

Boil milk and lemon juice to curdle and make into cheese. Then place in cloth bag and squeeze out all the moisture. Place under a weight for ½ hour to complete the process.

Mix the sugar with the cheese in a skillet, breaking and crumbling it with a spoon. Cook and turn over the mixture till thick. Then remove from heat and place in small individual molds or shells. Press some slivered pistachio nuts into each mold, with a few cardamon seeds, bruised, and a suspicion of nutmeg. Makes 3 or 4 molds.

Cool, and gently prize them from the shells to serve.

CHAPTER 14

Chutneys and Pickles

THEY SAY in India that wild elephants are caught by tame elephants. Food, the best food, is "caught" with the help of relishes: chutneys, pickles and other zesty preparations. These help out the flavor of food. They must, however, be taken in moderation and in small dabs.

Chutneys are of two kinds. Pickles, or *Achar* as they are called in India, are long-keeping. They mature slowly, and may be made from vegetables, fruit, game and fish. Chutneys are made mostly from fruits and vegetables. They differ from the Achar or pickles — inasmuch as they are made in paste or minced form. Although some chutneys require time to mature, more often than not they may be made fresh daily. This makes two distinct classes of chutney. The simpler ones, for daily use, can be made quickly and with comparative ease. With the help of the electric blender, the work can be concentrated into a few minutes.

Most of the chutneys and many of the pickles can be used with American and European cuisine. Many are hot and spiced enough to wring tears from you. Others are so mild that they will occasion initial disappointment (offset by a new recognition) at the lack of strength. This is as it should be. Hot pickles for zest, and mild for contrast of flavors. All the recipes are indicated: (H) for hot, and (M) for mild, and (S-M) for sweet and mild.

Treading carefully we approach our first.

PUDEENA CHUTNEY (*Mint Chutney, M*)

25 stalks of fresh mint
1 small onion
5 tablespoons parsley
3 tablespoons lemon or lime juice
¾ teaspoon salt
2 tablespoons sugar
¼ teaspoon cayenne

Wash, flick dry, and pull the leaves from the mint stalks, saving a few whole stalks. In the blender (or mortar and pestle) put the onion, mint, parsley and blend with lemon juice. Add salt, sugar and cayenne while blending. It is best served slightly chilled. Keeps for several days in the refrigerator.

RHUBARB CHUTNEY (*S-M*)

1½ pounds rhubarb
½ to ¾ quart good vinegar
2 cups sugar
1 tablespoon green ginger (⅜ teaspoon powdered)
2 tablespoons blanched almonds
1 teaspoon cayenne
1 tablespoon mustard seeds
1 tablespoon garlic

Clean and wash the rhubarb. Boil with vinegar and sugar. When it becomes a paste, mix in the ginger, finely chopped, almonds, slivered, cayenne, mustard seeds and finely chopped garlic. Simmer, adding more vinegar if necessary, till it is done. Pour into dry clean bottles, jars or earthenware crocks and expose to the sunlight; or keep in a warm place for about a fortnight. It will be ready and will keep a long time.

CARROT CHUTNEY (*M*)

2 pounds carrots
1 cup salt
2 cloves garlic
2 tablespoons mustard seeds
1 teaspoon cummin
1½ green peppers
2 tablespoons green ginger (⅜ teaspoon powdered)
½ teaspoon black pepper
vinegar

Cut the carrots into ¾ inch pieces (about). Salt them well and dry on a tray for 3 days, preferably in the sun. Use the oven if sun is not available. Keep for period of ½ hour in an expiring oven (heated to 250° and shut off) as long as the oven is warm.

On the fourth day, mix with pounded garlic, bruised mustard seeds, powdered cummin, thin-sliced green sweet peppers, sliced ginger and black pepper. Use enough vinegar to cover. Leave for a day or so, stirring often. Then use when the texture of the carrots is to your liking.

MINCED CARROT CHUTNEY (*M*)

1 pound carrots
1 teaspoon salt
½ medium onion
sprig of parsley
2 to 3 tablespoons lemon juice

Use the blender (or mortar and pestle). Put in diced carrots with salt, onion and parsley.

Use the lemon juice to liquefy it, adding more than the 3 tablespoons advised if necessary. Then chill slightly. This will keep a few days.

To work the blender, proceed with quick turns of the switch. Stop the motor and with a wooden spoon move the carrots about. Then start the blades working again. For a heavier chutney, blend a short time. For a more liquid chutney, blend for a longer time at top speed.

BURNT TOMATO CHUTNEY (*M*)

8 large tomatoes
½ lemon (rind of)
2 tablespoons chopped onions
2 tablespoons chopped green ginger (¾ teaspoon powdered)
⅛ teaspoon pepper
1 teaspoon salt
¼ teaspoon turmeric (optional)

Start the broiler at 425°. Place whole tomatoes on the tray and broil till skins are scorched. Peel and cut tomatoes in pieces. Place in blender. Cut the lemon rind, rejecting any white membrane (it gives bitterness) and add to tomatoes. Blend for 2 minutes and add the onions, ginger, pepper, salt and the turmeric if used. Blend well and remove. Serve slightly chilled.

HALF-AND-HALF TOMATO CHUTNEY (*H*)

2 pounds ripe tomatoes
1 pound green tomatoes
2¼ quarts vinegar
1 cup capers, or ½ pound tamarind
½ pound brown sugar
2 pounds raisins
¼ pound garlic
¼ pound green ginger (3 teaspoons powdered)
¼ pound onions
½ tablespoon mace (P)
½ tablespoon cayenne
1 cup salt
1 tablespoon coriander

Mash the tomatoes somewhat and boil them in 1 quart of vinegar till they are reduced to a paste. Boil remainder of the vinegar, and pour over the capers, or tamarind, placed in a mixing bowl. Immediately add brown sugar and stir with a wooden spoon. (Be sure that the tamarind, if used, separates from the fiber.) The capers need be stirred for ½ minute. Strain this second vinegar solution through a coarse cloth.

Mix pounded (blender or mortar) raisins, garlic, ginger and onion, finely chopped or pounded, with the caper or tamarind liquor. Heat again, without boiling. Mix the mace, cayenne, 1 to 3 more tablespoons brown sugar, salt and coriander; cook without boiling for ¼ hour. Then place in dry airtight jars, and keep for 5 to 6 months before using.

This chutney will show the difference between the "daily" chutneys and the long-maturing ones.

Here are a few more simple recipes for the chutneys that will keep for no more than a few days or a week.

NAREAL CHUTNEY

(*Coconut Chutney, M*)

4 ounces grated coconut
1 onion
2 teaspoons lemon rind (no white membrane)
1½ tablespoons vinegar
½ teaspoon chili (P)
pinch of saffron (P)

Pound coconut (blender does the work in a few seconds). Grate the onion and lemon rind in blender or in mortar. Mix and pound or blend together with vinegar, chili powder and saffron. Serve cold or chilled.

APPLE CHUTNEY (*M*)

4 green apples
salt
4 onions
4 tablespoons chopped green pepper
3 ounces shredded coconut
juice of 1 lemon

Pare and chop apples. Mix with salt and a little sprinkling of water. Leave for 7 minutes. Then drain well. Place in blender with onions, green peppers, coconut and lemon juice and blend well.

CUCUMBER CHUTNEY (*M*)

- 1 pound cucumbers
- ¼ clove garlic
- 1 tablespoon pimento
- ½ tablespoon heart of celery
- 1 sprig of parsley
- ¼ teaspoon black pepper
- pinch of cayenne
- 2 tablespoons or more lemon juice
- salt

Pare and salt the cucumbers, letting stand for 1 hour. Then wash off salt. Chop them and put in blender with the rest of the ingredients. Use as much lemon juice as required to make a thick paste of them. Chill a little before serving.

This can be finished off with equal quantities of yoghurt and lemon juice.

BANANA CHUTNEY (*M*)

- 4 tablespoons dates
- lemon juice
- 6 ripe bananas
- 4 ounces shredded coconut
- 2 onions
- ⅛ teaspoon mustard (P)
- salt
- ½ tablespoon mint leaves
- ¼ teaspoon chili (P)
- ¼ cup vinegar
- coconut milk (p. 55)

Stone dates; boil in lemon juice till soft. Peel bananas; remove all strings and hard parts. Place in blender with all the other ingredients. Blend with coconut milk, adding enough to get the desired consistency of a thick chutney. Use within a week.

Beet Chutney may be made in the same way.

PUMPKIN CHUTNEY (*M*)

- 2 pounds half-ripe pumpkin
- 5 onions
- 1 green sweet pepper
- 4 red peppers
- 1 cup thick coconut milk
- salt
- 2 tablespoons lemon juice
- ¼ teaspoon mustard seeds

Steam or boil the pumpkin, sliced. Then blend it with chopped onions and peppers, coconut milk, salt, lemon juice and mustard seeds. Chill slightly.

TOMATO AND RADISH CHUTNEY (*S–M*)

- 2 pounds green tomatoes
- 1 sweet green pepper
- salt
- 2 cups chopped radish or horseradish
- 6 chopped onions
- 2 tablespoons ground cloves
- 1 tablespoon ground cinnamon
- 1 teaspoon caraway seeds
- malt vinegar
- 1¾ cups brown sugar

Slice the tomatoes and shred the pepper. Sprinkle them generously with salt and leave overnight, or for 18 hours. Drain off water and pat the surface dry with paper toweling.

Cook the tomatoes with salt, radish (some prefer grated radish; can use blender here), onions, cloves, cinnamon and caraway seeds. Boil for few seconds. Then cover tight and simmer gently, adding enough vinegar from time to time to keep the consistency of chutney. Cook for 6 to 9 hours, using the lowest heat possible.

Brown sugar is added after three quarters of cooking time. The mixture may be thinned with more vinegar. No water must be used. Then cool and bottle the chutney for use. This can be used immediately, but is at its peak after 3 months maturing time.

PEACH CHUTNEY (*M*)

2 pounds peaches
1 pound brown sugar
1 pound raisins
1 quart vinegar
½ teaspoon saffron
salt
3 tablespoons green ginger (1⅛ teaspoons powdered)

Select peaches that are not quite ripe. Split open and stone, using a silver knife, not steel.

Boil the brown sugar in the vinegar with the saffron and add the peaches and raisins. Simmer very slowly till tender. Add salt to taste, ginger and more vinegar to keep the chutney consistency. Cook them well together for another ½ hour.

Then cool and bottle. Cork well or cover with airtight lids. Use when required.

TIPARE OR CAPE GOOSEBERRY CHUTNEY (*H*)

¾ pound mustard seed
1 pound salt
2¼ cups brown sugar
2 quarts vinegar
5 pounds gooseberries
2 tablespoons black pepper
1 tablespoon cayenne
¾ pound garlic
1 pound seeded raisins

Pound the mustard seeds. Make a syrup of salt, sugar and ½ quart vinegar. In another quart of vinegar cook the gooseberries with pepper, mustard seeds, cayenne, pounded garlic and raisins. Mix in the rest of the vinegar. Stir well and then cook to the proper consistency. Bottle and use after 5 to 6 months.

PINEAPPLE CHUTNEY (*M*)

1½ pounds ripe pineapple
salt
½ clove garlic
¾ tablespoons green ginger (¼ teaspoon powdered)
½ pound raisins (or substitute same quantity pineapple or peaches)
2 cups vinegar
¾ cup sugar

Pare and slice the pineapple. Cut out eyes, knots and woody stuff, if any. Chop pineapple, sprinkle with salt and set aside for 1½ hours.

Pound the garlic, ginger and raisins, or that quantity of pineapple (use blender). Mix well with rest of pineapple from which juice has been drained.

Boil the vinegar with sugar and add the pineapple with the other ingredients. Cover and simmer. When the right consistency has been reached, cool and pour into bottles for use.

SESAME SEED CHUTNEY (*M*)

6 tablespoons sesame seeds
2 cloves
½ medium-sized onion
1 red pepper
1 tablespoon sweet green pepper, chopped
salt
lemon juice

Roast the sesame seeds gently in a dry skillet. Then put in blender or mortar with cloves, onion, sliced, red pepper, green sweet pepper, salt and enough lemon juice to make a proper paste. Blend and serve.

SHRIMP CHUTNEY (*M*)

1 pound raw shrimp
1 teaspoon salt
2 teaspoons chopped onion
2 tablespoons watercress
2 red peppers
5 tablespoons grated or flaked coconut
1 lemon (juice of)
coconut milk

Clean, wash and boil shrimp. Shell and dry them. Cut into pieces and sprinkle with salt. Set aside for ¼ hour.

Mix shrimp with onion, watercress, red peppers, coconut and place in blender. Add the lemon juice and blend, using as much coconut milk as required to make a correct paste. Serve slightly chilled.

SPECIAL KISH-MISH CHUTNEY

(*With Raisins, M*)

3 medium tomatoes
1¼ tablespoons butter
½ pound seedless raisins
½ cup water
2 whole cloves
1 inch stick cinnamon
1 teaspoon salt
¼ teaspoon black pepper
½ cup sugar
1¼ tablespoons wine vinegar

Skin the tomatoes and chop them. Melt butter in a saucepan and toss in the raisins. Cook 2 minutes. Then add tomatoes. Cook on medium heat, uncovered, for 7 minutes. Stir all the while.

Transfer contents to double boiler. Add the water, cloves, cinnamon, salt and pepper. Mix well and cook uncovered over boiling water. After ¾ to 1 hour add the sugar and vinegar. Cook some more and serve hot or cold.

Now for some pickles. Mangoes have been mostly left out of the collection for chutneys, and here also. These are commoner in India than pebbles, having had their origin there, but are not so easy to obtain in the United States. Next to a pickle of tart green mangoes, there is nothing nicer than:

NIMBOO ACHAR

(*Lime or Lemon Pickle, H*)

5 limes or lemons
2 tablespoons salt
1½ tablespoons crushed red pepper
garlic
½ teaspoon ginger (P)
1 cup salad oil (*not olive oil*)

Wash and thoroughly dry the limes. Without peeling, cut into crosswise slices ¼ inch. Place the slices on a tray and sprinkle with salt, red pepper, garlic, crushed, ginger and mustard.

Heat oil to the boiling point, then cool. Put the seasoned lemons in a jar or bowl. Pour in the oil and let stand 5 to 6 days before using. Keep in warm place during maturing period — preferably in the sun.

LIME PICKLE IN LIME JUICE

(*S–M*)

2 pounds limes or lemons
2 teaspoons salt
¼ teaspoon turmeric
1 teaspoon chili (P)
8 tablespoons green ginger (3 teaspoons powdered)
2 cups fresh lime juice

Either slice or quarter the limes, removing all seeds. Mix the salt with the limes; sprinkle with the turmeric, chili, the ginger sliced thin and then cut in ½ to 1 inch pieces. Mix them and put them in a glass or earthenware jar. Pour in the lime juice and cover firmly. Keep in a warm place or in the sun — whichever is best — for several days. The pickle is ready to eat when the skins are tender. This takes about a week.

CAULIFLOWER PICKLE *(S–M)*

1 medium cauliflower
2 teaspoons salt
2 teaspoons coriander
½ teaspoon ground thyme
1½ cups salad oil
2 teaspoons crushed red pepper
2 teaspoons dried mustard
2 tablespoons vinegar

Wash cauliflower and break into 1-inch flowerets. Cook in boiling water for 5 minutes *and no more*. Drain well and place in a bowl or jar. Mix the remaining ingredients and pour over the cauliflower. Let stand for 5 days or so at room temperature. It will then be mellowed enough to serve.

Turnips, sliced ½-inch thick, may be made in similar fashion. Add Garam Masala (p. 264).

CABBAGE PICKLE *(M)*

3 small cabbages
salt
enough oil to cover cabbage
2 tablespoons black pepper
1 teaspoon turmeric
1 teaspoon mint leaves
4 tablespoons green ginger

Take only the hearts of the cabbages. Quarter them. Do not wash, or touch them with wet hands. Put cabbage pieces in a big jar, with salt between each layer.

Cook the salad oil with pepper, turmeric, ginger and mint leaves, bruised, very gently for ½ hour. Then cool and pour over the cabbage. Cover tight till ready in a few days.

This pickled cabbage may be made with 2½ quarts of vinegar instead of the oil. Cook the vinegar with spices for ½ hour also before adding to the cabbage.

PICKLED EGGS (*M*)

3 dozen eggs
2 quarts vinegar
4 tablespoons black pepper
1 tablespoon crushed red pepper
2¼ tablespoons green ginger (1 teaspoon powdered)
bunch of bay leaves
5 tablespoons coriander
3 tablespoons mustard seeds
pinch of saffron (P)
12 cloves
10 cardamons (seeds of)

Hard-boil the eggs. Prick slightly. Then boil the vinegar with all the ingredients. Make a layer of eggs, some bay leaves, a sprinkle of parsley. Pour on some vinegar. Repeat till all are arranged; then cool. Close lid and set aside for a fortnight before serving.

KASHMIR PICKLE

(This is actually a Chutney, H)

2 pounds brown sugar
vinegar
2 pounds green ginger
1½ pounds garlic
¼ pound red chilis
½ pound mustard seeds

Mix brown sugar with enough vinegar to dissolve it. Pound separately and then together, the green ginger, garlic, red chilis and mustard seeds. Mix them with 1 quart of vinegar. Add brown sugar dissolved in vinegar. Thoroughly blend and lay aside for 2 to 2½ weeks before using.

The vinegar may be increased or decreased to make proper chutney consistency.

SWEET GREEN PEPPER PICKLE

(*H*)

1 quart salad oil
2 tablespoons dry mustard
½ tablespoon chili (P)
1 tablespoon salt
2½ pounds green peppers
¾ pound fennel seeds

Heat the oil and stir in the mustard, chili and salt. Cook over a low fire for ¼ hour.

Slit the green peppers open on the side and scoop out all the seeds. Stuff with fennel seeds. Pour the warm oil over the peppers which have been arranged in jars. Cover with airtight lids. Open after 10 days and try for texture. When the peppers are soft they are ready to serve.

There are recipes in India for pickled oysters, pickled walnuts, and others that require the expert ministrations of a professional pickler, or at least firsthand experience. Leaving aside recipes for delicious bamboo shoots, and tantalizing combinations of peaches and dates, there is at least one from the myriad recipes for mangoes that can be easily made in the kitchen.

The real pickles are made in the Punjab: those with mustard oil, which is a prerequisite. Clean, unbruised, of best quality, these Punjabi pickles are examples of wizardry in pickle making, in comparison to which, chutneys are poor cousins. But this recipe for chutney is a favored one.

MANGO CHUTNEY FROM LUCKNOW (*H*)

- 6 pounds green mangoes
- 1 gallon vinegar
- 1 pound brown sugar
- 1 pound salt
- 1 pound mustard seeds
- 1 pound garlic
- 2 pounds green ginger
- 4 tablespoons red chilis
- 2 pounds raisins
- 3½ tablespoons turmeric

Slice the mangoes fine and boil in sufficient vinegar to cover till the mixture is smooth. Boil 1 quart of vinegar with the brown sugar and salt. Add the mangoes to the second mixture.

Blend the mustard seeds, using mortar and pestle or electric blender, with garlic, ginger (chopped), chilis, raisins and turmeric.

Mix all ingredients well and pour into 2 quarts of vinegar. Mix again and correct the consistency. Keep in sun or a warm place for 7 to 10 days. It is then ready to use. In a fortnight it will have matured fully.

FISH PICKLE

8 pounds finest fish, firm-fleshed
1⅛ pounds salt
¾ cup capers
2 quarts vinegar (approximate)
2 tablespoons turmeric
1⅛ pounds sugar
bay leaves

Clean fish well, being careful that no water touches it. Cut fish in slices ¾ inch thick. Sprinkle salt over the slices and set aside for 5 hours. Then wipe fish meticulously dry. Mash the capers in 3¾ pints of vinegar, adding turmeric and sugar. Strain the liquid.

Arrange the fish in layers with some bay leaves and add the vinegar mixture. Cover airtight and keep a month before using. An excellent pickle.

Appendix

GARAM MASALA

6 tablespoons black pepper
5 tablespoons dark caraway seeds
1¾ tablespoons cinnamon (P)
6 tablespoons coriander
1¾ tablespoons cloves (P)
1½ tablespoons cardamon seeds

Pick over ingredients and remove any husks, or strawy bits. Grind in the blender or a finely adjusted coffee grinder. Do not make the mixture too fine. Then place in airtight jars and keep for use.

This Garam Masala is fragrant and also strong. Its rather crusty flavor goes well with meat, fried and braised foods. I would not advocate the use in dishes with much liquid. There is no objection except for a loss of crispness.

Try the spice powder on fried potatoes, with a pinch of turmeric. Sprinkle a little on yoghurt, sour cream and other chilled dressings.

This is not a Curry Powder, and has certain limited uses.

YOGHURT

Bring 1 quart of whole milk to a boil. Let boil up once only. When the milk is *lukewarm* (never hot), mix into it 1 to 1½ tablespoons yoghurt. Leave in a warm place overnight, or 12 to 18 hours, to set.

It is important to use enameled saucepans, a glass or porcelain bowl and wooden or plastic spoons for stirring. No metal should come in contact with the milk once the yoghurt has been added. To keep it warm, the bowl containing the mixture may be wrapped in a piece of woolen blanket.

To ensure success the first time, let the yoghurt come to room temperature before using.

Indians eat yoghurt with sugar, syrup, or with salt and black pepper. Many people prefer the latter.

A delicious cooling drink can be made by beating or whipping a half carton of yoghurt and mixing with 2 to 2½ cups chilled water, adding salt or pepper, or sugar.

Indians also make butter, and a soft cheese, which has the texture of shellfish, from yoghurt.

For a hangover, or for overindulgence in alcohol, yoghurt is a capital remedy. It is generally soothing to the stomach and much more nourishing than milk. No sugar to be used, in this case.

Random Hints

For a red or rich brown color in Indian food, soak a little ground chili powder or whole red chili peppers in a little warm water for ½ hour. Then add to the dish.

If using limes for food that is being heated, add it drop by drop to avoid curdling.

When cooking apples, add a squeeze of lime or lemon juice to prevent them from blackening.

Always hang your onions. This will keep them from sprouting.

Put a slice of bread in the mouth when cutting onions. You will shed no tears.

Wax the stems (if any) of your tomatoes and they will keep much longer.

To remove excess of salt from a cooked dish, make some dumplings of flour and water. Throw these in the dish and leave them till the food is to be served. Then put the dumplings aside. If this is not enough, throw in some raw sliced potatoes. If these do not absorb enough of the excess salt try this remedy: cover the saucepan with a thick linen or double fold of muslin cloth, so it is stretched tight. Sprinkle a cup of flour on top. Repeat if necessary. The flour should absorb much of the salt with the moisture and steam.

Put a bowl of water in the oven if the roast is getting too dry. Try it for reheating old bread in the oven.

Preserve your cheese by keeping it first on one side and then on the other on alternative days. The fat contents will travel in opposite directions and keep inside the cheese.

When cooking fish add a little vinegar to the cooking water or the court-bouillon. This destroys the fishy smell. Also sprinkle river (not sea) fish with salt and then wash it before cooking. This rids the fish of the muddy taste river fish often have.

When cooking chicken rub it with a slice of lemon, especially on the breast. It will make the white meat even whiter.

When cooking rice, squeeze a little lemon juice in the boiling water. The rice will come out pure as driven snow.

When cooking red meats, rub lemon well into the meat. This will tenderize it somewhat.

I would keep away from the tenderizing powders and the

Ajinomotos. They give the same taste to everything and a day or two of this surfeit will pall. Good meat should need no tenderizer. If you are in a hurry use a pressure cooker.

If there is an excess of cayenne or chili in any dish, lemon juice will help to cut a little of it. Add it at the last moment, and stir.

Here is the way to cut parsley the way they do it in India: roll the parsley around the tip of your little finger, a pencil, or even something slimmer, and make a tight ball of it. Now slice it vertically. In this manner the green herb will come cut finer chopped than with the usual way. To wash parsley and prepare it for decorating a dish: take the sliced parsley, put it in the corner of a cloth (a napkin will do well) and roll the cloth around it loosely. Hold ten seconds under tap. Roll the cloth very, very tight, like a tourniquet, around the parsley. Give a good shake to get rid of the last water and open the cloth. The parsley will be fluffy and springy; quite unlike the spongy or soggy mess we often manage to serve ourselves.

If your lettuce is getting old, soak it face down, root up, in one inch of water. It will absorb the water and revive crisply — most of the time.

To get rid of that cabbagy smell when cabbage is in the cooking pot: place ½ slice of bread in a muslin bag or in cheesecloth doubled and put in the pan with the cabbage. This should take care of the smell.

When stoning raisins or similar fruit, butter your fingers slightly.

When chopping suet, dip the knife in powdered ground rice or in flour. It will not stick to the suet while cutting.

To blanch almonds the Indian way: soak almonds overnight. Next morning, or later, peel them. The skin will slip off easily. The almonds will be soft and somewhat tender. Blanched almonds dipped in boiling water are hard and quite tasteless.

Preserve any egg yolks in cold water; enough to cover.

If cream will not whip properly, add the white of an egg to *egg* it on to better heights. About one white to two cups of cream.

If you have a saucepan that smells of onions, and cleaning and soaping have not helped, then cook potatoes in it the next time. The spuds will take the smell away with *sang-froid.*

Remember that too many croquettes — either meat or vegetable — frying together will produce a common catastrophe: soggy and overfatted croquettes. The cooking medium tends to lower its temperature if too much food is in the skillet. Fat seeps in instead of forming a crust and cooking the food.

Steam potatoes with a cloth over them. They are rather common but shy, and like to work in privacy. In this way you will get tastier potatoes, and easier to peel too.

Brush your pie crust with egg white. This will improve its looks. Also, if the liquid in the pie has leaked out while cooking, brush it with egg white while the crust is hot. This too will help the crust to look virgin and clean for the table.

As pointed out earlier, use white or yellow onions for Indian food. The Spanish ones are big to look at but add little flavor.

Indian cooking requires a small fire or low heat generally. The Indian cooking techniques will explain why. But the virtues of slow cooking are self-evident in any cuisine . . . An anonymous saying from India would have it of Time that:

It makes the sad, shamefaced lions fail to rage,
Their captive spirits mastered by the cage;
And captive elephants' brows and pride
By drovers' goads are scarified;
Charm, in time, dulls the cobras; hopeless woe
Lays scholars flat and soldiers low:
For Time the mountebank enjoys
A juggling bout with chosen toys;
Only with food does it relent
And this is its virtue great.

A few things more: stir food in a saucepan with a fork rather than with a spoon or ladle, to prevent food from sticking to the bottom. I have not puzzled out why it should be better.

Use individual spices, not packaged curry powder.

Indian cuisine demands, like any other great cuisine, fresh and good meat and material. Leftovers, however, *can* be used and the book has some recipes for these.

Each Indian dish is a specific creation. Please *do not* toss in anything handy. While cooking, keep away from pineapples, sour apples, assorted citrus fruits, miscellaneous nuts and dried fruits unless called for in a recipe.

Harden your heart and simplify your cooking. Eschew the use, in Indian food, of wine, gelatin, French dressings, mayonnaise, grated cheese, Worcestershire sauce and consommé. You will take heart from the fact that no Indian uses them; in fact may never have heard of them.

Be discreet and don't overuse cayenne, chili and paprika.

The name in India for a stinging hot green chili is the same as that for a mettlesome but quarrelsome woman — a *laraki.*

Index